1978

STUDIES IN
SPANISH-AMERICAN
LITERATURE

STUDIES IN SPANISH-AMERICAN LITERATURE

BY

ISAAC GOLDBERG, Ph.D.

WITH AN INTRODUCTION BY

PROF. J. D. M. FORD
Smith Professor of French and Spanish Languages
in Harvard University

KENNIKAT PRESS, INC./PORT WASHINGTON, N. Y.

TO
MY PARENTS

INTRODUCTION

It is only the other day that cultured men in the Spanish motherland began to manifest any real interest in the literature of their one-time colonies in the Western World. Hardly at all before Juan Valera, the charming novelist and discerning critic, wrote his gossipy *American Letters,* (1888–1890) did well trained men and much less, of course, the ordinary reader in the Iberian peninsula realize the ambitious activity of the many writers of the 19th century, scattered throughout the countries lying between the southern bounds of the United States and Tierra del Fuego; and not until Menéndez y Pelayo prepared for the Spanish Academy his *Anthology of Spanish-American Poets* (1893–95) was there any considerable knowledge in Spain of the great output of Spanish verse in the New World from the period of settlement down to our own times.

Genial spirit though he was, Valera was unable to avoid a certain display of that condescending tolerance of the European critic for the products of the colonial mind which we in the United States have been so accustomed to find in the attitude of the British critics and essayists toward our own belles lettres. Still, Valera and Menéndez y Pelayo did prompt their Spanish compatriots to look with some degree of attention at the range of Spanish-American authorship, and then came the Modernist movement, which, emanating from the once ignored field of colonial letters, made its way into the Old World Capital, Madrid, and showed that the American children had something of value and of their own contrivance to bring back to the Iberian mother.

What the Modernist Movement means—of course it has nothing to do with the similarly named theological flurry of a little while ago—Dr. Goldberg aims to make clear in the pages of this book, and, doing this, he is also playing his useful part in the spreading of the evangel of intellectual Pan-Americanism. For we, the northern brothers of the Spanish Americans, have remained even more oblivious to the ideals and merits of Spanish-American literary culture than the Spaniards were until lately, and it is high time that we rouse ourselves to a sense of our backwardness in the case. When we do so and bestir ourselves to know properly the tendencies and achievements of Spanish-American writers—nor should we forget the Portuguese-American writers of Brazil in this connection—we shall perforce begin to conceive a high regard for their zeal, their motives, and their conscious artistry. Racial antipathy, if it exist at all, or, at least, racial indifference will certainly yield to some better feeling, when the thinking people of one racial origin are led to an adequate comprehension and a favorable estimate of the intellectual performances of a people whose provenience is quite other than their own. A sermon might well be preached on this subject, but instead of a sermon a book is now presented in the hope that it will help to break down barriers for the maintenance of which there is no just excuse of a racial, political, commercial, cultural or other nature.

J. D. M. Ford.

FOREWORD

The purpose of the present volume is to introduce to English readers a continental culture that they have too long neglected. Not that we have been alone in our neglect; Spain itself, the mother nation of Spanish America's growing republics, has until very recently ignored the letters of its numerous offspring.

Owing to the meager acquaintance that our reading public has with Spanish-American literature, a book of purely critical essays is at this time inadvisable; I have, therefore, in the following chapters, freely mingled excerpts, exposition and a modicum of criticism, in the hope of thus providing an incentive for further delving into the authors and the books commented upon. Whatever criticism I have written has been determined by a flexible attitude,— I have sought to suggest rather than to define.

Not entirely without reason, although in occasionally exaggerated fashion, Spanish Americans have frequently expressed suspicion of, and hostility to, the United States. Yet it is from a North American, Dr. Alfred Coester, that the first literary history of Spanish America has come (New York, 1916), and that valuable volume I recommend most cordially to any one desirous of securing an adequate historical background for studies in Spanish-American letters.

In later books I plan to present not only other Spanish-

American writers of distinction (and there is a host that might with equal profit have been treated in the present book), but also Brazilian authors of note,—such men as Machado de Assis, Olavo Bilac, Coelho Netto, Jose Verissimo,—to name but four out of a multitude. The spirits referred to are of value not only to a study of comparative literature, but in themselves.

For the chief impulse in assembling these studies I am indebted to Prof. J. D. M. Ford of Harvard University, a pioneer scholar of singularly communicative inspiration. I alone, however, am responsible for my opinions. I am glad to record also my thanks to Mr. Burton Kline, the short-story writer and novelist, who as magazine editor of the *Boston Evening Transcript* held his columns always open to articles upon Spanish and Portuguese American letters. And I am especially thankful to Miss Alice Stone Blackwell, the well known editor and suffragist, for numerous versions of the work of Spanish-American poets. Unless otherwise indicated, all verse translations are from her pen.

In a field so relatively new to this country, and in which the difficulties of intercommunication are great, (even in Spanish America), errors are more than likely to appear. The author may be addressed in care of the publishers with reference to suggestions that may be incorporated into a later edition.

Isaac Goldberg.

Roxbury, Mass., 1919.

CONTENTS

CONTENTS

STUDIES IN
SPANISH-AMERICAN LITERATURE

CHAPTER I

THE "MODERNISTA" RENOVATION

THE study of that phase of recent Spanish-American letters which has been rather loosely and inexpressively, if
popularly, termed "Modernism" forms one of the most interesting adventures in comparative literature. For in its
broader implications it is not a phenomenon restricted to
Castilian and Ibero-American writers of the late nineteenth
and early twentieth century, but rather an aspect of a spirit
that inundated the world of western thought during that
era. The English language contributed such influences as
Whitman, Rossetti, Swinburne, Stevenson, Wilde, Kipling;
in Germany, Sudermann and Hauptmann dominated the
stage, while Nietzsche launched forth to subjugate foreign
thought under the yoke of his super-philosophy, which was,
even more, poetry and vaticination; in Russia, Garshin,
Korolenko, Chekhov and Gorki came to the fore; Isben and
Bjoernsen spoke in different voices for Scandinavia; from
Italy sounded the song of d'Annunzio; above all, from
France, through which the Spanish-Americans absorbed so
much of the foreign influence, echoed the labors of the
Parnassians and the Symbolist-Decadents. And into the
subsequent productions of the "modernists," both the mere

1

imitators and the genuine spirits striving for self-expression, filtered something from all the schools and movements of the various nations.   It is an age of spiritual unrest; on all sides the word "free" flings its challenge to the breeze. Free verse, free love, free music, free woman; there is a riot of emancipation that crystallizes into the one great freedom,—a free self.   The quest for that liberty lies over treacherous paths and in its name are committed many crimes, literary as well as political.   This, however, does not invalidate the impulse itself; man everywhere seeks to release his mind as well as his body; the true deliverance is discovered to be spiritual as well as material.   The spirit of novelty and renovation in the air is but an evidence of the search for self.

"Modernism," as applied to Spanish-American letters (and later to the same impulse making its way into Peninsular literature in the year of Spain's defeat by the United States) was not, then, a school.   Perhaps the word movement is likewise inadequate to describe the tidal wave of reform and innovation that rose in the last quarter of the nineteenth century and, before it had spent its force, washed away the old rhetoric, the old prose, the old verse, and carried a fresher outlook, a more universal culture, a fuller, more sensitive means of expression to the former colonies of Spain.   Modernism was not a school for the simple reason that its divers tendencies were too various to admit of unified grouping.   It was decidedly eclectic in character and from the most antagonistic principles managed to select, with more or less confidence, those elements best suited to its purpose,—a purpose at first somewhat spontaneous, uncritical, hesitant, but gradually acquiring self-reliance, direction, vibrating consciousness. The word movement is for similar reasons not entirely satisfactory. It does not convey the dynamic conception at the bottom of modernism, which, more exactly speaking, is the synthesis of several movements. In the latter sense modernism, far from having run its course, has entered upon a continental phase which promises to bear fruitful and significant results. For the purposes of the present study, however, it will be advantageous to use the term modernism to mean that wave of renovation and innovation to which we have already referred; we must not forget, nevertheless, that human thought possesses a certain continuity which critical labels tend to conceal; the various phases of the modernistic impulse are natural outgrowths of one another; they are all petals of the same flower, with a stem that sinks deep into the fecund soil of modernity.

I

THE FRENCH BACKGROUND

FOR a more than superficial understanding of this important epoch it is necessary to glance at the course of French letters during the last half of the nineteenth century. The study of literature by periods, movements and nations is, after all, an arbitrary method,—necessarily so, since man must classify if he is to master in any degree the achievements of his predecessors and his contemporaries; yet none the less arbitrary, and often leading students and masters alike astray. This is particularly true in the study of literary influences, where too often one man is represented as affecting another, when in reality they are both being acted upon by the same, or similar, non-literary influences. "A great many sins," says one of the most penetrating and independent of our younger critics, "have been committed by the scholarly search for influences. A saner and more philosophic view of the history of literature regards the appearance of new sources of inspiration and new forms of expressions as outgrowths of those larger spiritual forces that are wont to affect at the same time or almost at the same time groups of people that have reached a like stage of development. The modern emergence of the free personality from the merely political individual—the voter who in his day succeeded the tribesman and the slave—accounts for the change in the passions and the forms of poetry in Goethe and in Shelley, in Whitman and Henley, in Richard Dehmel and in Henri de Regnier." [1]   It is a platitude that literature, in common with all art, has its roots in life, yet how often we forget, or even ignore, that life which indirectly creates it.   A more thorough consideration of letters, then, seeks to penetrate beneath merely personal influences; it seeks to understand those economic and social forces that underlie artistic manifestations; it seeks the environment behind the man and the age behind the environment, all the time remembering (what many scientific critics forget) that no age, however homogeneous it appears in the light of history, is a simple attitude, and that no man, however unified his life may outwardly seem, is an embodiment of calm logic unruffled by inner conflict.

In a larger sense, literary history is a series of actions and reactions.   That is why it is just as true to say that

[1] Ludwig Lewisohn. *The Poets of Modern France.* New York, 1918.

all things under the sun are new, or that nothing is; it all depends upon the point of view. The names we give to the recurrent ebb and flow suit our purpose with varying degree of utility, but all are alike harmful if they obscure the essential fluidity of human thought. Classicism did not die with the age to which that label is usually applied; indeed, it never died. Romanticism, likewise, is more than an epoch in the history of letters; it is a human attitude. Under various titles we have designated literary periods which show as their distinctive traits the one or the other spirit, but no age has lacked examples of both views of life and art. Later artistic history, indeed, reflecting the growing complexity of modern life, finds the task of labelling,—once so simple and matter-of-fact,—an increasingly difficult affair. This is but one of the consequences brought on by the resurgence of self in creative endeavor, by a more personal note (even in so-called impersonal art), by a life so rich in stimulus as to open up new worlds within as well as without.

If, then, I speak of literary influence, and make use of certain symbols of criticism it is with a strong feeling that the influence, though literary in manifestation, rests upon a firm foundation of that group-life out of which the creative artist must rise, yet from which he may never completely detach or isolate himself.

The main currents of French poetry of the second half of the nineteenth century have been variously grouped; common critical opinion recognizes as distinct manifestations the Parnassians [2] and the Symbolist-Decadents.

[2] So named from the title of the first anthology of poems by the group— *Parnasse Contemporain* (1866), which had been the name of a little review published by Catulle Mendès and Xavier de Ricard.

Like all new schools, the Parnassian was a reaction, finally growing to the proportions of an affirmation. Romanticism, by 1850, had run its course and the times were ripe for change. The scientific spirit of the age, as well as the oppressive character of the reign of Napoleon III, produced a tendency in favor of a more classic interpretation of art,—an interpretation that favored sobriety of conception, refuge in the ivory tower of lofty seclusion, an objective attitude toward life. It was not so much a preconceived program as a common refutation that brought together such varying spirits as the sombre, Olympic, Leconte de Lisle and the sympathetic, tender, charming François Coppée.

The contribution of the Parnassians to French poetry is well known; in opposition to the intensely personal touch of the Romanticists (itself a reaction against the impersonality of the classic school), they reintroduced the impersonal attitude, seeking objective reality and embodying it in a form of marmoreal beauty. The Symbolists, on the other hand, with whom the Decadents are frequently grouped, in turn rebelled against realism and the impersonality, the sculptural isolation of the Parnassians. They beheld the necessity of a radical change in both the form and substance of French poetry, and gathering a group of writers who were well-defined personalities rather than slaves to a formula, they initiated an era of expansion and experiment whose effects have extended into our own day. For inspiration they turned to such a relatively "old" poet as Charles Baudelaire, as well as to the vibrating lyricist Paul Verlaine and the tremulous, vague, enigmatic Stéphane Mallarmé.

Like the Parnassians, the Symbolists were more or less a reflection of the dominant attitude of the social environment. The day of self-expression was being definitely ushered in; the marble Galatea of Parnassianism was rendered gradually transparent, revealing the pulsing heart within, the complex soul; man was a universe in himself, aquiver with a being new-born, seeking for self-revelation means as subtle and suggestive as possible. The Symbolists turned as naturally to music,—the most subtly suggestive of the arts, as some composers of the day turned to the delicate nuances of symbolistic poetry for inspiration. More than one writer has commented upon the ill-chosen name of that group; the word symbolic suggests too much to suggest anything. The purpose of the Symbolists, however, was clear. They sought to sound the well of human personality, and to accomplish this aim by all the artifices of suggestion they could master. Where the Parnassians chiselled for the eye, they would chant for the ear. Like the "Art Poétique" of Verlaine, who for long did not realize the revolution he had brought about in verse, so they proclaimed

> De la musique avant toute chose
> Et pour cela préfère l'Impair
> Plus vague et plus soluble dans l'air
> Sans rien en lui qui pèse ou qui pose.
>
> —
>
> Rien de plus cher que la chanson grise
> Ou l'Indécis au Précis se joint
>
> —
>
> Car nous voulons la Nuance encor,
> Pas la Couleur, rien que la nuance!
>
> —
>
> Prends l'éloquence et tors-lui son cou!

These few excerpts from the famous poem of Verlaine give in themselves a fairly adequate summary of the Symbolist aim. Musical verse, delicate shades rather than definite color, absence of pompous verbiage, freedom of structure, independence in matters of rhyme,—which in the same poem is characterized as a penny trinket ("ce bijou d'un sou"),—the communication of what has been called "spiritual reality" (which is by no means a contradiction in terms),—these are symptomatic of symbolist matter and manner. Professor Lewisohn, in the compact but stimulating, suggestive book I have already quoted, rightly relates the movement as a whole to that "modern striving toward self-hood" which appears in varied form in all the leading literatures of the world.

That striving for self-hood, quite naturally,—since in the words of the great German, "man errs the while he strives," —vented itself, as it still does today, in fashions strange and often uncanny. These neo-idealists, as a voluminous Spanish critic [3] has termed them, early betrayed synæsthesiac tendencies. Gautier established a hierarchy of words, comparing them to precious stones. Mallarmé, the elusive interpreter of suggestion, thought that the name Emil possessed a green-lapislazuli hue. Arthur Rambaud's well-known neurotic sonnet of the vowels sought to reduce the vowel system to a palette, assigning to A the color black, to B, the color white; to I, red; to U, green; to O, blue, and carrying this fantastic foolery to absurd details. Not to be outdone, René Ghil, likewise an exemplification of the decadent persuasion, reported a different classification. To him I is not red, but blue; O, instead of blue, is red; U,

[3] Julio Cejador y Frauca. *Historia de La Lengua y Literatura Castellana, Comprendidos los Autores Hispano-Americanos. Tomo X.*

rather than green, is yellow; the same author carried his color impressions into the domain of the orchestra, and in his *Traité du Verbe* discovers that harps are white, violins blue, the brass instruments red, the flutes yellow, the organ black. "I have found crimson words to paint the color of the rose," says Theodore de Banville in one of his poems. And Baudelaire: "Perfumes, colors and sounds are interrelated. There are perfumes fresh as the flesh of babes, sweet as oboes and green as the prairies."[4]

To judge artistic schools by temporary aberrations of their representatives is to confess an uncritical attitude. Criticism itself, which is an art rather than a science (despite the unbending dogmatism of certain Rhadamanthine personalities) has been affected, as it always will be, by the same forces that have operated upon the creative intellectual world. It tends today to encourage individuality and to become itself more personal, and is gradually abandoning the position as taskmaster, labeller, preceptor and mere castigator; it seeks to interpret, rather than judge; to recreate, rather than embalm.

That modern French poetry which was destined to reform the poetry of Spain through the modernist spirit, which first

---

[4] The question of colored audition and related phenomena forms one of the most interesting phases of modern psychology. There is nothing new in René Ghil's orchestral coloring. Goethe, in his work on Color, says that Leonhard Hoffmann (1786) assigned colors to the tones of various instruments. The violoncello, for example, was indigo-blue, the violin was ultramarine blue, the oboe was rose, the clarinet yellow, the horn purple, the trumpet red, the flageolet violet. Later Germans have toyed with similar concepts. Recent investigations by neuropaths have revealed patients who are sensitive to the temperature and taste of color, as well as to the color of pain, etc. For a full statement of Johann Leonhard Hoffmann's color-sound comparisons, see, in Goethe's *Zur Farbenlehre*, the part devoted to *Materialien zur Geschichte der Farbenlehre*, under Hoffmann's name.

affected Spanish-America, was itself (in its later phase) influenced by Germanic philosophy. "Just as naturalism derives from the English spirt," avers Cejador y Frauca,[5] "so symbolism comes from the Germanic spirit." Lewisohn, enlarging upon the same idea, states that "The French Symbolists, . . . drew their doctrine of freedom in life and art partly, at least, from the doctrine of the post-Kantian idealists. The creative self that projects the vision of the universe stands above it and need not be bound by the shadows it has itself evoked. The inner realities became the supreme realities: Maeterlinck translated the *Fragments* of Novalis . . ."[6] M. Jean de Gourmont is quoted to sustain the thesis that "Symbolism was not, at first, a revolution, but an evolution called forth by the infiltration of new philosophical ideas. The theories of Kant, of Schopenhauer, of Hegel and Hartmann began to spread in France: the poets were fairly intoxicated by them."

Such, in bare outline, is the background of recent French poetry in so far as it is to affect the more immediate subject of our study. These elements, taking root in a soil prepared for them by politico-economic history (the evidences of which are so remarkably and indissolubly present in such a large body of Spanish-American literature) produce upon modern Castilian verse and prose an effect that has now been all the more exactly analyzed in its numerous manifestations since the wave of "modernism" has receded on both Spanish sides of the Atlantic; or at least, has accomplished its historic mission. Contemporary Spanish-American prose and verse at their best, are remarkable for their

[5] *Op. cit.* Page 28.
[6] *Op. cit.* Page 8.

lucidity, their ductility, their adaptation to the multifarious hues and humors of latter-day thought. The language can crackle and splutter beneath the fiery pen of a Blanco-Fombona; in the hands of a Darío it acquires Gallic luminosity; Santos Chocano achieves with it new sonorities that well match his volcanic, bi-continental utterances; José Enrique Rodó makes it the vehicle of pregnant essays that at times match those of Macaulay or Emerson.

The French influence, however, was more or less sporadic; or, if sporadic is not quite the right term, uneven and dependent upon particular circumstances. Spanish writers have been wont to chide Spain's former colonies for their intellectual dependence upon France—a phenomenon that is likewise to be observed in Portuguese Brazil—and Hispano-American writers (often with an exaggerated and unphilosophic hostility toward the mother country) have gloried in that same bond of cultural amity.

"Modernism" was, then, an intellectual as well as an artistic reaction, and signalled the definite entrance of Spanish America into European literary currents; from the Parnassians it learned to seek new beauties of line and form; from the Symbolists and Decadents it received the opposite contribution to French letters—a sense of color and nuance, a deeper susceptibility to the musical possibilities of words. To be sure, since Spanish Americans, more ardent than their trans-Atlantic brethren, are born reciting verses, they quickly showed themselves prone to exaggerations quite comparable to the vocalic chromomania of Rambaud and Ghil, and to the recondite, esoteric practises of better known Symbolists. That was to be expected; but it is a wrong attitude (such as is entertained by more than one Castilian critic) to charge these aberrations to Modernism. Modernism merely incited them, because it happened to be in vogue; bad poetry has always been written; and always will be, and I suppose there will always be critics who will blame the "new" movement rather than the poets themselves, forgetful of the fact that mere imitators will ever imitate, and that original spirits will break through all canons. Schools and movements do not produce poets; the reverse is more near the truth. Similarly, the study of schools and movements is a useful aid to the appreciation of the poet's work, but never a substitute for the poetry itself, which, if it be genuine art, rises above strict classification.

Although the date 1888 (during which year Rubén Darío's volume of prose and poetry called *Azul* appeared) has been taken as the starting point of the Modernist era, the movement had, like all great historical events, cast its shadows before it. Darío, though the standard-bearer of the reform (self-consciously and progressively so) was not the first of the "modernistas." He had been preceded by Manuel Gutiérrez Nájera in Mexico, by Jose Martí and Julián del Casal in Cuba, perhaps by José Asunción Silva in Colombia, and was ever alive to the new notes being sounded by such personal and outstanding figures as Díaz Mirón of Mexico and Santos Chocano of Peru.

When the new French influence first appeared (chiefly through the Symbolists and the Decadents) it marked what has been called the most important epoch in the history of Spanish-American letters. Speaking in terms of epochs rather than of single writers, this is fairly true. Henceforth Spanish-American letters are destined more and more to be produced by men with a broad outlook, trained directly or indirectly in the culture of contemporary Europe, endowed with a growing selective power that imbibes from foreign influences that which native needs may best employ and in turn supplies its personal, original contribution to the literature that crosses boundaries.

The beginning of the last quarter of the nineteenth century found the Spanish-American writers of originality in need of a new expressional medium and eager for new intellectual impulses. While these were received chiefly from France, they came, too, from sources as wide apart as our own Poe (whose *Raven* was most admirably translated by Pérez Bonalde, the noted Venezuelan "poet of Niagara," so named for an inspirational outburst that rivals the verses of the Cuban Heredia to the same handiwork of Nature) and Heine, rendered into Spanish by the same poet. The transitional period reveals characteristics that are familiarly recurrent in literary history,—a pantheistic mysticism, a new return to mother nature, a desire for simplicity coupled with an intense response to contemporary life and a note of query addressed to the enigma of existence.

To Spanish-American modernism there is something more, however; the age is complex and so are its literary manifestations; a writer like Gutiérrez Nájera, coming at an early stage of the new influences, and being, in reality, a transitory figure, appears simple beside the multi-colored poesy of a Darío; I say appears, because at bottom the Mexican is quite as intensely human as the Nicaraguan; moreover, we must view with reserve the statement as to modernist simplicity when we recall some of the symbolistic extravagances in France, Spain, Spanish America and the United States. Not all is simple that is symbolist; very recent developments in Hispano-American poetry (sporadic, though significant) reveal the fact that complexity of conception is not at all dead, and that poets of modernist provenance, like the modern individualistic spirits they are, reserve the right to confound critical pigeon-holing, and to climb up into the ivory tower of the Parnassians, there to write Symbolist verse in Modernist language.

The Parnassians exercised a powerful influence upon form in Spanish-American poetry; their impassivity, however, (or, at least, their desire to convey the impression of impersonality) did not, on the whole, appeal to an ardent youth panting for self-expression. It was only natural that a Gallic school, representing a group of highly refined spirits belonging to an old civilization, should undergo important change in the virgin soil of a new continent. Parnassian impersonality, then, was an exception rather than the rule. By the same token the Symbolist reaction appealed more to the nature of the Spanish-Americans.[7]

Verlaine, above all, drew to himself a host of poets who turned to him not because he was French but because his

---

[7] Cf. Ugarte, *La Joven Literatura Hispanoamericana*, Prefacio. "The 'decadents,' as they were at first called with scorn, and later with admiration, determined the most intense literary activity, and most fertile in results, that South America has ever known. Through them the language acquired a force, an accent, a precision and freshness which transformed it completely; through them, thought, which had up to then been concealed beneath the commonplaces of rhetoric, discovered innumerable paths of unexplored beauty; through them, above all, was inaugurated the era of literary individualism, and style was emancipated." For an excellent discussion of Ugarte's anthology, as well as for valuable comment upon Spanish-American letters in general, see Rodó's article, "Una Nueva Antología Americana" in *El Mirador de Próspero*.

deep humanity spoke to their groping souls. His religious leanings, his questioning of the unknowable, his neurotic afflictions, his weakness of the flesh,—these rendered him in a way a symbol of the age. To say, for example, that a poet like Darío merely imitated Verlaine, is empty phrasing; Verlaine was in every sense a kindred spirit. Unless we are ready to assent to the manifest absurdity that all priority is causality, we must be ready to see that behind both the French decadent poets and the young Hispano-Americans was an age-spirit that brought them together; as in the case of so much of what is called literary influence, we are in the presence, not merely of cause and effect, but in great degree, of earlier and later effect of a common cause. It is significant that one of the rare spirits treated in Darío's book *Los Raros*, is Ibsen. The age was growing cosmopolitan, and it is this groping cosmopolitanism, this yearning for broader horizons, that is myopically dismissed by some critics as a mere novelty-seeking exoticism. Exoticism, (in its prurient sense) there was; novelty-mongering there was; underneath, however, lay an age-spirit that vented itself in music, in art, in science, in economics.

We have, then, in Hispano-American modernism a phase of universal revolt, a double revolt, which is in reality a single one, since new technical procedure is but a concomitant of altered vision. The self-conscious personality of the new youth now looked to the conquest of spiritual as well as political and economic independence; more ample expression of self demanded more ample means of expresssion. The phenomenon is not French; it is not Spanish; racial or cultural inheritances color the manifestation, but do not determine it. The modernist influence (using the term in its broader sense, yet with all its connotation of new technique and expansion of personality) may be amply and profitably studied even in the Yiddish poets of New York City, who, partly through American influences, have absorbed and transformed the most varied manifestations of modernity.

II

SOME MODERNIST PRECURSORS

1. *Manuel Gutiérrez Nájera* (1859-1895)

Chief among the precursors of modernism who have already been mentioned was the noted Mexican, Manuel Gutiérrez Nájera.

The average educated American of the North, who has received his information about Mexico largely from the columns of the daily press, would be surprised, perhaps, to learn that the republic directly to the south of us is an ancient seat of culture. As much surprised, indeed, as the average South American, who has received his information about the United States from the columns of *his* daily press, would be to discover that in our country something more than lynchings, prize-fights, railroad wrecks and divorce trials is the order of the day. Yet Mexico's literary past is distinguished by glories little appreciated in other Spanish-speaking countries—Spain itself included—not to speak of the United States.

Before the middle of the sixteenth century Mexico had a "colegio" for the natives, at which were taught reading, writing, Latin, grammar, rhetoric, philosophy, and music.

In 1533, thirty years after Hernan Cortes arrived at Ten-
ochtitlan, the University of Mexico was founded by mandate of Carlos 1.   Here, also about 1536–7, appeared the
first printing-press.   During the sixteenth century, in fact,
no less than one hundred and sixteen books were published
in the City of Mexico; the first of these—*La Escalera de
San Juan Climaco*—was printed some one hundred and
three years before *The Freeman's Oath*, published by Harvard College.   Naturally, the first books were confined in
the main to religion, morals and works in native dialects.
At the beginning of the seventeenth century belles-lettres
and history appeared in print.

Two of the greatest names in Castilian literature belong
by nativity, if not by their products, to Mexican letters.
The noted dramatist Juan Ruiz de Alarcón and the world-
famous poetess Sor Juana Inés de la Cruz, both of the seventeenth century, reveal their Mexican origin in not a little
of their work.   Thus Luis G. Urbina, one of the leading
contemporary poets of Mexico, as well as a critic of engaging style and keen perceptions, reminds us in his *La
Vida Literaria de México* that the tender melancholy of
Alarcón is distinctively Mexican; the playwright himself,
writing in far-off Spain, felt this allegiance to the land of
his birth, as is shown by his frequent reference to it.   In
Sor Juana Inés de la Cruz—once upon a time heralded, in
terms that would bring a blush of inferiority to the cheeks
of our most enterprising press-agents, as "the Tenth Muse"
—Urbina discovered the first symptoms of Mexican folk-
lore as well as the first Mexican feminist.

Today, after almost three centuries, Mexico has regained
her literary pre-eminence.   That same melancholy atmos-

phere which Urbina advances as one of the characteristics
of his nation's art, and which his own poetry exemplifies in
so charming a manner, wafts through much of what is now
being written; yet contemporary poetry, particularly in such
original spirits as Amado Nervo and Enrique González
Martínez, achieves something more than intense personality
of mood,—something that maintains the new universality of
Mexican poetry, which was brought with flying banners into
the realms of pure art by Manuel Gutiérrez Nájera.

The contribution of Mexico to the renovation of modern
Spanish letters has, in a measure, been obscured by the
very universality of its chief poets, even as has been obscured its contribution of three centuries ago.   Not only
to Gutiérrez Nájera, to Amado Nervo and to Enrique González Martínez is the modernist school a debtor; the bold
eloquence of Salvador Díaz Mirón affected both Darío and
the powerful poet that has, in the minds of many, taken
his place,—Santos Chocano of Peru.   Nor is the position
of the latter undisputed; some would accord the pedestal
to Díaz Mirón.

Manuel Gutiérrez Nájera, by most reckoned as the greatest of Mexican poets, was born into a pious middle-class
family, and was educated chiefly at home, having been
early intended for the church.   Parental influence seems
to have been strong on both sides; from his mother he
acquired that delicate sensitivity which shines through all
his labors, and which, if but a single phrase were available,
would aptly characterize his varying productions.   Not
only is his love of her directly evident in his prose and his
poetry, but it appears in amplified fashion in his distinctly

feminine outlook, using that much abused word in its finer connotations; it is evidenced by a piety that rarely deserts him, although it is later translated into terms of an undogmatic mysticism not infrequently led to the brink of despair; to her is due his Catholic poetry, which was to raise false hopes in the breasts of some of his countrymen. Born into another age, Gutiérrez Nájera might have become the standard-bearer of a lyric Catholicism; he had come too late for that, and with the awakening of his personality turned to other radically different paths.

From his father came, perhaps, that desire to write which the son manifested at a very early age, at times in disconcerting fashion. For the older man was not only a lover of good poetry, but wrote verse himself and even tried his hand at dramatic pieces, which he later submitted to his son for approval. As one of the poet's commentators suggests, the taste of the child may have been influential in keeping the dramas from attempting success upon the stage. Both by racial surroundings and parental influence, then, Gutiérrez Nájera seemed destined to become a poet; to the melancholy that is characteristic of the Mexican spirit was added the piety of a devoted mother and the frustrated literary ambitions of the sterner parent.

Among the readings that shaped his initial thoughts were the mystic writers Juan de Avila, San Juan de la Cruz, the two Luises, Santa Teresa and Malón de Chaide; to this orthodox instruction was added a training in Latin; both elements are in evidence in his later work. Before he is thirteen we discover his running off to the editor of a Catholic paper, requesting that worthy to print one of his articles. Stranger still, the article is accepted and printed with no little praise. If, however, the poet's Latin lore helped to ripen his mind and store it with the feeling for classic form that never left him, it did not furnish him, as it still furnishes to many, a series of symbols by which his erotic poetry might always be disguised beneath a veil of mythological allusion; his love verses often contain a genuine, if precocious, passion and an ardent sincerity.

Then came the knowledge of the French language which was to transform the poet. "How," asks Urbina, "could Manuel, without having attended the official places of learning, have thus early learned French? The reason is that ever since the invasion of the soldiers of Napoleon III, Mexico experienced, in the upper and middle classes, the irresistible influence of this so communicative and suggestive people. When, after four years of living among us, and fighting us, the time came for the foreign troops to return, there remained in the country many Frenchmen who had assimilated our ways, and among these were some who devoted themselves to instruction and opened schools." . . . This, among other things, determined the propaganda of the language and the literature of the invading country. Gutiérrez Nájera, through the effect of these recent studies, turned his back upon Hispanism; he became Gallicized. But so innate was his good taste that, in his juvenile works (done at sixteen to seventeen years of age) though there is a preponderance of his enthusiastic predilections, there are still traces of his earlier admirations; even in the years 1876–77 he is found imitating Campoamor and Bécquer. It is to Bécquer, indeed, that some contemporary critics would relate the deeper spirit of the poet's complete labors, so that strangely enough, the same singer who introduced the new French influences into Spanish-American verse, is compared to the charming lyricist who himself was called the Spanish Heine.

Once the Gallic seed was sown it grew rapidly to maturity; it seems that a new world has been opened; there are changes in the poet's expression; he ventures certain freedoms of construction; he reveals his new readings by the nature of his citations; his ideas and his style are completely transformed. Through the new influence he is aided upon his path to the acquisition of an independent personality. Not only is this true of his poetry, but of his prose, in which he is no less the innovator, the precursor of Darío and the modernistas. Out of the mingled currents that affected his labors,—the oratory of a Castelar, the bitter-sweet philosophy of a Campoamor, the romantic extravagance of an Echegaray, the tenderness of de Musset,—he fashioned himself a language capable of expressing the finer shades of his feeling, the nuances of his thoughts. His most famous pseudonym—El Duque Job— seems to synthesize in two words, the dominant traits of his contradictory personality. A duke he was, with his leanings toward elegance, his innate aristocracy of feeling, his glinting humor of thought and phrase; and a sufferer as well, not with the patience implied in the biblical name, but with all the torments of a modern soul adrift on a sea of doubt.

When Gutiérrez Nájera came upon the scene, liberalism was triumphing in Mexico; added to that liberalism, the character of his French readings was not of the sort calculated to deepen in him the Catholic fervor he imbibed from his mother; yet at bottom the poet was a religious soul,

or if not quite that, a soul in need of rest, of faith, of resignation.   When, as early as 1877, he published his famous
Para Entonces, voicing his wish to die an early death—a
frequent wish of the modernists, and one too frequently
fulfilled, as in the case of Gutiérrez Nájera himself—he
was but eighteen years old.   Bearing in mind his orthodox
training, the nascent liberalism of the age, and his over-
whelming introduction to the new current of French
thought, it is easy to imagine that these youthful verses
are by no means the ordinary morbidity of the juvenile intellect suddenly cast upon the real world, but are symptomatic of the beginning of that conflict within him which never
was fully resolved into the resignation of the calm, philosophical outlook.

His first articles appeared in *El Federalista* under the
title "Confidencias"; there followed, in various periodicals,
such as the *Liceo Mexicano,* the *Revista Nacional,* and *El
Partido Liberal,* a series of chroniques, tales and poems,
written at times under various pseudonyms, which are il-
lustrative of the author's readings as well as his tastes:
*El Duque Job, Junius, El Cura de Jalatlatco, Puck, Re-
camier.*   The era of Mexican periodical activity was approaching; much of modern progress is heralded by the
array of magazines that sprang up on all sides.   One of
the most important of these—the *Revista Azul*—was
founded only a year before the poet's death, by him and
Carlos Díaz Dufóo.   To this new review flocked the leading intellects of the day.   And why a *blue* review?   "Because," explained the gracious duke, borrowing a leaf from
Hugo's notebook, "in blue there is sunlight; because in the
blue, there are clouds; and because in the blue, hopes fly

in flocks.   Blue is not merely a color, it is a mystery."
And lest it be thought that this cerulean outburst was due
solely to the widespread success of Darío's *Azul*, which
had been printed six years before, it is instructive to remember that as early as 1880, "the thought of the poet appears more refined still, in some strophes taken from *Del
Librito Azul.*   Do you not see in this title (the blue book) a
predecessor of the first revolutionary work written by
Ruben Darío, *Azul* . . . published years later, in 1888?"[8]
Gutiérrez Nájera, in fact, everywhere shows his fondness
for color names; his poem *De Blanco* (1888) is an orchestration of the color white that is more successful, in my es-
timation, than Darío's *Symphony in Grey Major:* [9]

What thing than the lily unstained is more white?
More pure than the mystic wax taper so bright?
   More chaste than the orange-flower, tender and fair?
Than the light mist more virginal—holier too
Than the stone where the eucharist stands, ever new,
   In the Lord's House of Prayer?

By the flight of white doves all the air now is cloven;
A white robe, from strands of the morning mist woven,
   Enwraps in the distance the feudal round tower.
The trembling acacia, most graceful of trees,
Stands up in the orchard and waves in the breeze
   Her soft, snowy flower.

See you not on the mountain the white of the snow?
The white tower stands high o'er the village below;
   The gentle sheep gambol and play, passing by.
Swans pure and unspotted now cover the lake;

[8] M. H. Ureña. *Rodó y Rubén Darío.* Havana, 1918. Page 92.
[9] Both poems were probably suggested by Gautier's *Symphonie en Blanc Majeur.*

The straight lily sways as the breezes awake;
　　The volcano's huge vase is uplifted on high.

Let us enter the church: shines the eucharist there;
And of snow seems to be the old pastor's white hair;
　　In an alb of fine linen his frail form is clad.
A hundred fair maidens there sit robed in white;
They offer bouquets of spring flowers, fresh and bright,
　　The blossoms of April, pure, fragrant and glad.

Let us go to the choir; to the novice's prayer
Propitiously listens the Virgin so fair;
　　The white marble Christ on the crucifix dies;
And there without stain the wax tapers rise white,
And of lace is the curtain so thin and so light,
　　Which the day-dawn already shines through from the skies.

Now let us go down to the field.　Foaming white,
The stream seems a tumult of feathers in flight,
　　As its waters run, foaming and singing in glee.
In its airy mantilla of mist cool and pale
The mountain is wrapped; the swift lark's lateen sail,
　　Glides out and is lost to our sight on the sea.

The lovely young woman now springs from her bed,
On her goddess-like shoulders fresh water to shed,
　　On her fair, polished arms and her beautiful neck.
Now, singing and smiling, she girds on her gown;
Bright, tremulous drops, from her hair shaken down,
　　Her comb of Arabian ivory deck.

O marble! O snows! O vast, wonderful whiteness!
Your chaste beauty everywhere sheds its pure brightness,
　　O shy, timid vestal, to chastity vowed!
In the statue of beauty eternal are you;
From your soft robe is purity born, ever new;
　　You give angels wings, and give mortals a shroud.

You cover the child to whom life is yet new,
Crown the brows of the maiden whose promise is true,
  Clothe the page in rich raiment that shines like a star.
How white are your mantles of ermine, O queens!
The cradle how white, where the fond mother leans!
  How white, my beloved, how spotless you are!

In proud dreams of love, I behold with delight
The towers of a church rising white in my sight,
  And a home, hid in lilies, that opens to me;
And a bridal veil hung on your forehead so fair,
Like a filmy cloud, floating down slow through the air,
  Till it rests on your shoulders, a marvel to see! [10]

The parallel between Gutiérrez Nájera and Darío does
not stop here, however; both were essentially aristocratic
natures; neither was a specimen of masculine beauty. The
Mexican was of medium height, with a large head; his face
was somewhat unsymmetrical,—a detail which would
doubtless furnish critics of decadence with a handy topic
for a sermon upon physiognomy and mental equilibrium;
his nose was ill-proportioned, "cyranesque"; his eyes were
slightly oblique; his mustache was sparse but bristly; his
mouth turned to one side, perhaps because of his inveterate
cigar smoking. A friend (Jesus Valenzuela) describing
him, wrote that he looked like

  A youthful Japanese in terra cotta.

Was it not Vargas Vila who saw in his friend Darío a
marked Mongolian expression? Was not Darío, like
Gutiérrez Nájera, like the later Amado Nervo and so many
other Spanish-Americans, tormented by the necessities of

[10] Version by Alice Stone Blackwell.

journalism?   Did they not both seek consolation in drink,
—their anæsthetic for life?

The chief service of Gutiérrez Nájera to Spanish-American prose and poetry was his introduction of melody into the structure of the language; after him the verse of writers flows more smoothly, more musically; the prose is more agile, more luminous, and gleams with a thousand pregnant suggestions, novel images, and evidences of a varied culture.   He did not, any more than his noted successors, denationalize Spanish style; he broadened it; fertilized it; increased its expressional power, and answered the objections of his critics, as his eulogizer Justo Sierra did after him, by telling them that since art lived a more intense life in France than elsewhere, thither must those who would cultivate art go for their supplies.   The statement looks more servile than it appears in his work.   We find in him something more than the precursor of a school or a movement; something more than a transitional figure who imbibed from France the soul of music that was to infuse new life into the pallid muse of Spanish-American poesy.   He was these things and more.   He was a vibrant personality who caught these various influences because he was ready for them; the French infiltration did not alter him fundamentally, however high the structure that it reared upon his romantic foundations; at bottom he remained the romantic, elegiac spirit.   What it did communicate to him, however, was a refinement of his natural grace, a subtlety of expression that was necessary to the expansion of a personality rich in nuance,—a lyric nature whose note echoes with new overtones.

It has been remarked of him,—and it should be noticed

of many another, since we are too prone to see in the objects of our study a regular development that is not always present—that his advance does not reveal a steady progress through the various dominant French schools to his own artistic self.   Parnassianism of a sort there is in Gutiérrez Nájera; but never of the type that seeks to take refuge in impersonality; Symbolism there is in him aplenty; a tinge of Decadence, if the familiar terminology must be employed.   But however consciously he absorbs these influences, they are metamorphosed into a product entirely his own.   Whether we read the Gutiérrez Nájera so intensely adored by the women—the poet of *Ondas Muertas* (*Dead Waves*) or of *Mariposas* (*Butterflies*) or the Gutiérrez Nájera of the playful conceits, such as that addressed to the *Duchess Job* (his wife), or to the man plunged into the vortex of modern doubt,—we come face to face with an aspect of the person himself; it was his ambition to transfuse the French spirit (Justo Sierra even says the French thought) into the Spanish form; he accomplished the purpose by making himself the crucible of that test.

A seeking soul, torn by doubt, a prey to a dominating vice, distilling his query into melodious beauty,—a vagrant spirit caught between a vanishing world and a nascent era, —a nature shedding his inner grace upon everything touched by his pen,—such was the suffering poet who died midway upon the journey of his life, mourned by the continent to which he had given the gifts of his own song and the impulse of fresh artistic conquests.

The various moods of Gutiérrez Nájera are not distinct stages in the transformation of a man's personality; they are the different aspects of a spirit compounded of a facile wit, an ardent nature, and that deep melancholy that so often hides beneath the outward smile.   Before his gifts as a poet he feels a simple wonder, as so fancifully expressed in the playful "ars poetica" which he entitles *Nada Es Mío*. Nothing is his, he tells the inquisitive Rosa, who wishes to learn how his verses are made.   "I myself do not know. Like your ignorance, Rosa, so mine comes from heaven! I do not write my verses, I do not create them; they dwell within me; they come from without; this playful one was formed by desire; that one, drenched with light, was born of Spring!"   At times he is aided by the magnificent ruby of the dawn; "I make a verse and unwittingly plagiarize some unpublished poet,—the thrush, the chattering sparrow, or the bee. . . ."

> No soy poeta; ya lo ves!   En vano
> halagas con tal título mi oído,
> que no es zenzontle ó ruiseñor el nido,
> ni tenor ó baritone el piano!

Beneath this poetical denial of his poetical gifts, so characteristic of the poet's whimsical temperament (a trait in which so many of his followers in other countries are sadly deficient, but which has been carried by the brilliant Amado Nervo to the heights of bizarre genius) lies a stratum of sincerity.   Poetry, no less than the poet, is born, not made.

The same whimsical note, sparkling with foreign allusion and metrical crispness, sounds from the well-known lines to the Duchess Job.   To English readers the rhymes and rhythms of their own Gilbert come to mind in such lines as

> Mi duquesita, la que me adora,
> no tiene humos de gran señora;

es la griseta de Paul de Kock.
No baila *boston*, y desconoce
de las carreras el alto goce,
Y los placeres del *five o'clock*.

This, however, is not the most popular of the author's
styles; it requires too wide an acquaintance with foreign
currents of thought; it represents a certain ease, an elegance, a grace, which however evanescent the product may
be, are rooted in a cosmopolitan culture.   More to the taste
of the Spanish-American lover of verse is the tender melancholy of such self-revealing poems as *Ondas Muertas*, in
which the poet's sadness does not plumb as deep as the de-
vastating despair of *Después* or the *Monólogo del Incrédulo*.   Miss Alice Stone Blackwell's English version of the
poem does not preserve the metrical structure of the
original—

En la sombra, debajo de la tierra,
donde nunca llegó la mirada,
se deslizan en curso infinito
silenciosos corrientes de agua—

but it affords a very adequate idea of the poet's thought, in
a characteristic effort to sound the depths of the soul that
never come to light.

In the deep darkness underneath the ground,
    That never has been reached by mortal sight,
There silent currents of black water glide
    In an unending course amid the night.
Some of them, by the shining steel surprised
    That pierces through the rocks to their dark home,
Limpid and boiling to the light gush forth
    In a vast plume of white and silvery foam.

The others in deep darkness evermore
    Glide silently upon their winding way,
Doomed to a course unending under ground,
    Failing to find an outlet to the day.

The noble rivers to the ocean flow
    Past field and forest, meadow-bank and lawn
Reflecting in their silvery, changeful glass
    The stars of heaven, the pale tints of dawn.
Veils of fair, fragrant blossoms make them glad
    Nymphs bathe in their clear current with delight;
They fertilize the rich and fruitful vales;
    Their waves are singing water, free and bright.

In the white marble fountain, lo! the stream
    Is mischievous and playful, sporting there
Like a young girl who, in a palace hall,
    Scatters the pearls that form her necklace fair.
Now like a shining arrow it shoots up,
    Now like a fan it opens in its flow;
It splashes glittering diamonds on the leaves,
    Or sinks to slumber, singing soft and low.

The waves that in the mighty ocean swell
    Assail the craggy rocks, upsurging high;
Their raging fury shakes the solid earth,
    And rises up in tumult to the sky.
Those waves are life and power invincible;
    The water is a queen with wrath on fire,
And against heaven like a rival fights,
    And wages war with gods and monsters dire.

How different is the sable current sad,
    Doomed to imprisonment which knows no end,
Living below the earth in sunless depths,
    Down deeper even than the dead descend!
That stream has never known what light may be;

It neither sings nor sobs, that sunless wave;
The subterranean stream is dumb, unknown;
It goes upon its way, a mute, blind slave.

Like such a stream, to all the world unknown—
Like such a stream, whose prisoned waters roll
Surrounded by thick darkness—such are you,
O dark and silent currents of my soul!
Who e'er hath known the course your waters take?
No kindly friend goes down where shadows sleep
To look upon you in the dark—and yet
Your captive waves reach deep, oh, very deep!

Should you be given an outlet to the day,
You would gush upward from your sunless home
As higher than the cedars and the pines
The water leaps, a column white with foam.
But no—you ne'er will feel the gaze of light;
Still through the night your rayless waves must roll.
Go on, forever gliding in the dark,
O deep and silent currents of my soul!

Similar in appeal and quite as symbolic in style, is the perennially popular *Mariposas*, which sings the disillusionment of life, the foundering of its hopes, in the forms of butterflies of different colors. For in many of the poet's verses the golden wings of the butterfly hover over the dark chasm of the unknown. . . .

Ya no viene la blanca, la buena!
Ya no viene tampoco la roja,
la que en sangre teñí, beso vivo,
al morder unos labios de rosa!
Ni la azul que me dijo: poeta!
Ni la de oro, promesa de gloria!

Ha caido la tarde en el alma.
Es de noche . . . ya no hay mariposas!

Night comes to the poet, and the butterflies are gone.   The
following is Miss Blackwell's version of *Mariposas:*

BUTTERFLIES

Whether white as flitting snowflakes,
Whether dark, or blue, or crimson,
They adorn the air in myriads
And amid the petals frolic.
Lightly springing from the blossoms,
Like the fleeing souls of roses,
They with winning grace are swaying
On the leaves, their verdant hammocks.
By a gleam their life is kindled
And a drop at eve can quench it.
They appear with dawn's first brightness,
And before the dark they perish.
Who knows where their hidden nests are—
Where they find repose at nightfall?
The coquettes, inconstant, fickle,
Have no home, no sleeping chamber.
They are born, love, shine, and perish;
In the air they change in dying,
Pass away and leave no traces,
Like the drops of some light shower.
Some of them are turned to blossoms;
Others, up to heaven summoned,
With their million gleaming winglets
Join to form the glorious rainbow.
Where is then thy nest, O rover?
Where thy harem, wee Sultana?
Who, coquette, thy favored lover?
Where, O butterfly, thy death-sleep?

Thus take wing, and pass, and perish,
The chimeras, love and glory,
Those bright pinions of the spirit,
Whether white, or red, or azure.
Who knows when and where we lost you,
Dreams like butterflies that glittered?
Ah, how swift your bright swarms vanish,
In the soul when falls the shadow!
Why dost thou not come, thou white one?
Wast thou not the orange blossom
Of my bride?   Ah me!   I made thee
Of a white drop from the taper
That I carried at the altar
Of my parish church in boyhood.
Thou wast artless, chaste, believing;
When thou on my lips didst tremble,
Thou didst murmur, rapture's herald,
"Now thy wedding night approaches!"
She, the white one, she, the good one,
Comes no more; nor yet the crimson,
Which I dyed in red—a live kiss
On some rosy lips pressed sharply;
Nor the blue, that called me poet,
Nor the gold, that promised glory.
In my soul the night has fallen;
All the butterflies have vanished!
Like that yellow waxen taper;
Now the others will come thronging—
Those with black wings, circling nearer,
Dancing a funereal measure.
Comrades, now the wax is burning;
Comrades, now the room is empty.
If ye for my soul wear mourning,
Come, O butterflies, come quickly!

This is more like the Gutiérrez Nájera that mirrors the

unrest of his age; the poet that realized the creative power of grief and who sang the sterility of happiness. How often one opens his pages for the sweetness of his song, only to shudder before the hopelessness of the melody! There is a fascination even to his most despairing poems,—the phase of his work that makes the strongest personal appeal to me, because I seem to divine in them the total man. To be sure this is not all of life; to be sure, the very creation of the poetry is itself a denial of the dark pessimism it embodies; but it is all so human, so unaffectedly human, and how much to be preferred to the artificial optimism that vitiates so large a proportion of verse in these United States! Even pessimism may be beautified by the symbols in which it is presented, and thus become, despite itself, a carrier of life and inspiration. Such is the expression of Gutiérrez Nájera's doubt. Like the later Casal, this poet desired an early death, yet unlike the strange Cuban, he was not afraid to taste life's joys for fear of becoming enamored of them and losing his unnatural desire of annihilation. This very thirst for death, in one man and in the other, is perhaps but an evidence of an overmastering yearning for a full, all-embracing life.

One more of the tenderly elegiac poems will suffice to present this phase of the artist's personality: the perennial *Serenata de Schubert*. This is more than an experiment in lending new music to Spanish verse; it is a lyric outburst of the eternal question:

> Por qué es preciso que la dicha acabe?
> Por qué la novia queda en la ventana,
> y á la nota que dice: "hasta mañana!"
> el corazón responde: "quien sabe?"

There is one of the secrets of the poet's verse: "Who Knows?" For happiness is of yesterday and tomorrow is "grief, obscurity and death." Beside the mere coquetry of a Herrick's *carpe diem*, such a poem as *A Un Triste*, from the author's *Odas Breves*, rings with a deadly earnestness that may not enjoy the fleeting pleasures of the moment even when they are captured, because of the rankling query that outcries the clinking of glasses, the laughter of maidens and the intoxication of wine. And it is but cold consolation that he proffers, with the parting encouragement that roses, like loves, die young.

We have sampled the whimsical, the elegiac and the tenderly melancholy strains in our poet; let us approach him in these moods where he seems shaken to the depths; where he is a prey to the inner conflicts so characteristic of an age that has not yet found itself,—that proceeds from scientific surety to a neo-metaphysical questioning,—that seeks to resolve doubt by resignation or affirmation,—that begins to wonder whether there is a sole truth, and has begun to sense the futility of dogma, whether clothed in religion or in science.

In this connection one of the keynote poems is the *Monólogo del Incrédulo*,—an important human document in which the despair of the poet treads upon the verge of what to him was blasphemy, and the brittle rhythm matches the subject, being well suited to the curt questioning, the sudden thoughts and the distracted debate.

> ¿La existencia no pedida
> que nos dan y conservamos,
> es sentencia merecida?
> decidme: vale la vida
> la pena de que vivamos?

The opening stanza plants the bold question: "We have not asked for existence; is life worth the trouble of being lived?"

If it is a punishment, what sin have we unknowingly committed?   If it is a reward, what was it awarded for? The life of the happy one is worth while, perhaps; let him watch over it if he finds felicity here below; but the sufferer, —why does he not escape it?   And like many a one before him, the poet reflects that although life was not a boon he asked for, death is in his own hands.   By the same token it is foolish to complain against fate; that would be excusable were not death possible, but since it is, he keeps silent.   But is that silence the product of fear?   Fear of what?   Of that God who gave him what he did not ask? If he should meet a God after taking his life, he could truly say to him, "I did not care for life; that is why I return it to you."   In any case, let none blame fate; the man of strong will does not call upon death; he goes out fearlessly to seek it.   And yet,—and yet,—like most suicidal philosophers, he maintains his grip upon life.   Why?   Is he happy?   Or is it that, once here, he is bound to his parents, and loves them?   If a man could think at his birth, he would surely destroy himself.

Now comes a transition in the thought.

> Tengo derecho á morir,
> mas no derecho á matar;
> y comprendo que al partir,
> si con la muerte he de ir
> me irá mi madre al buscar.
>
> Puedo matarme sereno,
> pero mi madre adorada

> creerá que entre llamas peno;
> así es que no me condeno
> y à ella dejo condenada.

He has the right to die, but not the right to kill; he knows that were he to commit suicide it would endanger his mother's life; not only that, but were she to survive that grief, she would believe that his soul was burning amid the flames of sinners.   Here is a strange phase of that love for his mother which so often appears in his work.

Life now looms up in the aspect of a wily deceiver. First pleasure leads us to engender existence, and then life chains us to duty.   And just as he was brought to earth by a woman who afterwards seemed to implore his pardon, so he, too, in turn, will create life and feel grief at having created it.   No, suicide were better.   But this time the thought of his sweetheart detains him.   Here, too, however, the canker-worm of doubt gnaws at his heart.   Is her love sincere?   Does he love her?   And later, will that love endure?   Then follows a verse in which the Tennysonian "it is better to have loved and lost than never to have loved at all," is echoed with a characteristic note.

> Amar y no ser amado
> no es la pena mayor:
> ver el cariño apagado,
> no amar lo antes amado
> es el supremo dolor.

"To love and not be loved in return is not the greatest grief. To see one's affection diminish and no longer love the one of yore is the supreme sorrow."

The poet would have death or the certainty of God's

power.   "Either hasten to me, oh Death, or rise from the shadows, oh God!"

I do not say that this is a great poem; I do not say that it contains any remarkable profundity of thought or beauty of language.   It does, however, reveal the man that wrote it and the experience of many another perturbed spirit of his day amid the storm of an existence that strives to rationalize joy and pain and give a meaning to life.

And when the poet does for a moment find a refuge from such thoughts, what sort of peace is it that hovers over his soul?   He himself tells us in his *Pax Animæ*, a bitter-sweet production in which the rebellion of the previous poem now and then storms to the surface, to be conquered more or less by resignation.   Be proud and gallant in the fall, he counsels the poet; "look with supreme disdain upon all the injustices of life!   Seek no constancy in love, nor ask anything eternal of mortals; make, oh artist, of your griefs, supreme sepulchral monuments. . . ."   He does not agree with the famous lines from Dante that there is no grief like remembrance of past happiness in present woe.

> En esta vida el unico consuelo
> es acordarse de las horas bellas. . . .

> In this our life the only consolation
> Is the remembrance of hours framed in beauty

In beauty alone,—impassive and immortal beauty,—is solace.

> Recordar . . . Perdonar . . . Haber amado . . .
> ser dischoso un instante, haber creído . . .
> y luego . . . reclinarse fatigado
> en el hombro de nieve del olvido.

The one lesson of his sorrow is to seek clarity and calm on the summits; love and pardon those around you; seek that love and pardon above.

The fragment *To Be* is associated naturally with the Monologue of the Unbeliever.

> A deep abyss is this our human grief!
> What eye has ever gazed into its depths?
> Lend but your ear unto the dismal pit
> Of vanished centuries. . . .
> Within there falls
> An eternal tear!

"A groan arises tremblingly from the white bones.   Life is grief.   And the life of the sepulchre may be a gloomy one, but it is life none the less. . . ."   Suicide would be vain. It would represent merely another phase of the essential, indestructible matter of being.   We live in grief; the great ambition of all that is, is to be lost in nothingness, to sleep without dreams.   To the poet's distracted soul, there is no "not to be"; it is all a grievous being with no outlet for the harassed victim of life.

It is in the poem *Después,* however, that the poet strikes his deepest note of despair.   Here the thought of the *Monólogo* is something more than mere complaint, mere blasphemous soliloquy.   To read the poem is not to be able to detach oneself from the work and analyze a mood; we are plunged into the very shadows that surround the frightened questioner and beat about the darkness without shore.

> El templo colosal, de nave inmensa
> esta húmedo y sombrío;
> sin flores el altar; negro, muy negro;
> apagados los cirios!

> Señor, ¿en donde estas?   Te busco en vano . . .!
>   ¿En donde estás, oh Cristo?
> Te llamo con pavor porque estoy solo,
> como llama á su padre el pobre niño . . .!
> Y nadie en el altar!   Nadie en la nave!
> Todo en tinieblas sepulcral hundido!
> ¡Habla!   Que suene el órgano!   Que vea
> en el desnudo altar arder los cirios! . . .
> Ya me ahogo en la sombra . . . ya me ahogo!
>   Resuscita, Dios mío!

In the presence of such a human outcry, it may be profitable to speak of the metrical skill with which the effects are wrought, of the symbolic beauty in which the poet drenches his work; but above and beyond this is the eternal flash of his query, like a tongue of flame pointing to the heavens. . . . Only he who had once been a believer could have written such a poem of unbelief. *Después* deserves a place among the great poems of the Eternal Query.

The prose of Gutiérrez Nájera, even more revolutionary than his poetry, is no less revelatory of the man who guides the pen. It is no less indicative of a highly sensitive nature that was certain to revivify the prose of his day because of the new things he had to say and the delicate shades of thought he tried to convey. His paradoxes, his numerous epigrams, his luminous imagery, his flowing line, are not so many disintegrated elements of a mosaic manner; they are organic parts of a whole. There is a new music to the phrases, a downy tenderness; now and then the note of pure horror, told in language that renders the horror all the more poignant,—not the horror of a Poe, however, and quite devoid of that technique so overprized by our own writers; the prose, indeed, is poetry of a sort,—a strange

commingling of substance and airiness, more crystalline
than that of Martí (who was likewise a master of epigram
and imagery) and no less a carrier of thought framed in
beauty than that of Darío.   His *Smoke-Colored Tales* are
notable not so much for their plot as for their melodic amplification of a lyric mood.   Everywhere is the brooding,
tenderly elegiac note; there is humor, too; the humor of the
facile *Duke Job*,—even a bitter, ironic, grim humor.   How
well named are his *Fragile Tales!*   The fragility, however,
is that of the finely labored ivory filigree; the humor is here
bitter-sweet, the epigrams are barbed thought that stings
like arrows.   The author is fond of quasi-philosophic or
reminiscent prologues to his tales, which, as we may be now
expect, are mood rendered vocal rather than self-sufficient
narrative.   At times, without any loss of virility in the essential conception, Gutiérrez Nájera writes prose that possesses the subtle charm of the violin's muted strings.
Everywhere is the lyric attitude; even in his travels he looks
at the cities out of eyes that gaze as much inward as outward.

What does he tell us in this music of language that is
music of thought?   What does this spirit, attuned to such
various influences as Leconte de Lisle, Verlaine, Baudelaire, Carducci, de Castro, d'Annunzio, Dante, Gabriel Rossetti, Anatole France, Ibsen, Tolstoi, Nietzsche, Renan, distil from the multifarious streams of world thought that
inundate his early provincial soul?   Almost wherever we
greet him, he offers us something peculiarly his own.   Let
us follow him for a few moments at random in his prose.

"I did not see this tale," he begins his homiletic version
of the Rip Van Winkle legend, called *Rip-Rip*, "but I believe I dreamed it."   This prepares us at the very start

for the dreamy atmosphere so proper to legends.   But if you imagine that we have been launched upon the story, you are mistaken.   "What things the eyes behold when they are shut!   It seems impossible that we contain so many persons and things within . . . for when the eyelids fall, the glance, like a lady closing her balcony-window, returns to see what is inside the house.   Very well; this house of mine, this house of the madame Glance that I possess, or that possesses me, is a palace, a city, a world, the universe . . .; but a universe which ever contains the present, the past and the future.   Judging by the things that I see in my sleep, I think to myself, and even for you, dear readers: Good Lord, what things the blind must see! These, who are always asleep,—what can they behold? Love is blind, they say.   And love is the sole beholder of God."   So, in his *Vestido Blanco*, that same attraction for the color white appears that is so noticeable and so notable in his sterling poem, *De Blanco*.   So, too, in his *Cuento Triste* (I am seeking now insights into his moods and parallels with his poetry rather than mere plots) he finds himself unable to sing, because "harmonies do not rise from the lute whose strings are broken, nor does chirping sound from the abandoned nest. . . . I have pursued love and glory like the children who run after the coquettish butterfly that mocks at their pursuit and their laughter.   All the roses that I found had thorns,—all the hearts, forgetfulness. . . . There was a moment in which I thought that love was absolute and unique.   There is only one love in my soul, as there is only one sun in the sky, I said to myself then.   Afterwards, studying astronomy, I learned that there were many suns.   I knocked at the door of many hearts and they did not open to me, because no one was within." The note of loneliness amid the crowd—our poet disliked multitudes—sounds most naturally from the man whose superiority isolates him. In his *Las Almas Huérfanas* (Orphan Souls), turning the famous biblical lines to lyric use, he tells us

> tienen ojos y a mi no me miran;
> tienen labios y á mi no me hablan.

> Eyes have they yet do not see me;
> Lips have they, yet speak not to me.

How far is this from the witty whimster who, in his account of a comet's progress (*Los Amores del Cometa*) can mingle fact and fancy in so striking a manner! And yet even here, amid a fascinating discourse of such nonsense as is relished by the best of men, he must strike his characteristic note, comment upon the fleeting aspect of things, and counsel us to seize the day while we may!

A turn of the page and we find our responsive spirit wandering into a circus tent. And what does he carry forth? A detestation for those spectacles in which he beholds human debasement. A horror for the utter denial of "the most noble gift of God: thought." A deep sympathy, above all, for the poor exploited children of the circus. His attention is soon centered upon a little "daughter of the air." . . . "Tell me, dear little girl, have you no mother? Were you, perchance, born of a night's passion, or did you come to earth upon a moonbeam? If you had a mother, —if they tore you from her arms,—she, with that incomparable divination which love gives us, would know that here you were weeping and suffering; crossing seas and mountains she would come like a madwoman to free you from this slavery, this torture! No, there is no such thing as an evil mother. The mother is the projection of God upon earth. You are an orphan." In the last sentence but one we find one of the dominant inspirations of the author: that mother through whom he knew God, and to whom, when firm belief deserted him, he still clung in thought and labor. In the same tale of the circus he shows himself capable of a most powerful, even if poetical, protest against the exploitation of the child in the acquisition of money.

He is, like all persons possessed of a sense of humor, capable of poking fun at himself and his fellow writers, to whom, in the delightful skit entitled *Historia de un Corista*, he refers as "men who, for lack of Champagne and Bourgogne, drink down in gulps that thick, dark liquid called ink." And such a chorus girl as this is! She quotes Greek mythology and Hugo with equal ease, and when it comes to veiling the dubious aspect of her career, what a mastery of innuendo she displays. His words on the evil effects of drink are doubly effective because of his own well-known weakness. "Man thinks that he is drinking the glass," he avers, in *Semana de Lázaro*, "but he is deceived, for it is the glass that drinks him. At first he drains it at a single gulp; but the glass recoups its losses, and the man must fill it with somewhat of his mind, with somewhat of his heart, with somewhat of his soul. A glass seems so narrow, and within it, nevertheless, so many sons, so many mothers, so many wives, so many lives have been drowned!"

His words upon music are likewise indicative of the man who brought music into the realm of modernism. "Music is a docile, obedient love that submits to all caprices, like the odalisk who, to please her master, places around his neck the divine necklace of her arms, or watches over his repose with discreet attitude, refreshing his atmosphere with her fan. It comes to us on tiptoe, so as not to waken us if we are asleep, knocks at our door and asks, 'What sentiments would you have me rouse in you?' Therefore yesterday we laughed to the same harmonies that today cause us tears. Music does not impose its will; it does not dominate; it is the language that adapts itself to all passions; the tongue of the lion which, by dint of caressingly licking the foot of his master, finally makes a wound. On the same note Faust meditates, Marguerite sobs and Mephistopheles laughs." Rarely has more been said of music in so few words. The metaphor of the lion, besides containing a most adaptable pun on the word tongue, is imbued with a deep truth; if we slay the things we love, the things we love slay us no less. By a single reference to the opera *Faust* he conveys the multiple appeal which is music's eternal charm.

Such is the charming personality that is hidden by the pseudonym *Duke Job.* Whether, with his deep fondness for children, he tells us a tender tale of sadness or death; whether, with his inquisitive nature, he engages in that strangest occupation for a poet,—the scientific elucidation of a fairy tale; whether he attends a murder trial and brings back a report that would grievously disappoint the prurient readers whom our own "star" reporters have been trained to pamper; whether he visits cities and summons most un-touristic thoughts; the essential Gutiérrez Nájera is visible.

Gutiérrez Nájera is, whatever his medium, fundamentally a poet; his prose, even his so-called journalism, is, in essence, poetry. He sees in images and thinks in terms of feeling. Deeply romantic in nature, he is by the spirit of the times plunged into the maelstrom of modern thought, amid which he attempts to preserve a yielding faith; this faith, like all departing creeds, seeks new altars. The query of that quest vibrates in his verses,—now soothed by resignation, now calmed by renunciation, now blasphemous with despair, and never completely satisfied. This is the real man beneath the verbal melodist, the revolutionary force in journalism, the inquiring soul that poured its beauty alike into the Parnassian urn and the neo-Hellenic vase, and plucked the strings of the Symbolist harp. He is a modernist precursor not through a mere pruriency for novelty, not through an affected exoticism, but because he helped fashion a new interpretative medium for a new outlook. Rise what may out of Pandora's box, mankind must peer within. . . .

2. *José Martí*

(1853–1895)

The resemblances among the more noted exponents of modernism are many; there is the note of growing cosmopolitanism, the morbid tendency, the pale cast of thought, the resurgence of self. From among these figures, however, that of Martí, "the gallant paladin of Cuban freedom," stands out as an exception. True, Martí shared, and even contributed early vigor to, the dominant characteristics of modernism. In him, however, no morbidity, no preoccupation with metaphysical mysteries; he is the rebel in action,—a volcanic force driven by fate, like a Wandering Jew of liberty, through many lands and to many hearts. Like so many of his fellows, he became early embroiled in journalism, and, imbued with a passionate desire for his country's independence, voiced that ideal with the rashness of Latin youth. Before he was well along in his 'teens, he was deported to Spain for his "insurrecto" spirit, and while there was allowed to study law; he completed the course at Zaragoza. Returning to Spanish America he married in Mexico (1873) and five years later went back to the scene of his early efforts, conspiring against Spain under the guise of practising law. There follows (1879) a second deportation; this time, however, he managed to escape to France, eventually reaching New York, making his way to Venezuela and returning to New York, where he engaged in journalism for *La Nación* (Buenos Aires), wrote for the *New York Sun* on art, incessantly strove to maintain the fires of Cuban liberty burning in the hearts of the Spanish-Americans there, and published two collections of verse: *Ismaelillo* and *Versos Sencillos*. And now his labors, which had taken him to Paris, London, Mexico, the United States,—began to bear fruit. The final result, however, he was destined never to behold, for on the 19th of May, 1895, he was shot at Dos Rios, on his native soil, while attempting to leave the island.

So much of Martí (and how much it is!) belongs to history. But there is much of him that belongs to letters,—a little of his poetry (not so much as the generous Darío would lead one to believe from his paper on Martí in *Los Raros*) and a great deal of his prose. Even more, perhaps, of that elusive emanation which we term a man's spirit, only because language is still inadequate to the conveyance of human feeling.

Martí, in his glowing eulogy of Pérez Bonalde, has left us an excellent declaration of his views upon poetry. He reveals himself as an out-and-out apostle of personality, aware of time's conflicting currents, plunged in the struggle for liberty (of which he has a most undogmatic conception, comparable with Rodó's vision of enlightened democracy), and hence with a trace of the utilitarian in his poetic demands.[11] "The first labor of man," he proclaims, "is to reconquer himself. Men must be returned to themselves. . . . Only the genuine is powerful. What others leave to us is like warmed-over food." One element at least, in man's surroundings, responds to his desires: the free choice of educative influences. He can behold neither literary originality nor political liberty without spiritual freedom. Note this insistence upon self; upon the linking of the literary and political aspects of human activity. The multiple self of which Gutiérrez Nájera speaks and for which Martí combats is to blossom into Rodó's masterpiece, the *Motivos de Proteo*, which is one of the most suggestive of modern probings into the many latent possibilities of personality.

To Martí, the poem is in the man and in nature. He is so eager for spontaneity that he considers perfection of

[11] Cf. the similar views of poetry entertained by another man of action, the versatile, restless Rufino Blanco-Fombona.

form as being purchased at the price of the fecundating idea. "A tempest is more beautiful than a locomotive." This spontaneity is what he so much admired in Bonalde's noted poem upon Niagara. "To polish is all very well, but within the mind and before the verse leaps from the lip." And if you object that such slavery to spontaneity injures the beauty of art, he replies, "He who goes in search of mountains does not pause to pick up the stones of the road. . . . Who does not know that language is the horseman of thought, and not its horse? The imperfection of human language,—its inadequacy to the expression of man's judgments, affections and designs is a perfect, absolute proof of the necessity for a future existence." Note, in passing, another difference between the active, optimistic, implicitly believing Martí and the foundering precursors of his day. "No, human life is not all of life! The tomb is a path, not an end. The mind could not conceive what it was incapable of realizing. . . ." And, returning to his manifesto of spiritual independence: "No, leave small things to small spirits. Lay aside the hollow, hackneyed rhymes, strung with artificial pearls, garlanded with artificial flowers. . . ." Away with affected Latinism and the bookish ills, counsels Martí. With lips tightly pressed, breast bare and clenched fist raised to heaven, demand of life its secret!

The translator of Helen Hunt Jackson's *Ramona*, the revealer of Walt Whitman, the man who imbibed law at Seville and Zaragoza, immersing himself at the same time in Santa Teresa, Cervantes, Calderón, Quevedo, did not manage to communicate the ardor of his theory to his verses, which are more simple and tender than would be expected. They are characteristically sincere, written "not in academic ink but in my own blood." At times they possess the suggestion of de Campoamor, as in the following excerpt:

Un beso!
—Espera!
Aquel día
Al despedirse se amaron.

Un beso!
—Toma.
Aquel día
Al despedirse lloraron.

A similar note of love and disillusionment rings from the brief drama that follows:

Entró la niña en el bosque
Del brazo de su galán,
Y se oyó un beso, otro beso,
Y no se oyó nada más.

Una hora en el bosque estuvo,
Salió al fin sin su galán:
Se oyo un sollozo; un sollozo,
Y despues no se oyó más.

It is not in his verse,—his paternal delights, his love plaints, his patriotic poems,—that we must seek the literary revolutionist, but in his prose. And such a prose! One countryman has called it the "symphony of a fantastic forest where invisible gnomes enchant our ears with a flock of harmonies, and our eyes with a tempest of colors." Despite an occasional involution of phraseology and a veritable cataract of images he makes delightful, yet impressive, reading. If Gutiérrez Nájera's prose is the graceful violin, alternately muted by hushed thoughts and swelled by passionate utterance, the prose of José Martí is a Wagnerian orchestra. It blasts with trumpet-like sonority; it scatters sparks; it is, indeed, as the man himself was, incendiary. His journalistic labors moulded a new standard; from him Darío learned much of the secret of such enduring correspondence as makes up the great poet's volumes of newspaper labors. Martí, too, is a notable wielder of the epigram; indeed, this aspect of his prose is strikingly illustrated by a recent collection,[12] made up entirely of chips from the statue of his prose. In all the one hundred and forty-six octavo pages of the book there is a surprisingly low number of platitudes.

"There are cries that sum up an entire epoch," Martí has asserted. Martí himself was such a cry. Was it not he who opened one of his speeches with the affirmation that "I am not a man speaking, but a people protesting"? And he spoke not alone for Cuba, but for all of Spanish America. He is looked upon by those advanced minds in whom he sowed the seed of clamant freedom as not only a precursor of modernism in its narrower sense, but as one of the founders of literary, as well as political, Americanism. He was the proclaimer of a continental fatherland,—a Magna Patria. He did not believe in Cuba's annexation to the Republic of the North; knowing both nations intimately, he saw that only a virile Cuba could win the re spect of a virile United States.

[12] *Granos de Oro. Pensamientos Seleccionades en las Obras de José Martí. Por Rafael G. Argolagos. La Habana. 1918.*

A remarkable union of the man of contemplation and the man of action, a vagrant pioneer in both mind and body, an innovator in language because of the new vision he beheld, Martí is enshrined in both the literature and the history of his people. His life was as noble as his writings; he died for that to which he had devoted his life, and Cuba is his monument.

3. *Julián del Casal*

(1863–1893)

The life of the Cuban Casal is as marked a contrast to that of his compatriot Martí as any life well could be. Exhibiting more than one of the traits of Gutiérrez Nájera, he more closely resembles, in his inner existence and his poetic product, the gifted Colombian, José Ansunción Silva, whom I shall take up after him. Julián del Casal, in his brief career (and how all too brief are the lives of so many of these agitated spirits!) underwent, like the modern child he was, a variety of influences that corresponded to his neurotic, morbid personality,—Jean Richepin, Heredia of the flawless sonnets, Judith Gautier of the Oriental flavor, Baudelaire of the flowers of evil, Verlaine of the lyric soul turned song. A stranger to what is commonly called life, his poems throb with a feverish intensity of internal existence. Cejador y Frauca refuses to place del Casal among the modernists. "I find no point of comparison," he asserts, "between Casal and the modernistas." He is "sound and robust, without the slightest decadentism in thought or expression." The opinion is a strange one indeed; either the Spanish critic's definition of decadentism is an exceedingly elastic one, (and it surely is an unsparing castigation that recalls Max Nordau at his best—or worst!) or else Casal is very much "decadent" indeed. It has been asserted that the Cuban poet never experienced the griefs of which he sung; if that be the case, we have in his productions one of the most remarkable examples of personal projection into alien moods that modern psychology can furnish.

His poetry reveals him as a faithful yet hopeless seeker after beauty; he is capable of looking upon nature not through rose-colored, but through blood-colored glasses (as in the poem *Crepuscular*, with its bold opening comparison of the sunset to a slashed stomach) or of commenting ironically upon it in a poem ostensibly dedicated to the country (*En El Campo*), but in reality asserting his "impure love of cities"; his morbid presentiment of that early death which overtook him as it did Gutiérrez Nájera and Silva, recurs with overtones of disillusionment, hopelessness, yet ever with sincerity; like Silva, he thinks for a moment of his childhood, only to tell himself that he will be the hangman of his own happiness, as indeed his verses show him to have been; like so many of his confrères, he knows the price of eating from the tree of knowledge; his morbid introspection is so faithfully recorded in any number of poems, that if it be true they were bookish inspirations rather than the product of actual events, I make bold to say that Casal's real life was the life that no one saw,— the life within. He never expects to attain to manhood, and despite his griefs, does not feel "the nostalgia of happiness"; indeed, his wandering soul yearns only for what he may not attain, whether that be ineffable beauty or distant lands.

> Ver otro cielo, otro monte,
> Ostra playa, otro horizonte,
>   Otro mar,
> Otros pueblos, otras gentes
> De maneras diferentes
>   De pensar.

Such is one of his *Nostalgias;* yet could he reach these other scenes, these other peoples, would he really go? "But I go not," he concludes. "Were I to leave I should promptly return. When will destiny be pleased to grant me rest upon my journey?" At times (*Esquivez*) he fears to be lured by the love of this world, because of his presentiment that he must so soon leave it, and in the same poem he speaks of his "infinite homesickness for the other world; his love of night (*Laus Noctis*) may be due to the fact that it most suggests the death he often longs for; for night to him, like death, is the door to a deeper life; at times, with a sort of masochistic touch (*Oración*) he prefers torment to rest, suffering to ennui; he knows the age-old struggle between the spirit and the flesh, yet cannot resolve it; he recommends a volume of Leopardi's poems with the lines that it will teach the recipient

> The wealth of greatness that is girt by grief
> The infinite vanity of everything.

Sending his photograph to the same friend he sees in his own features "the indifference of one who yearns for nothing, or the corporeal fatigue of the brute." *Pax*

Animae, one of his numerous sonnets (a form he manip-
ulated with great skill and uncommon beauty of form and
imagery) belies its title, which is the mocking grin of the
skull; his sonnet to his mother (which is really to himself)
represents her as dying at his birth,—a symbol of the
wretched life he is to lead; his spiritual landscape (*Paisaje
Espiritual*), like his *Nostalgias,* reveals a soul fearful alike
of life or death; more than once he displays the neurotic's
desire to escape from the world (*Tras un Enfermedad*);
everywhere, even in the eyes of his beloved, whom, characteristically enough, he has never known, he sees lurking
death,—"el terror invincible de la muerte." Who, after
reading Darío's autobiography, for example, can fail to
see in this mental phenomenon not the affectation of an
artist, but the agonies of a man transformed into art? It
is more than mere paradox to say that Casal's death, like
that of other poets of the same movement, before him and
after, proves his life. In the eight lines of his *Flores* he
runs the gamut from faith to blasphemy: "My heart was
an alabastrine vase, where grew in fragrant solitude, under the purest gleam of a star, a white lily,—prayer.
Withered is this flower of delicate perfume, like a virgin
consumed by anæmia. Today in my heart a purple rose-
bay grows,—blasphemy." Surely this part of his work
is decadentism of a refined type and in a non-depreciatory
sense; but decadentism none the less.

Like a true son of Cuba, Casal could not, with all the
exoticism that transformed his daily surroundings into a
Japanese world-in-little, keep his oar out of the political
waters. The poet of morbid presentiments was, in his
strange life, amid his evocations of ancient Greece and

modern France, a man of his day who clashed with official-
dom because of the nature of some writings. Had he
lived longer, this more public phase of his character might
have developed; such was the case with his friend and
admirer Darío, on the occasion of whose departure after
a visit to Cuba he penned his *Páginas de Vida*, a poem that
affords an insight into both poets. Casal pictures the deck
of the ancient vessel on which he is told the tale of the
other poet's life. The Darío he represents, though essentially the real man, appears somewhat over-optimistic, perhaps in contrast to Casal's black pessimism.

> ¡Ignea columna sigue mi paso cierto!
> ¡Salvadora creencia mi ánimo salva!
> Yo sé que tras las olas me aguarda el puerto!
> Yo sé que tras la noche surgirá el alba.
>
> Si hubiéramos más tiempo juntos vivido,
> No nos fuera la ausencia tan dolorosa.
> ¡Tu cultivas tus males, yo el mío olvido!
> ¡Tu lo ves todo en negro, yo todo en rosa!

It may be true that Casal saw everything in its dark aspect;
but certainly Darío's glasses were not always rose-colored!

Casal was an ultra-refined soul who sought escape from
life in beauty; the quality of refinement he shared with
more than one other spiritual contemporary. There may
have been an element of imitation in this hyper-æstheticism,
as there surely was of inadaptability to the environment,
but it should be recalled that we reveal ourselves often as
much in what we imitate as in what we originate. If lit-
terary influence consisted of mere imitation, art would be
an endless mirroring of primitive models; even in imita-

tion there is selection of a sort, and that is preferable to stagnant acceptance of sterile "models."

4. José Asunción Silva

(1865–1896)

The position of Silva as a precursor is somewhat problematical. Some Spanish-Americans omit him from the list of forerunners, but none can deny the man's gifts or his influence. The verses of this great Colombian echo the malady of the century; futile questioning of fate and life, unalloyed by the faith that mitigates the sufferings of a Gutiérrez Nájera or a Darío; a deep sincerity that goes further than the suicidal monologue of the former, ending that life which he could neither control nor understand. With what persistence the thought of death haunts these modernists, who have so enriched life! Through the poems of Gutiérrez Nájera, through Silva, through Darío, through Julián del Casal, stalks the sombre shadow of Death,—not the romantic pose of morbid youth, for these men are deeply sincere.

Silva was born in Bogotá, the capital of Colombia; whatever benefit he might have derived from paternal inheritance was consumed in one of the frequent revolutions that still agitate Spanish-American politics. His regular instruction, which was of short and fragmentary nature, was added to by personal effort to understand the new ideas of the age. As the result of an early trip to Paris he was impressed with such poets as Mallarmé, Verlaine and Baudelaire (the latter of whom he seems to have placed above them all), at a time when Hugo absorbed the attention

of South-American youth.   The loss of a large portion of
Silva's poems during the wreck of *l'Amérique* off the Colombian coast in the year 1895 was a loss to literature as
well.   Among the manuscripts thus destroyed was a collection of *Cuentos Negros* (Black Tales) which, according
to testimony, were little known outside of the intimate
circles to which he had read them; there were also various
other prose works as well as almost the entire *Libros de
Versos*.   To the natural melancholy of the young poet was
added one stroke of misfortune after another.   A few days
after having written his marvellous bit of prose *De Sobremesa* (Table Talk), in which he seemed to breathe out his
aristocratic soul, he shot himself.

Miguel de Unamuno has summed up Silva's life in three
words: "Sufrir, soñar, cantar."   Thus succinctly does
he epitomize not only the life of Silva, but of a Darío, of a
Casal, who out of their sufferings spin the web of dreams
and distil the beauty of song.   In his *Psicopatía* (again
the neurotic note of the age) Silva, expressing the futility
of philosophy, has diagnosed his own case:

> Ese señor padece un mal muy raro,
> que ataca rara vez á las mujeres
> y pocas á los hombres . . . Hija mía!
> Sufre este mal: *pensar* . . . esa es la causa
> de su grave y sutil melancolía. . . .

That is Silva's ailment, expressed with an ironic humor
more characteristic of Gutiérrez Nájera than of Darío:
"A rare disease that rarely attacks women and infrequently,
men . . . *Thought* . . . that is the cause of his grave and
subtle melancholy."

Silva, in a sense, is the eternal child.   In his woes the
thoughts of childhood are his one consolation.   He has
sung, in *Infancia:*

> Infancia, valle ameno,
> de calma y de frescura bendecida
> donde es suave el rayo
> del sol que abraza el resto de la vida.
> ¡Comó es de santa tu innocencia pura,
> Cómo tus breves dichas transitorias,
> Cómo es de dulce en horas de amargura
> dirigir al pasado la mirada
> y evocar tus memorias!

So, too, evoking the fairy tales of childhood, which
Gutiérrez Nájera was able to consider in so poetically
scientific a light, he finds them more substantial than science
and philosophy:

> cuentos más durables que las convicciones
> de graves filósofos y sabias escuelas,
> y que rodasteis con vuestras ficciones
> las cunas doradas de las bisabuelas.

May not much of his disappointment with love and life
be due to this unending childhood, which persisted in the
spirit even after it had departed from the flesh?   Everywhere the haunting note resounds.   His bride (in the beautiful poem *Nupcial*) hears death as well as hope in the
music that plays at her festivities.   His *Midnight Dreams*
(bearing the English title in the original) bring him visions
of hopes and joys that he has never known.   Voices from
the tomb call to him,—voices he has not heard for he
knows not how long.   Often it grieves him that the dead

should be so soon forgotten, as if already he reckoned himself among their number and made their complaint his
own. . . . The eternal quest is futile, he feels; he suffers
the nostalgia of everlasting darkness even as the moth seeks
the light that once gave it life, but now destroys it.

In a poem entitled ....?......... he asks the
stars why, if they live, they are silent, and why, if they
are dead, they give light. He despairs alike of his own
art (*La Voz de las Cosas*) and of his critics (*Un Poema*);
his *Lázarus*, four days after resurrection, wanders amid the
tombs in solitary grief, envying the departed. The poet,
in all he has written, has given us a spiritual autobiography which renders other details quite superfluous.

In common with the other innovators, Silva strove for
metrical freedom and the untrammeled expression of his
personality. He was born into surroundings in which the
routine view of art and criticism had long held sway;
against this his artistic nature rebelled. He possessed, in
as marked a degree as any of the precursors, a sense of
melody and form that naturally enough astonished, with
its literary and artistic originality and irreverence, the
pundits of the past.

As examples of technical liberty, we may select the simple, affecting *Los Maderos de San Juan*, the *Luz de Luna*,
the *Día de Defuntos* and the popular *Nocturnos*. Others
may view in such pieces as these a technical skill worthy of
admiration in itself. To me (and I confess freely, that of
the various modernist precursors Gutiérrez Nájera and
Silva are my favorite poets) the metrical element is an indissoluble one. It may be convenient for critics to speak
of form and content; art knows only the beautiful whole.

The first of the poems named above is an amplification
of a nursery rhyme,—one of the evocations of a childhood
that the poet never outgrew completely. The changing
metre corresponds to a definite change in thought; the very
rhythm, with its occasional abruptness, conveys the rocking
of the child upon the grandmother's weary knees. Child
and grandmother! For, to Silva, how evanescent is the
age between! Like the swaying child, so his poetry rocks
between infancy and death. . . .

Both *Luz de Luna* and *Día de Defuntos* are characterized
by that melancholy mood of Silva's in which he comments
upon life's forgetfulness of the dead. Here again the
pulse of the poem, even as of our own blood, changes its
beat with the various emotions; the lines are nervous, immediately responsive, in their differing lengths, to the
poet's fancy. The *Día de Defuntos,* suggested by Poe's
The Bells, may be read after the English masterpiece without experiencing any discordant effect. Through the
sounds of the

> . . . campañas planideras
> que les hablan á los vivos
> de los muertos

in a poem that avails itself of a striking variety of plangent
metres he communicates his dominant pessimistic mood.
How quickly are the dead forgotten by the living! And
how strikingly Silva uses a single bell that resounds above
the chorus of the others,—the bell of irony and mocking
laughter, which rings out his own thoughts. It is in the
Nocturnos that Silva's metrical contributions may best be
studied. Here we have, for example, free metre, based

upon a rhythmic unit of four syllables, as in the opening
of the third Nocturne:

> Una noche,
> una noche toda llena de murmullos, de perfumes, y de músicas de
> alas;
> una noche
> en que ardían en la sombra nupcial y húmeda las luciérnagas
> fantásticas. . . .

He plays, too, with typography, seeking to obtain effects
of shadow by arrangement and repetition of lines; this,
however, is not an essential element in verse or prose, nor
is it an essential part of Silva's innovations.

Every true poet is an excellent writer of prose, wrote
Darío in his essay upon the aristocratic poet Jean Moréas.
This is noticeably true in the case of the modernistas, old
and new,—if modernists may ever grow old!   The prose
of Silva is pregnant with subtle rhythms; it glows with intensity, and is saturated with that same bitterness, that
same ceaseless inquiry, that same haunting melancholy
which inform his poetry.

Read this line from his *De Sobremesa*, not only for its
insight into the poet, but for its vehement expression of in-
cipient madness:

"Un cultivo intelectual emprendido sin método y con
locas pretensiones al universalismo, un cultivo intelectual
que ha venido a parar en la falta de toda fé, en la burla
de toda valla humana, en un ardiente curiosidad de la
mal, en el deseo de hacer todas las experiencies de la
vida. . . ."   This is the very pulse of scornful renunciation.   *De Sobremesa* is one of the most striking pieces of
neurotic self-revelation in modernist letters.

"An intellectual cultivation undertaken without method and with mad pretensions to universalism,—an intellectual cultivation that has led to a complete abandonment of faith, to the jesting scorn of all human effort, to a burning curiosity of evil, to the desire of tasting all the possible experiences of life. . . ." Such is the pass to which Silva brought himself, face to face with lunacy, which said to him, "I am thine; thou art mine; I am madness." And in a last burst of self-expression that resolves upon a chord of self-rejection: "Mad? . . . And why not? Thus died Baudelaire, the greatest poet of the last fifty years for all truly lettered folk; thus died Maupassant. . . . Then why should you not die thus, poor degenerate who abused everything, who dreamed of ruling over art, of mastering science, all knowledge, and of draining all the glasses into which Life pours its supreme intoxication?" And thus died Silva, by a bullet from his own hand.

By a strange coincidence, the life of Baudelaire was so similar to that of this great Colombian admirer, that Antonio Gómez Restrepo (in his *Parnaso Colombiano*) found it possible to apply to Silva, the words of Andrés Suares indited to Baudelaire: "He was fond of rare dishes and rare books, of the stars of the Orient and of old wines, of ultramodern music and of editions that were impossible to locate. Everything about him was artistic: his hair, of blackest silk; his glance, glittering and piercing; his forehead and his neck of admirable shape and feminine whiteness; his noble acts. He seemed to be a Persian or an Arabian prince. At thirty he was ruined completely: he then sank into the bitter sadness of those who, not having been born into poverty, are forced to compare in every sensation the excellency of their desires and the ignominy of reality.   As a voluptuary, he was of those who nourish and caress their desires, and causing them to grow inordinately, not only lose the illusion of realilty, but reject it.   The desire of such as these lives upon dreams, and only dreams content them.   A fearful contentment, which exhausts one more than orgies.   He lived only upon imagination, and this used up his nerves and exhausted his strength.   In him, the flesh was cerebral."

The same Gómez Restrepo, in his *La Literatura Colombiana* (*Revue Hispanique*, XLIII, 103, pp. 185) says that if Silva had lived longer he would probably have disputed with Darío the scepter of modernist poetry not only in America but in Spain.

5. *Salvador Díaz Mirón*

(1853–)

Although Díaz Mirón is not generally mentioned as a precursor of modernism, for more reasons than one he is entitled to consideration with the forerunners.   His own long life spans the beginnings, the hey-day, and the later transformations of the epoch; his intensely personal manner, particularly that of the earlier poems which later, in a mistaken fervor of perfection, he disowned, affected not only the Darío of *Azul*, but Chocano of the proud gesture and the sonorous, bardic strophes.   How different is that early Díaz Mirón, however, from the poet of *Lascas*,— that collection of polished, chiselled, artfully wrought marble chips in which the exacting artist gathered the few products that he stamped definitely with his own approval.

The poet of *Lascas* is not that writer of quatrains whose verses Darío (in a well-known sonnet from *Azul*) compared to a four yoked chariot drawn by wild eagles who love the tempest and the ocean. Nor did this "son of the New World" let humanity for long hear the pomp of his "lyric hymns which triumphantly salute liberty." No; the Díaz Mirón of this style,—the "fireater," as he has been called (for did not his mind, in the words of the younger poet, have craters and eject lavas?)—underwent a change of poetic outlook; his mind turned to the rigor of harsh self-discipline; it was no longer the crater of a volcano, but the atelier of an Olympic sculptor, hewing statues from mountains of marble. . . .

The life of the poet leads us to such varied places as prison cells (which, it would seem, form part of the necessary training of a Spanish-American writer), the tribune of the council chamber, where his fiery oratory wins him new admirers, and to the directorship of *El Imparcial* (1913–14). Prison, politics, press, poetry,—the four steeds that so often we discover guiding the rolling chariot of Spanish-American writers.

Perhaps as famous a poem as Díaz Mirón ever penned is his youthful *A Gloria*, which for years was widely known and cherished in the anthology of Spanish America's poetic heart. And little wonder. For it spoke the language of defiant self-assertion, couched in the flamboyant quatrains that Díaz Mirón made peculiarly his own. Like Darío after him, the poet in his early efforts sang the great god Hugo,—Hugo, the perennial fountain-head of so many "new" orientations of poesy, whose influence is so potent even in the novel of today, as confessed by his worshipper

Blasco Ibáñez.   Not the Hugo of *Les Contemplations*, it has been pointed out, but the Hugo of *Les Chatiments*, whom Chocano studied to good advantage.

Read a few lines from *A Gloria*; listen, and see if you catch more than a strain of Chocano's *Blasón*, and his other poems of arrogant defiance.

> No intentes convencerme de torpeza
> Con los delirios de tu mente loca!
> Mi razón es al par luz y firmeza,
> Firmeza y luz como el cristal de roca!
>
> Semejante al nocturno peregrino,
> Mi esperanza inmortal no mira al suelo.
> No viendo más que sombra en mi camino,
> Sólo contempla el esplendor del cielo!
> —
> Erguido bajo el golpe en la porfía,
> Me siento superior á la victoria.
> Tengo fé en mi: la adversidad podría
> Quitarme el triunfo, pero no la gloria!
>
> ¡Deja que me persigan los abyectos!
> Quiero atraer la envidia aunque me abrume!
> La flor en que se posen los insectos
> es rica de matiz y de perfume.
> —
> ¡Alumbrar es arder!—Estro encendido
> Será el fuego voraz que me consuma!
> La perla brota del molusco herido
> y Venus nace de la amarga espuma!
> —
> Confórmate, mujer!—Hemos venido
> A este valle de lágrimas que abate,
> Tu, como la paloma, para el nido,
> Y yo, como el león, para el combate.

It has been said that all of the early Díaz Mirón is in this poem. Note the aptness of the imagery: "My reason is at once light and firmness, firmness and light, like the rock crystal!" . . . "There are plumages that cross the swamp and are not stained," he proclaims in a quatrain not here quoted. "Such plumage is mine!" Note, too, the strikingly epigrammatic character of the utterances: "Adversity may cheat me of triumph, but not of glory!" "The pearl blossoms from the wounded mollusc, and Venus is born of the bitter foam!" Such a type of poetry may lack the coherence and the climax of higher flights, being in reality a succession of inorganic, if inspiring, utterances. Yet there is the ruddy vitality of youth in its veins, with just a touch of Nietzscheism in the final quatrain.

Urbina has given us an excellent personal view of this solitary figure in Hispano-American letters. "He is still alive, expatriated, ill, sad,—this man whose arrogant youth has resemblance and affinity to the ancient heroes, in the flight of his passion as in the nobility of his deeds. An exceptional being, out of the chivalric legends, gifted with a temperament ever ready for action as is his intelligence for perception. He is of those who are loved and feared. He seems an artist of the Renaissance. He could endure comparison with the Italian cinquecentistas,—with Leonardo for the variety of his learning; with Benvenuto for the impulse to daring. In the parliamentary tribune and the political harangue he revealed his tempestuous, flashing eloquence; when in the council chamber he raised his tremulous right hand, it seemed that, like the Olympic god, he released the thunderbolt." Not only Chocano took his first inspiration from this nervous, impassioned orator of the frail body, the haughty countenance, the dark eyes and the flowing mane. The Spaniard Villaespesa, too, in a recent visit to Mexico, confessed that he received his initial poetic impulses from the author of *A Gloria.*

The change that so greatly affected Díaz Mirón's poetic outlook seems to have affected his output as well. His new conception of technique is perhaps as rigorous a program as any poet ever devised—and followed. I sometimes wonder whether non-Latins can really appreciate the seemingly exaggerated attention paid by Spanish-American poets to the matter of metric structure. Our own tradition is so much freer, so rich in precept and example, that often the Spanish preoccupation appears overdone. But since we have not been brought up on Academic prescriptions, with regular places assigned to accents, cæsuras and all the other high-sounding trappings that would embalm verbal beauty, we are prevented, not only by the difference in language, but also that in tradition, from entering intimately into this detail of the poet's task. Díaz Mirón now refuses, for example, to rhyme two adjectives, shuns articles in favor of a Latinized phrase, avoids hiatus and in general holds up to his poetry a most difficult conception of dissonance and harmony.

This phase of his labors, partly shown in the remarkable collection *Lascas,* represents the opposite of such a poetic canon of spontaneity as we have noticed in Martí. Díaz Mirón, indeed, has with his later work induced comparison with the methods of Luis de Góngora. His preoccupation with sculptural perfection and an impersonality utterly at variance with his initial verses, ally him to the Parnassians. Yet, since somewhat of our old self always remains, the early Díaz Mirón is discernible beneath the "statuary tunic." The volcanic lava has cooled, but one may divine its crateral origin. So, for example, the *Ecce Homo* in *Lascas*, proclaims a poetic art that recognizes humanity's deeper response to sorrow than to joy, and an intention to sing that response in verses which shun the subtle jongleur's intense, crude grace,—to adjust to truth his calculated taste, under the gloomy brush and the tragic etching needle.

> A la verdad adjusto
> el calculado gusto
> bajo el pincel adusto
> y el trágico buril

The *Epístola Jocoseria* of the same collection sings likewise a sort of ars poetica that seeks to combine grace and power. A touch of the old personality is there:

> En mi el cosmos íntima señales
> Y es un haz de impresiones mentales.
>
> Para mi, por virtud de objetivo,
> todo existe segun lo percibo.
> Y el tamiz proporciona elemento
> propio y lirico al gayo talento,
> Y es quien pone caracter y timbre,
> Novedad y valor a la urdimbre.

Our impassioned seeker after the exact expression may, as the above lines show, be not a little Symbolistic as well.

"After the publication of *Lascas*," writes José Juan Tablada, one of the foremost Mexican propagandists of the French spirit in Hispano-American letters, "—that marvellous book whose perfection of form has neither precedent nor continuation in Castilian, the poet has continued his glorious pilgrimage upon other paths." Such superlative judgments are common in Hispano-American criticism; they are indicative not only of a healthy enthusiasm for beautiful self-expression, but of a passionate nature that has received a more conventional but deeper literary training than our own average students and critics. With the later work of Díaz Mirón we are not here concerned; his general line of development has been indicated, however; his chastened technique, his new æsthetics, his aversion to appearing in the periodicals, his proud isolation, have all conspired to obscure his importance. As a precursor he was a potent influence upon the young Darío; as the survivor of the great modernist he was hailed by more than one as his legitimate successor.

Such are some of the modernist influences that the chief poetic figure—Darío—breathed as he approached adulthood. As we shall see in the study devoted to him, he was by nature suited to drink in the inspiration of the age,—an intellectual turmoil that for all its artificiality possessed a core of sincerity; that for all its exoticism, its neo-Hellenism, its eighteenth-century-ism, possessed a core of contemporaneity; that for all its early Teutonic inspiration, (which filtered in through Bécquer and translations from Heine, and likewise through the Germanic philosophic backgrounds of the Gallic innovators) and its fulsome worship of French art, possessed a core of Hispanism.

Darío's great historic significance consists in his having absorbed a multitude of conflicting elements and unified them in labors that reveal a steady progress toward self-conquest and self-proclamation. The history of modernism, with his appearance, becomes largely a matter of his biography. As rapidly as new influences appear, he assimilates them, inspired and inspiring in turn.

Before approaching the salient personalities of the studies that follow, let us glance at some later phases of modernism, which has really not so much run its course as altered, restrained and firmly redirected it.

III

LATER PHASES OF MODERNISM

1. New Orientations

By the year 1898 the times were ripe for the introduction of the modernist movement into Spain; the war with the United States and its disastrous outcome had produced among certain of the younger writers a spirit of pessimism that assumed the extremes of dissatisfaction with the native land. They, too, like their brothers across the Atlantic, looked to outside suggestion, and although there was a possible taint of denationalization in their views (nor is this always a taint) their attitude had the effect of bringing Spain into closer touch with Europe and the rest of the world. Even so prejudiced an enemy of modernism as Cejador y Frauca admits that its effects, in Spain, were upon the whole beneficial. This dominantly French influence entered Spain from Spanish America rather than from across the borders directly; history thus reversed itself, for early French influences entered Spanish America through Spain. The views of Cejador y Frauca upon modernism itself, which are representative of a large body of Spanish thought, are rather preceptive, to say the least. To him the France that produced it is a decadent, positivist, effeminate France; a France eager for novelty for novelty's sake; he holds Parnassianism up to scorn because it sacrifices matter to manner; he gives a horrible picture of the Decadent artist as a sort of nervous wreck whose various senses have become telescoped into a mass of sensory confusions; modernist literature appears to him not only effeminate, but erotomaniac, falsely mystic, psychiatric and what not else, and he approaches the limits of the ridiculous by quoting Marcel Reja, who in his *L'Art Chez les Fous* (a study of art among children and lunatics) discovers that mad art coincides with the art of the decadents! Symbolism becomes a mixture of romanticism and gongorism; a decadence of decadence. Modernism, which grows worse as the critic writes on, at last sinks to the level of the mere desire to attract. "This and nothing more, is modernism."

I believe this is a most erroneous manner of considering any movement. The epoch is an historical fact; it was not merely willed into existence; it produced extravagances that literature has known before modernism and that it will know long after. The amount of bad writing produced by any movement is always far in excess of the great, for the simple reason that writers, being human, perform but average work no matter what banner they labor under. A movement that produces a Darío in Spanish America and helps to shape a Baroja or a Benavente, a Jiménez or a Rueda in the old Spain, has performed its mission and may well claim its due on that score alone. The same Cejador y Frauca, in condemning the exoticism of the modernists (which owes not a little to a similar phenomenon among

the romanticists, and goes to show that we retain more than
a little of all things that we reject), forgets that this may be,
as well as a sign of neurotic unrest or affectation, a broad-
ening of the human spirit, an interpenetration of races too
long separated by the barriers of language and that prejudice which attaches to the unknown and the misunderstood.
From the very confusion of the early stages of modernism
a more homogenous world-view was destined to arise.   Dis-
solution, reformation, reintegration—this has been the
course of the movement in Spanish America, where, in its
later phases, as we shall soon see, the movement turned to
a closer consideration of contemporary affairs, to a sense
of continental solidarity, and a broad Americanism which
may not be the final step.   The early exoticism of the modernists is sure, sooner or later, to be transformed by this
growing Americanism into a genuine universality.   There
are distinct promises of this in Santos Chocano,[13] who refuses to be called merely the poet of America, a title which
was held to be unmerited by Darío.   Darío's glory, however, consists, among other things, in the fact that he was
too vast to be included by such a conception, even as was
our own so different poet, Whitman.   And when a critic
exclaims "The great stupidity of Rubén Darío, who might
have been a great American poet, and reduced himself to
the position of one more in the cortège of Parisian
metecos. . . ." I feel strongly that the stupidity was not
all on Darío's part, and that surely no man is prophet in
his own language!

   The very fact that so many cosmopolitan influences
played upon the modernists of this continent and abroad re-

[13] See the special chapter devoted to him.

veals the interpenetrating spirit of the age.   From foreign lands came the labors of d'Annunzio, Dickens, Poe, Whitman, Tolstoi, Ibsen, Brandes, Nietzsche, not to speak of the roll of Frenchmen.   And Valle-Inclán approaches a subtle truth when he declares that a renaissance is simply "the fecundation of national thought by foreign thought."   I can understand, even when I cannot sympathize with, laws against immigration.   But the application of laws against literary immigration on the grounds of a national literary exclusivism is a retrogressive force in letters.   We have spoken too much about nationalist art, forgetting that though the roots may lie in nationality and personality, the results, independent of school and nation, should overleap boundaries and enter the universal heart.   Such results have been attained by the modernists, in common with the great writers of all schools and of no schools; such results, if justification of a historic fact were necessary, justify modernism.

The new path of modernism tends in Spanish America to abandon early extravagances and to produce a genuinely continental product.   Chocano's glorification of *Alma América* (the title of one of his most significant collections, and a beautiful variation of the phrase alma mater), awoke a legitimate continental pride that had been dormant, rather than absent.   Nervo's well-known *Epitalamio* to Alfonso XIII is looked upon as having proclaimed a definite turning point in the history of the modernist movement, by the assertion of the former colonies' spiritual service to the Spanish king.   Read by the author in the Madrid Ateneo, on April 28, 1906, it told the youthful king that

> Sois rey
> aún, en cierto modo, de América, como antes.
> Rey, mientras que el idioma divino de Cervantes
> melifique los labios y cante en las canciones
> de diez y ocho Repúblicas y cincuenta millones
> de seres; mientras rija las almas y la mano
> el ideal austero del honor castellano.[14]

Nervo (1870–1919) carried on the potent French influences that have revivified Spanish poetry on both sides of the ocean, without becoming a victim to the less artistic forms of that renovation; like the new spirits of Spanish America, he had reached a stage where he recognized no arbitrary schools or rules in art; he had found himself and expressed his personality in poems that glow with a strange, new beauty.   Through a dazzling succession of literary labors he advanced to a point where he could write

> Yo no sé nada de literatura
> Ni de vocales atónicas o tónicas,
> ni de ritmos, medidas o cesura,
> ni de escuelas (comadres antagónicas),
> ni de malabarismos de estructura,
> de sistoles o diástoles eufónicas. . . .

A splendid independence, a wise ignorance, that may be purchased only at the price of so much slavery to the quest of beauty, so much study of its elusive structure!   "I know nothing of literature, nor of accented or unaccented vowels, nor of rhythms. . . ."   Nothing,—except what only the wise know how to forget!   And what a deep remark of

---

[14] The spirit of Nervo's verses is plainly present in Darío's much earlier poem *Al Rey Oscar* (in *Cantos de Vida y Esperanza*) and in Chocano's still earlier *Canto del Siglo*.

Darío's it was, when, in referring to Nervo's skill, he mentioned a "modernism—let us call it such, that benefited
only those who deserved it!"

"I was born," Nervo has told us, "in Tepic, a small city
on the Pacific coast (Mexico), on the 27th of August, 1870.
My real name should have been Ruiz de Nervo, but my
fathered shortened it.   His first name was Amado, and
he gave it to me.   Whereupon I became Amado Nervo, and
what appeared to be a pseudonym—which was what many
in America believed to be the case—and what was in any
event a rare combination, was of no little worth to my literary fortunes.   Who knows what might have been my fate
with the ancestral appellation of Ruiz de Nervo, or if I
had been called Pérez y Pérez (that name is, among the
Spaniards, as common as Smith in English).   I began to
write when I was a mere child, and on a certain occasion
my brother discovered the verses that I had furtively written; he read them to the family gathered about the dining
table.   I escaped to my corner.   My father frowned. . . .
For the rest, my mother, too, wrote verses, likewise furtively.   Her sex and her great griefs spared her in time,
and she died without knowing that she possessed talent.
. . . I have never had, nor have I, any particular tendency.   I write as I please. . . . I support only one school,
that of my deep and eternal sincerity.   I have written
innumerable bad things in prose and verse; and some good
ones; but I know which is which.   If I had been wealthy,
I would have written only the good ones, and in that case
perhaps there would be today only a little volume of my
writings—a book of conscientious art, free and proud.   It

was not to be! I was compelled to make a living in a country where almost nobody reads books and where the only form of diffusion was the periodical. Of all the things that grieve me, this is the greatest: the small, precious little book that my life did not permit me to write—the free and only book."

Nervo was early destined to follow the career of the churchman. Very soon, however, he broke away from the surroundings, although the influence remained with him for years afterward, becoming transformed into a penetrating mysticism. His struggles to achieve his ambitions were many and discouraging; the pattern of his career, which included travels in both hemispheres, was a checkered one indeed. From literary success in Mexico City he attained to reputation in Paris and Italy; he flitted from journalism to translating, poetry, tales, education, to diplomacy, and along the path of his wanderings he culled the flower of a variegated poesy. Profoundly affected by French influence, he did not permit it to rob him of his poetic self; he was possessed of an inquisitive mind that now shook him in his religious beliefs, introducing the canker-worm of doubt; now enticed him into bold conceptions that ranged freely in space and time, dwelling in dreams of superhumanity; yet, as one of his noted fellow-poets, Urbina, has put it, "his autumn is filled with roses." Much of his poetry possesses an ineffable tenderness, especially such as appears in the first part of his collection called *En Voz Baja* (In a Soft Voice). Not only are the thoughts such as may be spoken only in a soft, sweet voice, but the very hush of passionate confiding, the soft breath of airy wishes, the deep sense of holy silences, the poignant, haunting memories of a past suddenly evoked, rise like incense from its pages.

Nervo, in some of his aspects, possesses a lyric introspection that seems, by some fourth-dimensional gift of thought, to penetrate into lives we only half dream of living; he feels the feverish hurly-burly of modern life, yet is a man of his times and has faith in his age.   His comparisons are not only things of beauty, but conveyers of beauty as well. He is not the empty, if beautiful urn of so many Parnassians; he can fashion beautiful urns and fill them with intoxicating wine.

For an example of Nervo's poetry—and it is hardly necessary to add that an example or two cannot hope even to suggest the innumerable beauties of his varied productions—we may choose a notable and a noble poem which is of especial timeliness today, when the air is so peopled with modern Columbuses en route to new discoveries. *Pájaro Milagroso* (Miraculous Bird) was written in 1910, after a flight in an aëroplane.   To Nervo's soaring imagination (the unintentional pun possesses substance!), the aëroplane becomes a colossal white bird that realizes the dream of generations, reconquering for man, the fallen angel, the wings that he lost in his struggle with the gods.   I quote a few lines from the original to give an idea of its metric and stanzaic structure:

> Pájaro milagroso, colosal ave blanca
> que realizas el sueño de las generaciones;
> tu que reconquistaste para el angel caído
> las alas que perdiera luchando con los dioses;

pájaro milagroso, colosal ave blanca,
jamás mis ojos, hartos de avizorar el orbe,
se abrieron más que ahora para abarcar tu vuelo,
mojado por el llanto de las consolaciones.

At last, cries the poet, man has grown wings.

"Fathers who sought this anxiously, and died without beholding it—poets who for centuries dreamed of such gifts—lamentable Icaruses who provoked laughter,—today, over your tombs, there flies, buzzing, the miraculous bird of the snowy wings that crystallizes the dream of the ages. And your dead eyes open to behold it, and your dry bones are garlanded with flowers! Oh, God! I, who, tired of the sad and frivolous journey of life, longed for eternal night, today cry to Thee, 'More life, oh Lord, more life—that I may soar like an eagle over all vanities and beauties, winging above them in vast flight!' We poets have now a new Pegasus. And what a Pegasus, friends, does Jove return to us! Let a divine exultation flood our spirits, and a Te Deum Laudamus burst from our lips, and let old melancholies perish, strangled by virile hands! Let us live! Let us live! Nations, in vain do you wish to make a weapon out of that which is a sign of peace among peoples! Stain not the celestial bird with missions of war; it thrusts them aside; it was born for the message of friendship and sows kisses of peace among men!"

Four years later Nervo's buoyant hopes were for a moment dashed to earth by the outbreak of the world war. Only a short while ago the poet returned to the subject, to his poems and to his hopes. He had not lost faith in the miraculous bird; rather it had been strengthened. After the war he could behold visions of the nocturnal sky illumined by signs upon vast wings, bearing the legends: "Paris to New York," "London to Mexico," "Madrid to Buenos Aires." . . . "The aëroplane," he said, in the same article, "will give back to us the lap of night, the majesty of the forgotten stars . . . and it is already well known that the stars are pale and ardent instructors that teach us many things.[15] . . . They civilized the Chaldeans, the Egyptians and the Greeks, the Mahuas and the Mayas.   They have given back to many men, in the clear nights of the trenches, the feeling of eternity. . . . In them is our hope of salvation."   It takes a Spanish-American to be a poet even in his magazine contributions!

Miss Blackwell has made versions of some of Nervo's love poems; two of the best known follow.   Just before his death, a charming collection of his latest work was issued in Buenos Aires under the title *El Estanque de los Lotos* (The Lotus Pond).

TO LEONORA

Black as the wing of Mystery thine hair,
Dark as a "Never" where deep sorrow lies,
As a farewell, or as the words "Who knows?"
Yet is there something darker still—thine eyes!

Two musing wizards are those eyes of thine;
Sphinxes asleep in shadow in the South;
Two beautiful enigmas, wondrous fair;
Yet is there something fairer still—thy mouth!

Thy mouth! Ah, yes! Thy mouth, divinely formed
For love's expression and to be love's goal,

---

[15] Nervo was a student of astronomy.

Shaped for love's warm communion—thy young mouth!
Yet is there something better still—thy soul.

Thy soul, retiring, silent, brimming o'er
With pity and with tenderness, I deem
Deep as the ocean, the unsounded sea;
Yet is there something deeper still—thy dream!

EVOCATION

From the deep mystery of the past I called her,
Where now a shade among the shades is she,
A ghost 'mid ghosts—and at my call she hastened,
Pushing the centuries aside for me.

The Laws of Time, astounded, followed after;
The Spirit of the Graves with mournful cry
Called to her, "Stop!"   Like unseen hooks, the Epochs
Grasped her rich, faded robes when she went by.

But all in vain!   She came, with red hair floating,
That red hair fragrant of eternity;
With wings loose hanging, clad like a chimera,
That strange queen, following my will, drew nigh.

I said to her, "Do you recall your promise
Made in the year One Thousand, to my bliss?"
"Remember, I am but a shade!"
                                "I know it."
"And I was mad."
                        "You promised me a kiss!"

"My kiss has by the chill of death been frozen;
Long has my life been hid in Time's eclipse."
"Queens do not break the word they once have given!"
'Twas thus I answered.   And she kissed my lips.

By no means has there been loss of personality among

the poets, but rather an increase that is mirrored by the tendency of the Republics to proclaim a literary autonomy not inconsistent with continental aspirations. Such sonnets as that by the most popular of living Mexican poets, Enrique González Martínez, in which the swan of Darío (overemphasized as the poet's heraldic bird, owing to Rodó's brilliant analysis of the *Prosas Profanas*), is sentenced to have its neck wrung and be replaced by the contemplative owl, indicate a more sober inspiration, yet one none the less modern. "Wring the neck of the swan with deceitful plumage," he counsels in a notable sonnet. "It merely parades its grace, but hears not the soul of things nor the voice of the landscape. Flee from every form and from every tongue that does not harmonize with the latent rhythm of profound life; adore life intensely, and let it understand your homage. Look upon the wise owl, how it spreads its wings from Olympus leaving the lap of Pallas, and rests its taciturn flight upon that tree. . . . It has not the grace of the swan, but its restless eye, peering into the dark, interprets the mysterious book of nocturnal silence."

Was it not Verlaine who began all this neck-twisting, in his *Art Poétique?* Do you recall the first line of the sixth quatrain? "Prends l'éloquence et tors-lui son cou!"

In the reaction of González Martínez against the swans of Darío may be discerned a double effect of the Mexican's milieu and his personality. This poet comes at a time when Mexico's need is for stern self-discipline, solid culture and widespread education, rather than for effete æstheticism and ultra refinement. The verses that he wrote as a child were probably of the same character as is produced by most gifted children; his training as a physician, however, with the necessary scientific application to concrete phenomena, must have had not a little to do with his substitution of the owl for the swan. Social need and a scientific discipline aptly merged with a poetic pantheism furnished the background for the physician-poet's new orientation of modernism.

He was born in 1871 in Guadalajara, the capital of the state of Jalisco, where he attended the Seminary. In 1893 he had won his physician's degree and was made an associate professor of physiology. For fifteen years he followed his calling in the State of Sinaloa, where he published his first four books. For a time he edited *Arte* with Sixto Osuna. The year 1911 saw him in Mexico City; here he founded the short-lived *Argos* (1912), and contributed editorially to *El Imparcial;* now, too, began his public career as President of the *Ateneo* (1912), Undersecretary of Instruction and Fine Arts for a short period (1913), professor of French literature in the *Escuela de Altos Estudios*, head of the literature and grammar department, and professor of Mexican Literature in the *Escuela Preparatoria*.

A host of contradictory influences have played upon the idol of young Mexico's poetry lovers. Lamartine, Poe, Baudelaire, Verlaine (the ubiquitous Verlaine!), Heredia, Francis Jammes, Samain. Yet here we find no morbidity, no dandyism, no ultra-refinement. Where other poets feel the passing nature of joy and cry out, admonishing mortals to "seize the day" ere it fly, González Martínez ("a melancholy optimist" de Icaza has termed him, in a paradoxical phrase that seems to sum up modern optimism) feels rather the transitory character of grief. He is what I may call an intellectual pantheist,—his absorption of nature is not the ingenuous immersion of the primitive soul into the sea of sights and sounds about him; it is the pantheism of a modern intellect that gazes at feeling through the glasses of reason, and having looked, throws the glasses away. . . . In all things, as he tells us in the beautiful poem *Busca En Todas Las Cosas*, from his collection *Los Senderos Ocultos*, he seeks a soul and a hidden meaning. The modernist poets are prodigal with poems upon their artistic creeds and practises. In this series of melodious quatrains González Martínez enlightens us upon his poetic outlook:

> Busca en todas las cosas un alma y un sentido
> Oculto; no te ciñes a la aparencia vana;
> Husmes, sigue el rastro de la verdad arcana
> Escudriñante el ojo y aguzado el oído.
>
> Ama todo lo grácil de la vida, la calma
> De la flor que se mece, el color, el paisaje;
> Ya sabrás poco á poco descifrar su lenguaje. . . .
> Oh, divino coloquio de las cosas y el alma!
>
> Hay en todo los seres una blanda sonrisa,
> Un dolor inefable ó un misterio sombrío
> ¿Sabes tu si son lágrimas las gotas de rocío?
> Sabes tu que secretos va cantando la brisa?

That is the secret of the poet's charm. His pantheism is as much wonder as worship; as much inquiry as implicit belief. As he has told us in *La Plegaría de la Noche en la Selva:* "Now I know it, now I have seen it with my restless eyes, oh infinite mystery of the nocturnal shadows! To my engrossed spirit you have shown the urn in which with jealous care you hoard your deepest secrets." If poets must have heraldic birds, if Poe must have his raven, Darío his swan, Verlaine his hieratic cat, González Martínez has his owl and night is his ambient,—not the *Tristissima Nox* of a Gutiérrez Nájera, but that night which unto night showeth knowledge.

To Miss Blackwell I am indebted for versions of some characteristic poems by González Martínez. These reveal the poet's mood of communion as well as his peculiarly contemporary pantheism. The first selection is one of the most popular of modern Mexican poems and almost at once found its way into the anthologies:

LIKE BROTHER AND SISTER

Like brother with dear sister, hand in hand,
We walk abroad and wander through the land.

The meadow's peace is flooded full tonight
Of white and radiant moonlight, shining bright.
So fair night's landscape 'neath the moon's clear beam,
Though it is real, it seems to be a dream.
Suddenly, from a corner of the way,
We hear a song. It seems a strange bird's lay,
Ne'er heard before, with mystic meaning rife,
Song of another world, another life.
"Oh, do you hear?" you ask, and fix on me
Eyes full of questions, dark with mystery.
So deep is night's sweet quiet that enrings them,
We hear our two hearts beating, quick and free.
"Fear not!" I answer. "Songs by night there be
That we may hear, but never know who sings them."

Like brother with dear sister, hand in hand,
We walk abroad and roam across the land.

Kissed by the breeze of night that wanders wide,
The waters of the neighboring pool delight,
And bathed within the waves a star has birth,
A swan its neck outstretches, calm and slow,
Like a white serpent 'neath the moon's pale glow,
That from an alabaster egg comes forth.
While gazing on the water silently,
You feel as 'twere a flitting butterfly
Grazing your neck—the thrill of some desire
That passes like a wave—the sudden fire
And shiver, the contraction light and fine
Of a warm kiss, as if it might be mine.
Lifting to me a face of timid fear
You murmur, trembling, "Did you kiss me, dear?"
Your small hand presses mine. Then, murmuring low,
"Ah, know you not?" I whisper in your ear,
"Who gives those kisses you will never know,
Nor even if they be real kisses, dear!"

Like brother with dear sister, hand in hand,
We walk abroad and wander through the land.

In giddy faintness, 'mid the mystic night,
Your face you lean upon my breast, and feel
A burning teardrop, falling from above,
In silence o'er your languid forehead steal.
Your dreamy eyes you fasten on me, sighing,
And ask me very gently, "Are you crying?"
"Mine eyes are dry. Look in their depths and see!
But in the fields when darkness overspreads them,
Remember there are tears that fall by night,"
I say, "of which we ne'er shall know who sheds them!"

The two poems that follow are a delicate variation of a
similar mood; note the attitude of wonder in the first, as well
as the sense of repose in both.

A HIDDEN SPRING

Within the shadowy bowl of mossy valleys,
Afar from noise, you come forth timidly,
Singing a strange and secret melody,
With silvery dropping, where your clear stream sallies.

No wanton fauns in brutal hunting bold
Have muddied you, or heard your voice that sings;
You know not even of what far-off springs
The unseen veins created you of old.

May rural gods preserve your lonely peace!
Still may the sighing leaves, the sobbing breeze,
Down the low murmurs of your scanty flow!
Forgive me that my momentary glance
Of your unknown existence learned by chance;
And hence, with noiseless footsteps, let me go!

TO A STONE BY THE WAYSIDE

O mossy stone, thou pillow small and hard
Where my brow rested, 'neath the starlight's gleam,
Where, as my weak flesh slept, my life soared up!
I give thee thanks for giving me a dream.

The gray grass gleamed like silver fair, bedewed
By a fresh-fallen shower with many a tear.
A bird upon the bough his music sighed
Beneath the twilight, hueless, thin and clear.

Yearning, I followed evening's concert sweet.
The shining ladder by a star-beam given
I climbed, with eyes fast closed but heart awake,
And ascended to the heights of heaven.

Like Jacob, there the marvel I beheld.
That in a dream prophetic glowed and burned.

In the brief space for which my sleep endured,
I sailed a sea, and to the shore returned.

O mossy stone, thou pillow small and hard!
Thou didst receive, beneath the starlight's gleam,
My aimless longing, my sad weariness;
I give thee thanks for giving me a dream.

His soul is quiveringly responsive to nature's every mood, which is his own.

Sometimes a leaf that flutters in the air,
Torn from the treetops by the breezes' strife,
A weeping of clear waters flowing by,
A nightingale's rich song, disturb my life.

And soft, sweet languors, ecstasies supreme,
Timid and far away, come back to me.
That star and I, we know each other well;
Brothers to me are yonder flower and tree.

My spirit, entering into grief's abyss,
Dives to the farthest bottom, without fear.
To me 'tis like a deep, mysterious book;
Letter by letter I can read it clear.

A subtle atmosphere, a mournful breeze,
Make my tears flow in silence, running free,
And I am like a note of that sad song
Chanted by all things, whatsoe'er they be.

Delirious fancies in a throng press near—
Hallucination, or insanity?—
The lilies' souls to me their kisses give,
The passing clouds all greet me, floating by.

Divine Communion! for a fleeting space
My senses waken to a sharpness rare.

I know what you are murmuring, shining fount!
I know what you are saying, wandering air!

I loose myself from all things, free myself
To live a new life—and I should not say
If I through all things am diffused abroad,
Or all come into me, and with me stay.

But all things flee me, and my soul takes flight
On heavy wings, 'mid faint and chilly breezes,
In an aloofness inconsolable,
Through solitude which terrifies and freezes.

Therefore, amid my pangs of loneliness,
The while my senses sleep, I bend mine ear,
O Nature, to receive thy lightest words—
I tremble at each murmur that I hear.

And that is why a falling, fluttering leaf,
Torn from the tree tops by the breezes' strife,
A tear of limpid water flowing by,
A nightingale's rich song, disturb my life.

González Martínez, indeed, is a strange union of the
social spirit and the lonely contemplator of the universe.
His loneliness is not, however, the seclusion of the hermit
fleeing mankind, as of the spirit in advance of his fellows.
"Genius," said Martí, "is simply anticipation; it foresees
in detail what others do not behold even in outline, and as
the rest do not see what the genius sees, it regards him with
amazement, wearies of his splendor and persistency and
leaves him to feed upon himself, to suffer." Something
of this sense of isolation is in González Martínez's "Sower
of Stars":

Thou shalt pass by, and men will say, "What pathway does he
    follow,
Lo, the somnambulist?"   But thou, unheeding murmurs vain,
Wilt go thy way, thy linen robe upon the air out-floating,
Thy robe of linen whitened with pride and with disdain.

Few, few will bear thee company—souls made of dreams and
    visions;
And when the forest's end is reached, and steeper grows the track,
They will behold the wall of rock that rises huge before them,
And they will say with terror, "Let us wait till he comes back."

And all alone thou wilt ascend the high and crannied pathways,
And soon the strange procession of the landscapes will file by,
And all alone it shall be thine to part the cloudy curtains,
There where the lofty summits kiss the splendors of the sky.

Upon some night of moonlight faint, and sad, mysterious shadows,
Thou wilt come downward slowly, descending from the height,
Holding thine hands up, laden full, and, with a giver's gesture,
Sprinkling around thee, one by one, bright roses made of light.

And men, absorbed, will gaze upon the brightness of thy foot-
    prints,
And, many-voiced, that multitude will raise a joyful cry:
"He is a thief of stars!"   And then thy generous hand forever
Will keep on scattering through life the stars from out the sky.

Is it strange, then, that he should have his moments of
temptation to climb up his ivory tower and renounce the
world?   This is the spirit of *The Castle.*

> I built my castle on a summit high,
> One of those peaks where eagles love to nest.
> One window I left wide toward life's unrest;
> The sounds, as of the far sea, rise and die.

There I shut up my dreams, beneath the sky—
Poor wandering caravan that haunts my breast.
Cloud girt, like some old mountain's hoary crest,
That far, strange stronghold greets the gazer's eye.

My dreams wait there till I shall close the door.
They will behold me from my home of yore
Cross the still halls, to be their guest for aye.
Latching the doors, the bolts I shall let fall,
And in the moat that girds the castle wall
Some night shall proudly cast the keys away.

"The thing which hath been, it is that which shall be;
and that which is done is that which shall be done; and
there is no new thing under the sun." Thus spake the
Preacher. But then, was it not Paul in his second epistle
to the Corinthians who said that "old things are passed
away; behold, all things are become new"? Between the
two statements might be placed all the battles that are forever being waged around the newest of the new standards
in art. "Newness," after all, is a matter of spirit rather
than of chronology. The unimaginative poetaster of today
who shrieks his little theories and seeks to exemplify them
in chopped lines that are neither literary fish nor flesh, is
ancient even as he writes, while the great authors of all time
are freshly new because true to something more durable
than a love of novelty for novelty's sake. Nothing ages so
quickly as novelty. This, however, is no reason for condemning an entire movement, for the new *spirit* is always
right, unless progress is to resolve into classic stagnation.
A Rémy de Gourmont may say that "the new is always good
because it is new," and a Villergas that "the good is not
new and the new is not good"; both, in their excessive ad-

herence to a school rather than to an idea, over-emphasize the point; above all the rivalries of school and precept (often merely verbal) there is a kinship among all true poets and creators. That modern view which tends to break away from schools, that inherent unity between the "new" and the "old," is deeply felt and effectively expressed by González Martínez in his sonnet *The Poets, Tomorrow.* . . . ,wherein he sings the same eternal questioning under different forms.

Tomorrow the poets will sing a divine verse that we of today cannot achieve; new constellations will reveal, with a new trembling, a different destiny to their restless souls. Tomorrow the poets will follow their road, absorbed in a new and strange blossoming, and on hearing our song, will cast to the winds our outworn illusion. And all will be useless, and all will be vain; the task will remain forever—the same secret and the same darkness within the heart. And before the eternal shadow that rises and falls they will pick up from the dust the abandoned lyre and sing with it our selfsame song.

Extremes meet. In such a beautiful sonnet as this is in the original, it seems that the new and the old join in a golden circle. Great art is neither old nor new; it is ageless.[16]

2. *"Literary Americanism"*

The growing national literary consciousness of the Span-

[16] A fuller treatment of modernism should include such widely admired spirits as Leopoldo Lugones and Leopoldo Díaz (Argentina), Guillermo Valencia (Colombia), Ricardo Jaimes Freyre (Bolivia), and Julio Herrera y Reissig (Uruguay) among the poets, as well as Francisco García Calderón (Peru) in whom many see the logical continuator of Rodó, and Manuel Díaz Rodríguez (Venezuela), a novelist and essayist of outstanding merit. I shall deal with these and others in a forthcoming volume.

ish-American republics, which early appeared, may be shown by two extracts from Mexican writers; the attitude is important as leading up to the natural evolution of a continental consciousness, now strongly evident in the labors of a Blanco-Fombona, a García Calderón, a Rodó.

Says Justo Sierra, the noted Mexican, in his study upon Manuel Gutiérrez Nájera: "No people, engendered by another in the plenitude of its culture, and to whom there have been perforce transmitted language, customs and religion, has ever been able to create an intellectual or literary personality together with its political personality; this has been, whenever it occurred, the slow work of time and circumstance. To tell us American sons of Spain that our rational literature has not yet appeared hardly smacks of good criticism. Does the illustrious Academician (Sierra is replying to the reproach of Menéndez y Pelayo directed to the new Mexican poets for their intense devotion to later French literature) believe that the history of our literature does not reveal an evolution toward a certain characteristic form,—one which singles the Mexican group out from all those who speak Spanish? Yes, there has indeed been an evolution, and assimilation was necessary to that evolution; at first, imitation without selection; then, imitation by selecting, and reproducing the model; and this is what is called assimilation, which is what we have gone through. And whom could we imitate? The Spanish pseudo-classicism of the beginnings of the (nineteenth) century? That was an imitation of the French. The Spanish Romanticism of the second third of the century? That, too, was imitation of the French. Nevertheless, we imitated them; Quintano and Gallegos, the Duque de Rivas and García Gutiérrez, Espronceda and Zorrilla,—these were our father's masters."

This line of reasoning has been further developed by another Mexican, in a recent book dedicated to the author of the lines just quoted.[17]

From the very beginnings of his investigations into Mexican letters, the poet Urbina tells us, he was assailed by the old plaint that Mexican literature, and in general all Hispano-American literary production, was but a reflexion of Peninsular letters, and was as yet unable to sustain itself; that they were late in development, vague in physiognomy, and being incapable of creation, had recourse to imitation, following the changes of literary style in Spain, becoming a shadow of that body,—the echo of that voice.   He does not deny the element of truth in this old notion; "the Spanish language is the sole form that has given us, and will give, a literary personality in the universe of ideas"; to speak Spanish is, in a certain manner, to think and feel in Spanish moulds.   Yet the very idea of transplantation connotes modification, circumstantial alteration, variation from the primal model; he sees that the mixture of the natives and the conquistador has produced a Mexican type; anthropological investigation shows that the bodily structure of the Mexican differs from the Spanish type as much as from that of the primitive American.   "Physiologically we are neither one nor the other; we are a well differentiated ethnic type, partaking of the nature of both progenitory races.   And one and the other strive to coexist, to survive in our organism." Undoubtedly, is Urbina's conclusion, there has been a psychological change commensurate with the physiological,—

[17] *La Vida Literaria de México.* Luis G. Urbina. Madrid. 1917.

a change to be noted not only in literature (for nature does not recognize our classifications of human activity) but in such pursuits as architecture and its fluid sister, music. Mexico's particular contribution in the spiritual world of Spanish speech is a certain all-pervading melancholy. "To the Sancho-Panzan jollity and the Quixotic delirium there is added in our hearts the sadness of the Indian, the ancestral submissiveness of the subject, the gentleness of the aborigine. And if we are Mexicans in life, we are Mexicans in speech, in dreams and in song."

The continental aspirations known by the name Americanism (since the term America to Spanish Americans denotes only their portion of the western hemisphere) are more or less bound up (as is the poetry of the politico-modernist writing) with a fear of the United States as possible aggressor. There is no advantage in blinking the fact that while our attitude has been one of indifference, the Spanish-American position has on the whole been hostile. Spanish America, judging from its literary representatives, looks upon the United States as inferior to itself in culture, and has preferred to model itself upon France. At best (always speaking generally) we are in their eyes as yet too engrossed in material ambitions to give attention to spiritual considerations; at worst, we are an intriguing nation that despoiled Mexico of Texas and California, despoiled Spain of Cuba, despoiled Colombia of Panama,[18] and who now, under the shield of the Monroe Doctrine and

[18] Prof. J. D. M. Ford of Harvard, in his recent *Main Currents of Spanish Literature* (chapter on "Spanish-American Literature") properly indicates that not our nation, but certain politicians, are here responsible. Unfortunately, the political and economic interests they represent are still powerful.

an alleged Pan-Americanism, cherish imperialistic designs upon the entire southern continent. It is unnecessary to dwell upon these matters in a book of primarily literary appeal, except that Spanish-American letters are so deeply tinged with the political (and even economic) hue that these opinions are certain to appear in some of the best poems that have been written in Spanish on this side of the Atlantic. To be sure, there is a tendency to modify such an extreme view; it would be saying too much to assert that it is making great headway as yet. Not only this, but our neighbor critics of the south recognize in the new Hispano-American literary and cultural movement a force for general progress; their proposed literary, continental solidarity is but a phase of the politico-economic unity to which more than one of their leaders aspire.

The general trend of the all-American movement is in the first place eclectic in nature; that is an inevitable result of the age-spirit,—the one possible position for creators of strong personality plunged into the whirlpool of kaleidoscopic modernity. The artist, whether he believe it or not, is eclectic.from the very nature of that selection which lies at the bottom of art. Self-made men and self-made literatures are alike contradictions in terms; therein lies the fallacy of "schools" in art, as of the narrow conception of "nationalism" in literature and music, for example. Modernism, which in its restrictive sense has passed into history, still persists in its effects; even as it proceeded from antagonistic elements like Parnassianism and Symbolism, it has produced a fusion of the best in Classicism and Romanticism. The new writers reserve the privilege (and exercise it!) of absorbing all the "isms" that float in the literary ambient and turning them to advantage for an autonomous product. Such is "literary Americanism" that is at present in its early stages. The purely national, while by no means overlooked, is relegated to a secondary position; and here, not even critics who insist upon the national note in all literary products may with validity object to the larger vision that seeks to merge the various republics into a common continental voice. For a common history, a common languge, a common problem and common aspirations naturally seek a common art.

It has been questioned whether the term literature may be properly applied to the letters of Spanish America. It may be noted in passing that Coester does not call his book a history of Spanish-American literature, but a literary history of Spanish America. He seems to have adopted the view of Bartolome Mitre, the famous Argentine poet, historian, and ex-President of his country, who, when some years ago a professor desired to initiate a course in Spanish-American literature, opposed the plan on the grounds that such a thing did not exist. The position of Mitre (similar to the one Sierra combated) was that literature is something more than a collection of books,—that the volumes written by Spanish Americans, though all in the same tongue, lacked logical coherence and the evidence of evolution toward a definite goal. He admitted, however, that their "literary productions might be considered, not as models, but as facts, classified as the expression of their social life during three periods, the colonial epoch, the struggle for freedom, and the independent existence of the social republics." To some it would seem that this statement approaches very near to self-refutation; there is certainly logic, if not unity or coherence, to Spanish-American letters, and there is just as certainly evolution; as to whether that evolution tends toward a definite goal is another matter, for literary evolution need not be conscious, and least of all, self-conscious.   Even this definite goal, however, seems to have appeared with what may be termed the post-modernist group, in their aspirations to intellectual continental unity, under the inspiration of a broader concept of union derived from Bolívar's audacious, unfulfilled dream.

It is interesting to compare with Mitre's position that of the recently deceased José Verissimo, one of the foremost Brazilian critics,—a man of broad views, wide reading (how often the one seems to grow from the other!) and incorruptible fearlessness of expression.   In regard to the letters of his native country Verissimo expressed doubts similar to those of Mitre.   "I do not know," he writes, in his essay *O Que Falta A Nossa Literatura.*[19] "whether the existence of an entirely independent literature is possible without an entirely independent language."   In this sense Verissimo denies the existence of an Austrian literature, as well of a Swiss or Belgian.   He finds that Brazilian letters lack perfect continuity, cohesion, the unity of great literatures, chiefly because at first they depended upon Portugal, then Europe (particularly France) and only lastly

[19] *Estudos de Literatura Brasileira.* Vol. II. Cf. however, the speech delivered before the Brazilian Academy of Letters by Joaquim Nabuco. "The truth is that, although they speak the same language, Portugal and Brazil will have, in the future, literary destinies as profoundly distinct as their national destinies. . . . The formation of the Academy of Letters is an affirmation of the fact that, in literature as in politics, we are a nation with a destiny and a character of its own—a nation that can be directed only by itself, developing its originality through its own resources and wishing only that glory which can come from its own genius."

referred to Brazil.   In such a sense, too, it would be possible to deny (or, at least, it would have once been possible)
the existence of a North American as distinguished from an
English literature.   Yet despite the subtle psychic bonds
that link identity of speech to similarity of thought, the
environment (which helps to shape pronunciation as well as
the vocabulary and the language itself) is, from the standpoint of literature, little removed from language as a de-
termining factor.   Who would pretend, on the basis of linguistic similarity, to say that there is no United States literature as distinguished from English literature?   Is it not
national life, as well as national language, that creates literature, especially in the broader sense as used by both
Mitre and Verissimo?   Time here, as elsewhere, plays a
leading rôle, creating new languages out of old, new literatures out of old, even new worlds out of old.   And although Rémy de Gourmont's characterization of Spanish-
American speech as "neo-Spanish" is rash, it recognizes
the innovating power inherent in a change of environment
and outlook; perhaps he spoke the word too soon rather
than too thoughtlessly.[20]

After all, the question as to whether the word literature

20 In this connection, with reference to the transformations English has
undergone in the United States, it is worth while to point out an exceedingly useful and vivacious volume entitled *The American Language*, by
Henry L. Mencken, New York, 1919. Mr. Mencken is a sober thinker, for
all his occasional levity, and is one of the few stimulating critics writing
in our country today. He is very much alive to the changes going on daily
in the structure, pronunciation and vocabulary of the English tongue as
spoken (and even written) in this land, and has in his own book suggested
more than one path that our more academic spirits would do well to follow.
There is something incongruous about the eagerness with which we study,
for example, the evolution of the Romance tongues out of Vulgar Latin,
neglecting similar phenomena in our very surroundings.

may be applied to the literary products of Spanish and Portuguese America is largely academic; few readers, when roused by the strophes of some modern Tyrtæus or entranced by the sheer musical beauty of a Guitérrez Nájera, a Julían del Casal, an Amado Nervo, or a González Martínez, stop to ask themselves whether they are reading part of a well-defined literature or not; the query is philosophical rather than literary.

Yet if the term literature, in the philosophical sense, be denied to the past productions of Spanish Americans, the very reasons for that denial seem to be disappearing; for none could ask a clearer statement of conscious purpose than comes from spokesmen of literary Americanism today. That literary Americanism is an artistic precursor of a political unity. "If this unity is impossible in political affairs," says F. García Godoy in his group of essays entitled "Americanismo Literario," "let us labor to impart a common orientation to what is worth more and is more durable than the political: the harmonic, coherent cultural vibration of peoples identified by blood, by speech and by history."

The conditions of Mitre are thus well on the road to fulfillment, and the vast dream of Bolívar is born anew in the cradle of art.

CHAPTER II

RUBÉN DARÍO

(1867–1916)

THE life of Rubén Darío itself, quite apart from the poems which flowered out of it, reads with all the interest of a fictive account. In his own day he became, to more than one admirer, a god with a legend all his own. He is with little doubt, both as person and as artistic creator, one of the most attractive figures in modern poetry. Perhaps such adulators as Vargas Vila have done him as much harm as good; he may not have been, as was asserted during his lifetime, the greatest poet that ever used the Castilian tongue. Such worship, however, is significant; the man impressed his personality upon the writers and readers of two continents; he was a servitor as well as a master of beauty; he has written works of dazzling technical perfection and of penetrating vision; he is the outstanding representative of modernism in poetry; he is a chiseler of luminous, glittering prose rich alike in imagery, melody and substance. He is not merely a Spanish-American poet, nor a Castilian poet; he is of the consecrated few who belong to no nation because they belong to all.

I believe that many Spaniards, on both sides of the Atlantic, have stressed Darío's technical perfection and innovating significance at the expense of his essential humanity. I believe that despite his aristocratic search after flawless

form, despite his hatred of the crowd, despite his intellectual sybaritism, he was as human in a great part of his poetry
as in his life.   This wanderer sought to distil beauty from
joy and sorrow, and at the bottom of this beauty the joy,
the sorrow, the vain questioning, the doubt, the vacillations
of the age are vibrant.   There is another Darío, I know,—
the Darío of the marquis's hands, of the pastels à la Wat-
teau, of the insubstantial symbolism wafted to the reader
upon winged words,—the Darío that had the weakness
for vain display, for the anodyne of drink, for creature com-
forts.   Yet is it another Darío, or the same?   In our creations of beauty we transform ourselves as well as life.   And
has not a very wise Frenchman said that we differ mostly
from ourselves? . . .

At the root of Darío's work as a whole lies agitated, multifarious life; without a knowledge of that life we may appreciate the beauty of his productions, but we miss much of
their humanity.   And without taking sides with Art for
Art's sake or Art for Heart's Sake, it is easy to understand
that beauty shorn of its human aspect is only half beautiful.

Darío has left us a personal account of his career, written
four years before his death; it is not a complete account,—
there are intentional omissions and strange caprices of
memory, yet by collating his own record with that of his
contemporaries it is possible to arrive at a fairly complete
knowledge of the man's career.

I

The poet's personal account *(La Vida de Rubén Darío,
Escrita Por El Mismo)* is on the whole a book of engaging
candor, revealing the man behind the poet; Darío puts on

no airs, he assumes no rôle of an inspired prophet, nor does he, on the other hand, impart to his frankness a suspicion of parading pose, of sensational confession. He is aware of his faults, but takes them for granted and wastes no time in futile repentance or ostentatious "peccavis." He is generous in his appraisal of others, and charitable to those who have sought to do him harm. He displays a deep sense of humor, which, like most deep humor, has overtones of sorrow. His prose is simple, unpretentious, conversational, yet melodious and rich in colorful words and happy phrases. It is not the prose of an *Azul* or a *Los Raros*, yet it is well matched to its direct purpose. Here, as elsewhere, we come upon a spirit that is surely cosmopolitan, with a touch of the exotic, yet more than these, restless and migratory.

In the cathedral of León, Nicaragua, he tells us, may be found the baptismal record of Felix Rubén, legitimate son of Manuel García and Rosa Sarmiento. Following the Spanish custom of composing the family name from that of both parents, his name should have been Felix Rubén García Sarmiento. Why, then, Darío? A great-grandfather of his had borne that name, and was known in the hamlet as Don Darío; hence all his offspring were called the Daríos. Rubén's own father did business under the name of Darío, so strongly had it become embedded. The marriage of Rubén's parents had been a loveless match of convenience; the couple had separated eight months later; the following month the child was born. He soon passed under the care of his maternal grandmother, Doña Bernarda Sarmiento de Ramírez, whose husband had come to Honduras for him, and he was brought up as the child of Colonel

Ramírez and his wife. Darío thus knew nothing of his mother; her image was early effacèd from his memory; his earliest school books, indeed, contain as his signature Felix Rubén Ramírez.

He was a child prodigy, it seems; he knew how to read at the age of three. At the death of the colonel, the child's education passed into the hands of his grandmother. The old house inspired the impressionable tot with terror. Added to the lugubriousness of the surroundings was the character of the superstitious tales he listened to from his grandmother's mother, an aged, quivering creature who told him stories of headless monks and mysterious hands, of sinful women carried off by the devil. "And thence my horror of nocturnal darkness, and the torture of ineradicable nightmares." The poet's fears, indeed, follow him all through life; he fears the darkness, he broods over death, he suffers neurotic torments.

At elementary school he takes courses in which the principle of the rod is unsparingly applied, together with hazy notions of arithmetic, geography, a pinch of grammar, religion. As early as this he betrays a weakness for feminine companionship, and his one whipping from the schoolmaster comes from being discovered "in company with a precocious little girl."

Among the first books he read (he came upon them in an old closet) were *Don Quijote*, the works of Moratín, the *Thousand and One Nights*, the *Bible*, the *de Officiis* of Cicero, Mme. Staël's *Corinne*, some classic Spanish plays and a hair-raising novel called *La Caverna de Strozzi*. It was, indeed, as he says, a strange mixture for a child's brain. And how symbolic is this early conjunction of the Arabian

Nights and the Bible! Was not the poet's life a continuous oscillation between the two? . . .

"I never learned to make verses," he asserts, in recounting his earliest attempts. "It was organic, natural, innate in me." His first fame came to him as a writer of versified epitaphs. But the thoughts of the juvenile poet of death were far indeed from the graveyard. Soon his first sensations of love were wakened in him by a distant cousin of his who came to live with the widow Ramírez, whom Darío considered his mother. "The call of the blood!" exclaims the autobiographer. "What a shabby, romantic figment! The only paternity is the habit of affection and care. He who suffers, struggles and watches over a child, even though he has not engendered it, is its real father."

The future poet's melancholy character became rapidly evident. He was fond of solitude, fond of gazing meditatively at the sky and out to sea. Together with these recollections of juvenile sadness mingled memories of horrible scenes. Perhaps Darío's explanation of his fears is but half the story or less; most children hear fairy tales and experience similar shocks, yet react to them more sturdily. Whatever the case, this neurotic sensitivity remains with Darío for the rest of his life, as does his amorous susceptibility, with which it may have had organic relation. Both these aspects are prominent in his poetry and he is early attracted to spirits of a similar nature.

A third element now appears, the religious—and it is significant that the youngster is at first more impressed by the awe of the ceremonies than by their beauty. During his passionate adolescence he writes many love verses and suffers more than one disillusionment at the hands of the "inevitable and divine enemy," love. One of these juvenile flames so scorched him that even with the passing years he could remember the name of the little North American circus girl,—Hortense Buislay. Unable at that time to obtain the price of admission, he wormed into the friendship of the musicians and gained surreptitious entrance by carrying their music or their instruments into the tent.

Before he had reached his thirteenth year one of his verses had already appeared in a daily called *El Termómetro,* published by José Dolores Gómez, in the city of Rivas. The poem was one of the rhymed elegies for which our Rubén had become locally famous; he recalls a stanza for us:

> Murió tu padre, es verdad,
> lo lloras, tienes razón,
> pero ten resignación;
> que existe una eternidad
> do no hay penas. . . .
> Y en un trozo de azucenas
> Moran los justos cantando. . . .

How blithely youth sings of eternity, and how sadly old age chants childhood!

With the publication of more verse Darío became known throughout the republics of Central America as the boy poet. He took his calling with intense seriousness, allowing his hair to grow long and neglecting his studies. The poet who was to work wonders with complicated metres and have such an epoch-making effect upon the mathematical bases of poetics, failed disastrously in mathematics!

The "boy poet" was soon called to the editorial office of

the political sheet *La Verdad*, where began his long companionship with journalism.   But this was an opposition
paper, and before long Darío was confronted with the inevitable police,—inevitable because they figure, it seems,
in the life of almost every Hispano-American writer of recent note, and not a few of Spain.   The fourteen-year-old
journalist left the position and became an instructor in
grammar in a colegio.   Here he happened upon a book
of free-masonry and acquired a certain prestige among his
companions because of his caballistic lore.   His early melancholy continued to torment him; he experienced, with the
coming of adolescence, a bodily and spiritual transformation.   "I felt an invisible hand thrusting me toward the
unknown."   And toward the known, too, for he was now
visiting a large-eyed girl every Saturday.

Induced to go to the capital, Managua, he soon acquired,
through influential friends, a position in the National Library.   "There I spent long months reading everything I
could lay hands upon, and among these readings were—
horrendo referens!—all the introductions in *Rivadeneira's
Biblioteca de Autores Españoles*, and the chief works of
almost all the classics of our tongue.   Hence it comes that
. . . I am really very well versed in Spanish letters, as
any one may see from my first published productions. . . .
It was, then, deliberately that I later employed manners and
constructions of other languages, exotic words and phrases,
not purely Spanish, with the desire of rejuvenating and
rendering flexible the language."   The excerpt is important; it helps to bear out the contention that the exoticism
of the modernists was not mere affectation, but a more or
less conscious (and here, as in the case of Gutiérrez Nájera,

very conscious) desire to enrich a language in need of expansion.   It is worth while noting, too, that the iconoclastic, or rather, innovatory program was based upon a knowledge of the old.

These readings were varied with fresh amatory adventures.   This time it was a green-eyed, chestnut-haired maiden of a gentle pallor.   Wherefore new verses, some of which found their way into the public print and later even into some of his books.   He was told that the girl had already loved before,—loved no other than one of his own dying friends.   Part of this torrid love and the consequent jealousy found its way into *Abrojos,* a rare predecessor of *Azul,* published in Chile.   At fourteen years of age he announces his intention to marry, and his friends, taking him at last in earnest, present him with a travelling bag and see him off to Corinto, where he takes the boat to El Salvador! Here he was charged with writing an ode in celebration of Bolívar's centenary, which, "according to my vague recollection was naturally very different from all my later productions."

He returns to Nicaragua; love-affair follows love-affair, verse follows verse, journalistic experience grows, political duties multiply.   Comes an especially bitter love-disappointment and he resolves to quit the land.   Whither? The United States.   But a friend induces him to go to Chile, and thither he sails, during an earthquake, on the good ship *Kosmos.*   "At last the ship reaches Valparaiso. I purchase a paper.   I read that Vicuña Mackenna has died.   In twenty minutes, before disembarking, I write an article.   I land.   The same thing as in El Salvador. What hotel? the best."   This short paragraph reveals the

ready journalist in Darío, as well as the man with the
"hands of a marquis," who loved luxury with a fondness
that made him hate money. His article is printed in the
Valparaiso *Mercurio;* he gets a place upon the Santiago
Le Epoca and becomes a member of the young intellectual
group. From the *Epoca* he wins a prize of two hundred
pesos for the best poem on Campoamor, offered by the director to the members of his staff. Darío's poem is a skil-
full *décima* well concentrating the essence of a poet whom
it is now the fashion to depreciate, but who exercised a potent influence and knew the secret of saying much in little.
This was the winning poem:

> Este del cabello cano
> como la piel del armiño,
> junta su candor de niño
> con su experiencia de anciano.
> Cuando se tiene en la mano
> un libro de tal varón
> abeja es cada expresión,
> que volando del papel
> deja en los labios la miel
> y pica en el corazón.

Those who have enjoyed the concentrated, epigrammatic,
piquant, worldly-wise, genially philosophic *Humoradas*
and *Doloras* of Campoamor will agree to the vivid characterization, in the very style of the man whose literary por-
trait he drew.

From the *Epoca* Darío went to the Valparaiso *Heraldo,*
there to write his first article on—sports! Which he did
so very well that he was invited to leave. He had long cherished a desire to figure as correspondent of *La Nación*

(Buenos Aires).   It was this newspaper that taught him,
he tells us, his journalistic style, and at the time of which
we are speaking three divers influences affected him in his
perfection of prose: Paul Groussac, Santiago Estrada, José
Martí.   In these existed the spirit of France, and of the
three, "Groussac was my real intellectual guide."   Through
the influence of his friend, the Chilean poet Eduardo de la
Barra, he was accepted on *La Nación*.

This, however, is but the beginning of Darío's literary
and amorous pilgrimage.   He is attacked by small-pox,
but left with few marks.   He falls into one of his numerous
early love affairs and is somehow or other invited to a party
given to the maiden by his successful rival.   Suddenly he
commences to improvise verses in which the blackest things
are said about the rival, the girl's family, and whom not
else, and is packed off.   He finds himself at the head of a
unionist newspaper.   He makes an important friend in
Francisco Gavidia, "who is perhaps one of the most solid
humanists and certainly one of the first poets of South
America."

Through Gavidia he had, on his first visit to El Salvador,
been introduced to Hugo; from their joint reading of the
master's alexandrines, "which Gavidia, certainly, first
wrote in Castilian in the French manner," he received the
idea of the metrical renovation that he was later to develop.

On the 22d of June, 1890, he was at last married, in civil
form, to Rafaela Contreras; the religious ceremony, which
was to take place shortly after, was postponed by a revolution that broke out in Salvador that same night.   Becoming
involved in a political issue, Darío fled to Guatemala,
where he was named through President Barillas (a friend

of President Menéndez of Salvador, who had been betrayed) director of *El Correo de la Tarde*.   A half year
later the religious ceremony of marriage took place.

He was sent to Spain shortly afterward (1892) as Nicaragua's delegate to the celebration of the Columbus centenary.   The assignment was so sudden that he had time
only to write to his wife and embark at once.   There he
made important friendships with Menéndez y Pelayo, Castelar ("the first time I went to the great man's home I felt
the emotions of Heine arriving at Goethe's house"), Nuñez
de Arce, who tried to keep him in Spain, Valera (who had
welcomed his *Azul* with such perspicacious comment and
unerring prophecy), Campoamor, Zorrilla.

It was on his return from this commission that he visited
Cuba and spent a few hours in Santiago de Cuba.   This is
not mentioned in his autobiography "despite the fact that he
then made the personal acquaintance of Julián del Casal.
Only in an article entitled *El General Lachambre* and in a
public letter directed to Enrique Hernández Miyares *(La
Habana Elegante,* Ano. X. No. 24.   Habana, 17 de Junio
de 1894) has Rubén Darío recalled this visit to Cuba and
his friendship with Casal.[1]

Reaching León he was informed of his wife's death.
For a week he resorted to the forgetfulness of drink in the
face of the terrible blow.   He does not seem, however, to
have possessed any more paternal affection than his own
father, for the bringing up of his child was entrusted to
other hands; thus it had been for nineteen years at the time
he wrote his biography.

Now comes a strange episode in which the poet, recover-

[1] M. E. Ureña. *Rodó y Rubén Darío.* Pages 128–129.

ing from his alcoholic lethargy, went to Managua to collect a half year's back pay from the government. "I arrived at Managua and took a place in a hotel. I was surrounded by old friends; I was given to understand that my salary would soon be paid, but the fact is, I had to wait many days; so many that during these days there occurred the most novel-esque and fatal episode in my life, but to which I may not refer in these memoirs, for powerful reasons. It is a sad page of violence and deception, which has prevented me from forming a home for more than twenty years; but there still lives the person who, like me, suffered the consequence of a familiar impetuous step, and I do not desire to increase a protracted grief with the slightest reference. The Mexican diplomat and writer, Federigo Gamboa . . . has for many years had this romantic, bitter page in writing, but has not published it because I was opposed to its inclusion in one of his books of memoirs. So that a gap is here necessary in my life's narrative." Conjecture is naturally rife about the episode; Gamboa has not yet made his knowledge public; the lines refer to Darío's second marriage, to Rosario Murillo. Was the marriage, as Max Henríquez Ureña suggests, the product of an alcoholic overindulgence and later pressure? At any rate, Darío's other son, Rubén Darío Sánchez, was the fruit of the poet's happy union to Francisca Sánchez, with whom Darío lived in Europe.

We soon find Darío named Consul from Colombia to Buenos Aires. What a weakness the great man had for outward trappings and uniforms! He did not proceed at once to Buenos Aires, however; his wish was first to go to New York, then to visit Paris, and only then to go to the capital of Argentina. So he took the boat to New York, where he met José Martí in the Cuban colony; the revolutionist was then at the height of his effort. Darío's impressions of Martí's conversational powers are very vivid. "Never have I met, even in Castelar himself, so admirable a conversationalist. He was harmonious, intimate and gifted with a prodigious memory,—swift and ready with quotation, reminiscence, fact, image. I spent several unforgettable moments with him, then left . . . I never saw him again." Before sailing for Paris the poet visited Niagara, but how different are his impressions from those of Heredia and Bonalde. "My impression before the wonder, I confess, was less than might have been imagined. Although the miracle dominates one, the mind pictures it so much greater that in reality it possesses no such fantastic proportions." He does, however, recall Heredia's verses before the sight. How, indeed, should Niagara have impressed the Darío of *Azul?*

Paris, on the contrary, is sacred soil to him. "I had dreamed of Paris since I was a child, to such an extent that when I said my prayers I prayed to God not to let me die before I saw Paris. Paris, to me, was a sort of Paradise in which the essence of earthly happiness was breathed. It was the City of Art, of Beauty and of Glory; and above all, the capital of Love, the realm of Dream. And I was about to know Paris, to realize the greatest desire of my life. When I stepped on to Parisian earth in the station at Saint Lazare, I felt as if I were treading holy ground." Here he met, during his short stay, Verlaine, Jean Moréas, Maurice Duplessis and others. His picture of the great Faun is short, but vivid. He was introduced to Verlaine by Alejandro Sawa, as "poeta americano, admirador . . .

I murmured in bad French all the devotion I could express, and finished with the word 'glory'. . . Who could tell what had happened that afternoon to the unfortunate master? The fact is that, turning toward me, and without ceasing to thump the table, he said to me in a low and pectoral voice: *'La gloire! . . . La gloire! . . . M. . . . M. . . . Encore!'* I believed it prudent to withdraw and await a more propitious occasion." This was to prove hardly possible, for Darío always found the poet in the same besotted state. *"Pauvre Lélian!"*

At Buenos Aires the consul was most cordially received. It was at this time, upon the occasion of Queen Victoria's anniversary, that he dictated in the café of *The Fourteen Provinces* a small poem in prose to the sovereign. For lack of paper it was written upon the backs of four envelopes. If I translate it here, it is not because of its intrinsic worth as a piece of art, which is not great, as for its indirect light upon the Darío of that epoch, just before the publication of the *Prosas Profanas* that were to create such a powerful impression on both sides of the Atlantic. The poem is entitled *God Save the Queen* (in English) with the English words as a refrain. At the time his autobiography was written, the poem had not yet appeared elsewhere in print.

GOD SAVE THE QUEEN

To my friend C. E. F. Vale

Because you are one of the most powerful lands of poesy;

Because you are the mother of Shakespeare;

Because your men are strange and bold, in war and in Olympic games;

Because in your garden blooms the best flower of springtide and in your heaven shines the saddest of winter suns;

I sing to your queen, oh great and proud Britain, with the verse
    that is repeated by the lips of all your children:

God Save the Queen.

Your women have the necks of swans and the whiteness of the
    white roses;
Your mountains are drenched with legends, your tradition is a
    mine of gold, your history a mine of iron, your poesy a mine
    of diamonds;
On the seas your banner is known by every wave and every wind,
    so that the tempest might have asked for English citizenship;
Because of your strength, oh England;

God Save the Queen.

Because you sheltered Victor Hugo on one of your islands;
Because, above the seething of your laborers, the drudgery of
    your sailors and the anonymous toil of your miners, you
    have artists that clothe you in silk of love, in gold of glory;
    in lyric pearls;
Because on your escutcheon is the union of fortitude and dreams,
    in the symbolic lion of the kings and the unicorn, friend of
    virgins and brother of the dreamers' Pegasus;

God Save the Queen.

For your shepherds who say the psalms and your fathers who, in
    the tranquil hours, read aloud their favorite poet by the fire-
    place;
For your incomparable princesses and your secular nobility;
For Saint George, conqueror of the Dragon; for the spirit of the
    great Will, and the verses of Swinburne and Tennyson;
For your lithe maidens, made of milk and laughter, as fresh and
    tempting as apples;
For your sturdy youths who love physical exercise; for your
    scholars, familiarized with Plato, rowers or poets;

God Save the Queen.

Envoi

Queen and empress, adored by your great people, mother of kings, Victoria favored by the influence of the Nile; solemn widow garbed in black, adored by the beloved prince; Mistress of the sea, Mistress of the land of elephants, Defender of the Faith, powerful and glorious dame, may the hymn that greets you today be heard around the world: God save you!

Now, too, he commenced the publication, in *La Nación*, of the series which was later to be published in volume form as *Los Raros*. He later agreed that there was too much enthusiasm in his criticism of the writers here represented, but very sensibly he recognizes the creative power of enthusiasm.   The verses penned during this epoch were likewise to be gathered later under the famous title *Prosas Profanas;* the volume was first brought out at the expense of Darío's friend Carlos Vega Belgrano.   It is at this period, indeed, that modernism may be said to have been definitely launched.

At the end of the Spanish-American war the poet was sent to Spain by *La Nación,* and out of his correspondence for that periodical grew the volume *España Contemporanea;* his later visit to the Paris Exposition of 1900 likewise resulted in his book *Peregrinaciones;* these continental travels were continued for the same enterprising organ, through England, Italy, Germany, Belgium, Austria-Hungary.   The traveler Darío in his work shows the same spirit we have noticed in the more circumscribed travels of Gutiérrez Nájera; once more he proves the old dictum that one receives no more from foreign visits than he brings to them; and Darío brought much.   Darío has left us a close view of Oscar Wilde, as the English poet appeared to

him when they met at the Paris Exposition.   ". . . Somewhat robust, shaved gentleman, with an abbatial air, very
engaging in manner, who spoke French with a marked
English accent. . . . Rarely have I met a person of greater
distinction, a more elegant culture, a more genteel urbanity.
He had lately come out of prison. His former French
friends, who had showered him with adulation in his days
of wealth and triumph, now ignored him. . . . He had even
changed his name at the hotel where he stopped, calling
himself by a Balzaquian title, Sebastian Menmolth.   All
his works had been placed under the ban in England.   He
was living with the aid of a few London friends. For reasons of health he needed a trip to Italy, and with all respect
he was offered the necessary expense by a barman named
John. A few months later poor Wilde died, and I was
unable to go to his burial, for when I learned of his death
the unfortunate fellow was already under the sod.   And
now in England and all over the world his glory begins
anew."

Darío himself, as he appeared at the Paris Exposition,
has been pictured by his friend Vargas Vila: "He was still
young, well built, with a genius's glance and a sad air.   It
seemed that all the races of the world had placed their seal
upon that countenance, which was like a shore that had
received the kisses of all the waves of the ocean.   It might
have been said that he had the countenance of his poetry—
Oriental and Occidental, African and Japanese, with a perpetual vision of Hellenic shores in his dreamy pupils.   And
he appeared, as always, sculptured out of Silence; he was
his own shadow."

Returning from his European travels, Darío was named

Nicaraguan consul to Paris, after having learned of a false report of his death.   The poet, indeed, was twice falsely reported dead; one of the rumors brought forth a hardly flattering obituary notice from some irate priest, in the *Estrella de Panama:* "Thank God that this pest of Spanish literature has already disappeared. . . . With his death we have lost absolutely nothing. . . ."

Being named, in 1906, Nicaraguan delegate to the Pan-American Congress at Rio de Janeiro, he proceeded to that country; the mission accomplished, he went to Buenos Aires, feeling the need of a rest.   Thence he returned to the perennial Paris of his dreams,—"the center of neurosis," he calls it, in a poetic letter to the wife of the noted Argentine poet, Leopoldo Lugones.   The letter, by the way, was written from Majorca, whither the sick poet had gone to avoid the Parisian winter, and where he visited spots consecrated by the memory of George Sand and Chopin, and the cave in which Raymond Lully prayed.

Disgusted with the outcome of the boundary dispute between Nicaragua and Honduras, which had been referred to Alphonso XIII as arbiter, and on which Darío, together with Vargas Vila, had been appointed members for Nicaragua, the poet resolved to return to his native land, after an absence of eighteen years.   He was received with the utmost enthusiasm and President Zelaya now named him Minister Plenipotentiary to Madrid, whereupon the eternal wanderer returned to Spain, where the King, after the official ceremony of receiving him, discussed his poetry with him.   With diplomatic honors flying in the air, there now came an appointment to Darío (who may have deceived himself that he was a diplomat, even as Voltaire did that he

was a playwright) as Envoy Extraordinary to the government of Mexico on the occasion of the centenary of Mexican
independence. However, Darío had once written a poem
called *To Roosevelt*, in which the United States was looked
upon as a possible invader of Spanish America; complica-
tions were feared, and Darío never fulfilled his functions as
envoy. Provided with the necessary funds, the poet returned to that Europe which was really more his home
than America, for all his calling Argentina his second
nation.

Shortly after his return he founded the review *Mundial;*
founding reviews is one of the literary amusements of
Spanish-American poets. He was received by such emi-
nent Frenchmen as Paul Fort, Anatole France, and Rémy
de Gourmont. Once again he made a tour of the continents, being welcomed enthsiastically in Spain, Brazil and
various nations of South America; then came the great war
to interrupt the publication of his review and to accentuate
the illness that was coming over the poet. Once again he
turned to that Majorca which has been enshrined in one of
Blasco Ibáñez's best novels—*Los Muertos Mandan*. His
final days were filled with an intense fear for France's
fate. It would not be difficult indeed, however unfruitful
all such discussions are, to show that Darío was intellect-
ually French rather than Spanish.

Darío's final homecoming is a gloomy one. Broken in
health, he journeyed to New York on his way to Nicaragua;
his coming was little noticed outside of intellectual circles.
He was presented by the Hispanic Society of America—
itself too little known here—with its coveted medal of
honor. Darío was stricken in New York with double pneu-

monia; he was able, however, to make his way to Guatemala, thence to León, where he died on the sixth of February, 1916.

Such was, in outline, the life of that strangely wrought
figure who symbolizes the age of modernism in Castilian
poetry.   His inner existence is fully as agitated as his outward.   "There was, in Darío," Vargas Vila has written,[2]
"the tendency, almost the necessity, to believe, which is inherent in all weak creatures; he believed in everything,—
even in the most absurd things; the supernatural world
attracted him with an irresistible fascination, as did all the
aspects of mystery.   He believed in God; he believed in the
Devil. . . ."   Darío, in fact, at one time of his life, desired to become a monk, and there is an interesting photograph of him taken in the monastic cowled gown.   Indeed,
with his photographs, as with his early readings, a significant juxtaposition might be made.   Place this priestly picture beside the vainglorious gold braid, plumed hat and
sword of the photograph that adorns the Maucci edition of
his autobiography, and you have the two dominant influences between which Darío wavered all through his life:
Paganism and Christianity, epicureanism and religion, the
body and the soul, agitation and repose, eroticism and contemplation.   This oscillation between contradictory impulses, so characteristic of the age itself as well as of its
literary figures, is well portrayed by Vargas Vila in his
lyric biography of his friend.

"He never matured.   He never became what we call a
man, in the dolorous, brutal sense of the word. . . . He
might have lived for centuries, and would have died the

[2] Vargas Vila's *Rubén Darío*.   Madrid.   Page 55.

same sad, radiant child we all knew.   Life wounded him,
but did not stain him.—His soul possessed the oiliness of
the wings of his beloved swans, over which the slime glides
without adhering to them. . . . Never in a soul so pure
was there lodged a body so sinful. . . ."[3]

It is from such a soul and such a body that Darío's poems
proceed; now one aspect is uppermost, now another, now
both aspects are fused in art's highest manifestations.   But
everywhere they are a human product,—the outpourings
of a spirit that wandered through art as well as through
life, and was, as much as a standard-bearer of innovation,
a plastic personality who revealed humanity to itself in
his own self-revelations.[4]

[3] Vargas Vila. *Op. cit.* Pages 150–151.
[4] Valuable autobiographic material is present in Darío's unfinished novel
El Oro de Mallorca (published in the February, 1917, number of *Nosotros,*
Buenos Aires).   Benjamin Itaspes, the hero, is recognized as Rubén Darío.
This Itaspes "recited his paternoster every night, for despite his restless,
aggressive spirit and his wandering, agitated life, he had preserved many
of the religious beliefs that had been instilled in him in his childhood."
Itaspes is as little sociable as Darío, and as much aristocratic except in
dealings with folk of untainted simplicity.   It is "the fifth and third of
the capital sins" that have most possessed, from his earliest years, his
"sensual body and his curious soul." . . . "If a diabolic drink or an ap-
petizing food or a beautiful sinful body brings me in advance . . . a bit
of paradise, am I to let this certainty pass for something of which I have
no sure notion?"   (Note the characteristic mingling of faith and epicureanism in that passage.)   In the same unfinished novel Darío speaks of the
hero's "erotic temperament, incited by the most exuberant of imaginations
and his morbid, artist's sensitiveness, his musical passion, which exacerbated
him and possessed him like a divine interior spirit.   In his anguish, at times
without foundation in reason, he sought support in a vague mysticism. . . .
His great love of life was placed against an intense fear of death.   This,
to him, was a phobia, a fixed idea."   Itaspes, like Darío, is portrayed as
a man with "the instincts and the predispositions of an archduke" (in the
Palabras Preliminares to *Prosas Profanas* he spoke of his marquis's hands).
The final years of Itaspes mirror Dario's concluding days,—neurotic, half
athritic, half gastritic, haunted by inexplicable fears, "indifferent to fame

II

The poetic career of Rubén Darío is another striking proof that the great artist may not be hooped in by critical symbols. The progress of his labors exemplifies what I may call a creative eclectism. Is that not, too, Nature's method of improving upon herself, which we call natural selection? . . . From the study of Darío's poetry we may discover the spiritual counterpart of his wandering existence, ranging from the earliest romantic efforts, through a renovation of prose technique, poetic technique, the acquisition of a more human outlook, and the final emergence of these combined powers in masterpieces that belong to world poesy.

1. Early Efforts.

Darío's earliest efforts are contained in the collections *Epistolas y Poemas* (1885) and *Abrojos* (1887). In the first his great god is Hugo; in the second his affections have shifted to Bécquer, Campoamor, Nuñez de Arce and Zorrilla, particularly the last. As may be expected, there is little in these lines from the pen of a youth between his eighteenth and twentieth years to reveal the dominant personality of the future. He is as yet diffident as to his powers and asks the Muses (*El Poeta á Las Musas*) whether his humble plectrum is better suited to martial hymns, or to harmonious eclogues. He knows surely that he longs for

and loving money for the independence it confers; desirous of rest and solitude, yet tense with the desire for life and pleasure. . . ." Weary, disillusioned, the tool of self-seeking exploiters of his gifts, the target of false friendship, adulation,—such is Itaspes, and such Darío at the end.

fame, and the crown it awards to the priests of beauty.   He
feels the influence of the past, yet is tempted by the modern:

> Decidme si he de alzar voces altivas
> ensalzando el espíritu moderno,
> o si echando al olvido estas edades
> me abandone á merced de los recuerdos.
>
> Hoy el rayo de Jupiter Olímpico
> es esclavo de Franklin y de Edison;
> ya nada quede del flamante tirso,
> y el ruín Champagne sucedió al Falerno.
>
> Todo acabó.   Decidme, sacras Musas,
> como cantar en este aciago tiempo
> en que hasta los humanos orgollosos
> pretenden arrojar á Dios del cielo.

A most reactionary beginning, this, for the priest of modernist beauty.   The very fact that he should address such
a question to the Muses shows that he inclines to the past, as
does his complaint that science is attempting to rob the Lord
of heaven.   Young Darío's faith, however, does not prevent
him from becoming unwittingly blasphemous when he
voices his worship of Hugo in *Victor Hugo y la Tumba*,
from the same initial collection.   Hugo is represented as
dying and seeking entrance into the abode of rest.   He is
refused admission.   "Wait!" speaks the Tomb.   "I know
not whether you may enter my regions."   For Hugo is
more than mortal.   The Tomb asks advice of the winds,
and the stars.   The genius must not die, is the universal
response.

> ¿Por que se va el profeta que al mal siempre hizo guerra?
> ¿Teme Dios que le aclamen y adoren como á el?

There is something comically juvenile about the image of
God fearing Hugo's competition.   At the same time the
young poet reveals a deep appreciation of the great Frenchman, who to him appears in the guise of a universal savior
of slaves, the singer of John Brown, "The great hope of
the cursed race, the new Messiah who brings infinite light
and a new decalogue for humanity."   Though conservative
in style, it is torrential in praise and gives us a glimpse of
the deep inner life of the youth.

But Hugo is not the sole influence in the *Epistolas y
Poemas*.   Such epistles as that to Juan Montalvo have been
recognized as possessing genuinely Hellenic balance and
sobriety.   Andrés González Blanco in his voluminous, ex-
haustive, exhausting, wandering, yet indispensable *Estudio
Preliminar*, quotes part of the epistle (the works of Darío
prior to *Azul* are very difficult to procure) and compares
it for classic decorum and serene elegance to the work of
Menéndez y Pelayo, who was much read by the young
Nicaraguan.   This phase of Darío's first book is illustrated
by the following excerpt:

> Noble ingenio: la luz de la palabra
> toca el ánimo y dale vida nueva,
> mostrándole ignoradas maravillas
> en el mundo infinito de los seres.

> La eternidad preséntase asombrosa
> astrayendo al espiritu anhelante,
> y el ansia crece en el humano pecho
> al resplandor lejano de la aurora.

> Tu inspirado y, deseoso, alzas la frente,
> y con el diapasón de la armonía

sabio sigues sendero provechoso,
extendiendo la pauta del idioma,
y formando el fulgor del pensamiento,
si subes melodías uniformes
como el ritmo immortal de las esferas.

Thus early do we find indications of a certain "Americanism," as in the poem *El Porvenir;* it is of interest as a germ that lies many years undeveloped. Thus early, too, do we discover the poet's Horatian hatred for the crowd, which is to him a mere beast to be discouraged every time it tries to raise its head. "The people is dull, filthy, evil; clap on the yoke; it complains of the taskmaster, then give it drubbings and more of them." . . . To this little sociologist (whose juvenile ideas are still unfortunately shared by more than one professor of economics), the common toiler was born for the yoke, must remain content with it and eat his bread and onions in silence.

Equally enlightening are the poet's early views on women. Of course there is nothing cryptic in this misogyny. We know Darío now better than he knew himself then; it is easy to see that his woman-hatred was symptomatic of his excessive love of them, as is most misogyny. That is why, when we read some of his early lines with the music and passion of his later ones ringing in our ears, we smile at such platitudinous condemnations as the verses in which he refers woman's beauty to alien aids, and tells them that though he covets their kisses, they are nothing but flesh and bone. "Carne y huesos!" The very words which he was later to deify as the best incarnation of the Muses!

Abrojos, as its name—Thistles—indicates, represents the varied reactions of the melancholy, love-sick adolescent

to the bitterness, grief and desires of his youthful career.
It is now cynical, now humorous in the Campoamorian
sense.   It is aware of man's envious nature and his cruelty
to his own species.

> Eres artista?   Te afeo
> Vales algo?   Te critico.
> Te aborrezco si éres rico
> Y si pobre te apedreo.

> Y de la honra haciendo el robo
> e hiriendo cuanto se ve,
> sale cierto lo de que
> el hombre del hombre es lobo.

What are some of these thistles?   Let us bind a few
together into the Darío we know from his own confessions.
"Consider whether so unfortunate a love was deep, when
it hated an honest man and was jealous of a dying one!"
. . . "I am a wise man, I am an atheist; I believe in
neither god nor devil (. . . But I'm dying. Send for a
confessor.)" . . . "Speak no more to me, for another word
like that could kill me!" . . . Platitudinous, naturally.
But isn't the later Darío here, too, as well as the impressionable youngster?   In his eagerness for fame he is sensitive to life's ironic attitude toward genius, and embodies
his sarcastic views in a sparkling eight-line antithesis:

> Vivió el pobre en la miseria,
> nadie le oyó en su disgracia;
> cuando fué á pedir limosna
> le arrojaron de la casa.

> Despues que murió mendigo
> le elevaron una estatua. . . .

Vivan los muertos, que no han
estómago ni quijados!

This is not poetry; it is, however, doubly instructive. It gives us to know the poet in his initial outpourings, and also helps us to understand that not all genius springs from the head of Zeus, full born.

There are, however, in *Abrojos*, touches of beauty as well as of youthful cynicism and disillusionment. Some of these touches· have been coupled with the names of de Musset and Heine. On the whole, however, the collection is what its name implies; the verses, of uneven worth and of easily recognized parentage, are based upon the young poet's daily experiences. They indicate the storing up of an immense hoard of emotions in the bosom of an ideally-minded, little communicative, intense youth. Only gradually does Darío fully disburden himself of his inner life; his early Parnassianism, indeed, may have been an artistic symptom of his characteristic aloofness. Yet that inner life was too intense to dwell in the ivory tower; now and again it sought refuge there, but always it looked through and, seeing the world, came down. . . .[5]

[5] In *Epistolas y Poemas* (first called *Primeras Notas*) Darío under the influence of his friend Gavidia, makes ventures in adapting the French Alexandrine to Spanish meter. The innovation is really due to Gavidia, who first adapted the free form of the Alexandrine in a translation from Hugo. (See M. E. Ureña, *Rodo y Darío*, page 102.) Regarding the *Abrojos*, Darío, in his *A. De Gilbert*, explains that they were genuine outpourings of bitterness actually experienced. "As for their technique, they were born of Compoamor's *Humoradas* and above all, from Leopoldo Cano's *Saetas*. . . . As a first book, as a card of entrée into the literary life of Santiago, it was hardly à propos. Above all, there is in it a skepticism and a black desolation which, if it be certain that they were true, were the work of the moment. To doubt God, virtue, good, when one is at the very dawn of life,—no. If what we believe pure we discover to be sullied;

2. *Azul*.

What's in a name?   And yet the name of this famous little book, a collection of poems and quasi-tales in poetic prose, has had much ink spilled about it and about.   "Why this title Blue?" asks Darío in his *Historia de Mis Libros*. And then, in response to the erroneous attribution of Hugo's influence (the French master had said "l'art c'est l'azur") he adds: "I did not at that time yet know the Hugoesque phrase . . ., although I was acquainted with the musical stanza from *Les Chatiments:*

> Adieu, patrie,
> L'onde est en furie!
> Adieu, patrie,
> Azur!

But blue was to me the color of dreams, the color of art, a Hellenic and a Homeric color, an oceanic and a firmamental color, the 'coeruleum' which in Pliny is the simple color resembling that of the heavens and the sapphire. . . ." And why should art be blue rather than any other color? asked

if the hand that we judged friendly wounds or deceives us; if, enamored of light, of holiness and the ideal, we come face to face with the sewer; if social misery produces in us the terror of vengeance; if brother curses brother; if son insults father; if mother sells daughter; if the claw triumphs over the wing; if the stars above tremble for the hell below . . . thunders of God! here you are to purify everything, to arouse the dormant, to announce the thunderbolts of justice. . . . Today, however much deceptions have destroyed my illusions, as a worshipper of God, a brother of men, a lover of women, I place my soul under my hope. . . ." How strange to hear a youth of twenty-two, already widely known for *Azul* when the above letter was written, speak of disillusions on the brink of a life that was to be filled with them, as well as with gnawing doubt and moments of despair!

Juan Valera, in his classic criticism of the collection. Why, indeed? And why not? Art is whatever color one will have it. And it must have been very blue indeed to the rising generation of the day, for two years after the death of Gutiérrez Nájera, when the name Blue Review (which had been endeared to the youth of Mexico by the late master) was given to a magazine that opposed the new poetic tendencies, there was an intellectual uprising which resulted in the withdrawal of the usurper. And did not that same tender poet write in one of his prose chronicles: "I cannot compare the sensation which the recollection of that lake produces in me with anything except that which is produced upon me by the poetry of Lamartine: it is a blue sensation. Why not attribute color to sensations? It is color that paints, that speaks in loudest voice to the eyes, to the spirit. And I feel a rose color when I recall my first morning in the torrid land, the sunrise contemplated from the window of the palace of the Cortes; I feel a silver color when I recall my moonlit night on the sea, and I feel a blue color when there comes to my memory the lake of Patzcuaro." A late critic professes to see in *Azul* . . . an entire program of ideological revolution. It is a skilful transmutation of the objective into the subjective. Something of this may have been present in Darío's mind when he chose the title; he was always skilful in naming his works. The title, however, is the least important matter connected with the work; if another Darío can produce another book of the kind in the firm conviction that art is heliotrope, why,—art is heliotrope, and that is all. . . .

Valera saw much further than the title. He noted at once the Gallicism of the author,—mental Gallicism, he called it,—and his cosmopolitan spirit. He saw, too, the young man's essential originality, and freely predicted his advancement. To be sure, he feared the Gallic element, even as more than one other Spanish critic fears Gallicism in thought on the part of a Spaniard, through an exaggerated notion of national values in literature. Whatever the faults with Valera's review of *Azul*—which is one of the important critiques to be read by all students of Darío,—despite a certain conservatism of outlook, a certain preceptive attitude,—he saw far more clearly into the prose and poetry of the book than more than one "modernist" critic after him. His opinions have been stamped more or less deeply upon all subsequent criticism. This is not merely because of his priority, but because the genial old man knew too much about good literature not to recognize it in whatever form it presented itself. Darío's book came at a time when the cosmopolitan spirit was needed by the letters of Spanish America; the work was revolutionary less in matter than in manner; it was the spark that ignited the modernist conflagration.

In the prose tales of *Azul* . . . may be discerned the intense idealism of their youthful author. Whether the scene be the fabled land of *The Bourgeois King*, the realms of *The Deaf Satyr*, or the garret of the starved artists over which floats the *Veil of Queen Mab*, the real background is the land of the ideal,—a land where art reigns in the telling, even though it be defeated by the tale. And how much self-revelation there is in these seemingly impersonal, delicate, airy traceries of language! When, in *El Rey Burgués*, the stranger addresses the King of the commonplace, is it not Darío speaking?

"I have caressed great nature, and I have sought the warmth of the ideal, the verse that is in the stars, in the depths of the sky, in the pearl, in the profundities of the ocean. I have tried to forge ahead! For the time of great revolutions is approaching, with a Messiah all light, all striving and power, and his spirit must be received with a poem that shall be an arch of triumph with strophes of steel, strophes of gold, strophes of love" . . . The stranger tries to impress a higher standard of art upon the ruler. "Sir, as between an Apollo and a goose, choose the Apollo, even though the one be of terra cotta and the other of marble."

A similar situation, with a similar defeat for the standard-bearer of the ideal, occurs in *El Sátiro Sordo*. Before the satyr-ruler comes a poet to plead his right to remain in the forest Kingdom. The poet sings of the great Jove, of Eros, of Aphrodite; the plea is listened to by the ruler's counsellors, the lark and the jackass.

When the poet concludes, he says to the satyr: "Do you like my song? If you do, I will remain with you in the forest." The satyr turns to his advisers, and from the mouth of the lark, the author addresses us:

"Lord," said the lark, trying to produce the strongest voice from her throat, "let him remain with us who so well has sung. His lyre is beautiful and potent. He has offered you the greatness and the light that you behold in your forest today. He has given you his harmony. Sire, I know of these things. When the naked dawn approaches I mount the high heavens and from the heights pour down the invisible pearls of my trills, and amid the morning brightness my melody fills the air and is the joy of all space.   And I tell you that Orpheus has sung well,—that he is one of the chosen of God.   His music intoxicated the entire forest   The eagles have descended to circle above our heads, the blooming bushes have gently swayed their mysterious censers, the bees have left their cells to come and listen.   As for me, oh Sire, if I were in your place, I would yield him my garland of tendrils and my thyrsus. There exist two powers: the real and the ideal.   What Hercules would do with his wrists, Orpheus accomplishes with his inspiration. . . . Of men, some have been born to forge metals; others, to wrest from the fertile soil the ears of corn; others to fight in bloody wars, and others, to teach, to glorify and to sing."   But there is the ass still to be heard from; he is not even heard; he shakes his head in negation, and the satyr cries "No!"

This pessimistic note is somewhat tempered in *El Velo de la Reina Mab*.   To be sure, we find the sculptor, the painter, the composer and the poet all starving in their lonely garret, but the blue veil of illusion is cast over them, and "ever since then, in the garrets of the gifted unhappy, where floats the blue dream, the future is thought of as an aurora, and laughter is heard that banishes sadness, and strange farandolas are danced about a white Apollo. . . ."

El Canción de Oro (The Song of Gold) is spiritually related to the foregoing pieces.   It is a bitter psalm, ironical and not without an alloy of sincerity, sung to the corrosive power of gold.   The note is one that is often sounded by Darío at various stages of his life; he was always in need of money, yet usually a hater of it.   *La Muerte de la Emperatriz de China* (The Death of the Empress of China) is notable for at least two things; in the first place it contains exquisite bits of exotic description that outdo even the Nipponese day-dreams with which Casal sought to surround himself in daily life; it reveals, incidentally, that perhaps Darío, like more than one of his predecessors and followers, received his idea of the Orient from Loti and Judith Gautier rather than any more intimate acquaintance, just as their neo-Hellenism was a Greek spirit that had filtered in through Italy and France. The tale seems, too, to represent, symbolically, the interference of woman in man's creative life. The empress in question is a gift statue to the artist husband; wife Suzette slays the statue, to which she fears her mate is becoming too closely devoted, and once more happiness reigns in the household, as a result of the ruined masterpiece.

It is not part of my purpose to summarize the various productions under consideration; what is important, however, is to seek the spirit that informs them. This, I believe, is a glowing idealism, attended by the passing pessimism that all idealism must inspire. There is a mingling of styles,—Hellenism, realism even,—but at bottom it is the idealistic note that rings out loudly, whether the particular bell, so to speak, be such a hymn to Mother Earth as occurs in *El Rubí* or such a neo-Greek evocation as *La Ninfa*. There is an important autobiographical element which speaks very plainly from *Palomas blancas y garzas morenas*, in which the author's love affairs come to light. In addition to the prose tales, the non-poetic section of the book contains a dozen brief impressions of Chile, where the volume was printed.

From the revolutionary standpoint, it is the prose part of *Azul* . . . that is more important; the language had become swollen, limited in resources, artificial and stagnant in expression; in these tales of Darío (which, if one must tell the truth, are of delicate fibre and contain little to set the literary world afire for either depth or intrinsic significance) the language flows with remarkable clarity.   Not so much for what they say as for how they say it are the tales of *Azul . . .* worthy of notice.   They represent an innovation in style, not in thought.   The coming master is preparing his tools for the sculpturing of the new statue. . . .

The poetic section of *Azul . . .* is named the Lyric Year, from the four chief poems there included, one to each season.   In each a varying phase of love is felt, even as the spirit of the ideal breathed in the prose tales.   In *Primaveral* we are introduced to the month of roses; love is fresh and sweet, and life is given up entirely to it:

> No quiero el vino de Naxos
> ni el ánfora de esas bellas,
> ni la copa donde Cipria
> al gallardo Adonis ruega.
> Quiero beber del amor
> solo en tu boca bermeja,
> oh, amada mia, en el dulce
> tiempo de la primavera.

With *Estival* the springtide idyll becomes the ardor of the rutting season.   And into the love of tiger and tigress intrudes the Prince of Wales, on a hunting expedition, which results in the death of the tigress; the tiger returns to his den to dream of wreaking vengeance upon the tender children of man.   The poem, in consonance with its subject, departs from the even rhythms of *Primaveral;* it seems, in part, the poetic dramatization of a fraternal feeling for

nature's creatures and a sense of man's brutal treatment
of the brute.   The third of the seasonal poems, *Otoñal*,
bears as its epigraph, in Latin, the words Love, Life and
Light.   It is the afternoon of the year, and of life as well;
a fairy friend whispers tales to the poet,—tales filled with
poesy, with what the birds sing and the zephyrs bear, what
floats in the darkness, and what maidens dream.   His thirst
for love cannot be sated; to every vision that the fairy reveals, he has but one reply: "More!"   It is the thirst of the
ideal, that may not be quenched.   Higher and higher they
fly, until, reaching the heights above all human yearnings,
he rends the veil of mystery.

> Y allí todo era aurora,
> En el fondo se veía
> Un bello rostro de mujer.

"A beautiful woman's face"—the vision that so often
greets Darío as he seeks to rend the veil of life's mystery.

Not even winter *(Invernal)* can extinguish the master
passion.   Let the winds howl without, so long as love
reigns within!

> Dentro, el amor que abrasa;
> fuera, la noche fría.

Of the four seasonal pieces I find it easy to select a
favorite: *Otoñal*.   It is the most original in conception and
execution; it is most prophetic of the poet's later progress;
it is most human.

Of the remaining poems in the collection, it will be worth
while to indicate a few, for their revelation of the poet
as well as their variety of construction.   Take, for example,

such a piece as *Anagke,* which the good Don Juan Valera found so blasphemous that he had to omit the final lines in his quotation. The poet is in a characteristic mood of pessimism—the mood of *Estival,* only one that expresses itself with less artistry if more point. A dove is singing an exultant song, whereupon a hawk swoops down and swallows the beautiful singer. And the Lord in heaven, meditating upon the scene, tells Himself that when He created doves he should not have created hawks. The indicative thing about the poem is not the shallow, the callow atheism, which was not characteristic of the mature poet, but the ideal element,—that same element which is so prominent in the prose tales of the volume; the young artist is obsessed with the ideal, and with the fear of its extinction by the hawks of life. There are sonnets worthy of attention, particularly that on *Caupolican*[6] which González-Blanco is anxious to make out as a testimonial of the poet's early "Americanism"; it is true, none the less, that the sonorous lines are worthy of Chocano, and seems to show that in later following the Peruvian poet, Darío was returning to an earlier style of his own that had long lain dormant. There is also a collection of five sonnets grouped under the title *Medallones,* and the men to whom these medallions are penned indicate various influences that the poet was undergoing: Leconte de Lisle, Catulle Mendès, Walt Whitman (to whom he reverts time and again), J. J. Palma and Díaz Mirón.

Darío has himself told us in what manner he considers *Azul* . . . a work of innovation: "I abandon the usual order,

[6] Cf. Chocano's later sonnet on "Caupolican" in his "Tríptico Heróico" (*Alma América*).

the conventional clichés; I give attention to the interior melody, which contributes to the success of the rhythmical expression; novelty in the adjectives. . . . In *Primaveral* . . . I believe I have sounded a new note in the orchestration of the *romance,* even though I count with such illustrious predecessors in this respect as Góngora and the Cuban Zenea. In *Estival* I tried to realize a tour de force." Among the metrical innovations critics have found the following: the verse of fifteen syllables (cf. the sonnet *Venus*); the verse of twelve syllables (cf. sonnets to Walt Whitman and Díaz Mirón; M. E. Ureña points out that this combination had been employed, tentatively, by Gertrudis Gómez de Avellaneda); the free sonnet, without subjection to the traditional distribution of rhymes nor the invariable measure of the hendecasyllable.

"What was the origin of the novelty?" asks Darío, in the short but highly instructive History of My Books. . . . "The origin of the novelty was my recent acquaintance with French authors of the Parnassian school, for at that time the Symbolist struggle had scarcely commenced in France and was not known outside, much less in our America. My real initial inspirer was Catulle Mendès,—a translated Mendès,—for my French was still precarious. Some of his lyrico-erotic tales, and one or another of the poems in the *Parnasse Contemporaine,* were a revelation to me." Darío mentions, too, Gautier, the Flaubert of *La Tentation de St. Antoine,* and Paul de Saint Victor, who brought him a new, dazzling conception of style. "Habituated to the eternal Spanish cliché of the Golden Age, and to Spain's indecisive modern poetry, I found in the Frenchmen I have quoted a literary mine to exploit: the application of their manner of employing the adjective, of certain syntactic methods, and of their verbal aristocracy, to Spanish. . . . And I, who knew by heart Baralt's *Dictionary of Gallicisms*, understood that not only an opportune Gallicism, but also certain peculiarities of other languages, were most useful and of incomparable efficacy when appropriately transplanted. Thus my knowledge of English, Italian and Latin was to serve me later in the development of my literary purposes. But my penetration into the world of French verbal art had not begun in Chile. Years before, in Central America, in the city of San Salvador, and in company of the good poet Francisco Gavidia, my adolescent spirit had explored the vast forest of Victor Hugo and had contemplated his divine ocean, in which everything is contained."

It is important to remember that the innovations of *Azul* . . . were not so revolutionary but that Darío was most cordially received four years later, upon his first visit to Spain, by the standard bearers of conservative literature. During all this time he was making a study of foreign letters, particularly the French moderns, and their influence was to appear not only in his critical collection called *Los Raros,* but in the next volume of poems, *Prosas Profanas.*

Of the *Rimas* by Darío, which were published in 1889, it is necessary to say but little; there is the same breath of Bécquer as hovers over his earlier poetry; for the rest the publication is exceedingly difficult to procure.

3. Prosas Profanas.

(1896)

Darío has been singularly fortunate in his critics. The name of Valera is indissolubly linked with *Azul* . . . ; the name of José Enrique Rodó is similarly inseparable from *Prosas Profanas*. And just as the first title roused a cerulean controversy, so the second, with its double contradiction, disturbed most and enchanted a few. I say double contradiction: first, because apparently the name means profane prose, which is disconcerting, to say the least, when applied to poetry; second, because in reality the title is of far deeper significance. "In his study of the Old Spanish poets Darío became familiar with their use of *prosa* in the sense of 'poem in the vernacular.' He knew, too, the sequences, or *proses*, Latin hymns that resulted in the setting of words to the music following the Alleluia in the Roman Catholic liturgy, a practise that became popular in the early 10th century. That the title was suggested by these sacred *proses* of the liturgy is clearly indicated by the second element, *profanas*, that is, 'not sacred.' . . . Just as the liturgical hymns, the 'sacred proses,' broke away from the quantitative meters of Latin verse and came to depend for their rhythms upon accent, so the 'profane proses' of Darío broke away from conventionality in form and content."[7]

Rodó, like the tolerant, broad spirit he was, enters remarkably into the spirit of the poet; he follows him, and does not seek, like Valera, to lead; he analyzes with a

[7] George W. Humphrey. *Rubén Darío*. Hispania, March, 1919. Vol. II. No. 2.

loving minuteness and out of the evaluation of a work of art, himself produces a genuinely creative masterpiece of criticism, such as virtually disarms later commentators. He seems to have said all that could be said, felt all that could be felt. Only because there was a later Darío, one that grew beyond the apostle of sheer grace and beauty whom Rodó knew in *Proses Profanas,* has Rodó's critique become, not out of date, but incomplete.

To Rodó, in a phrase that has become famous, Darío was not the poet of America. But *must* poets have homes? The poet is moreover revealed as a lover of luxury, as a select spirit destined never to achieve popularity and as perhaps being little bothered by that probability. "Art is a fragile object and Caliban has rough, brusque hands." The crowd, however (and Rodó's point is of primary importance) may be abominated in art and yet loved in most Christian-like manner in reality. To tell the truth, however, Darío, although later recognizing his need of the multitude, was always inclined to an aloofness that was mirrored in his work. And if it be true, as Rodó declared, that Darío loved the people neither in art nor in reality, there was a change on the part of the poet, as we shall see very plainly when we consider his next volume of poetry. Not only did Rodó's critique stamp upon Darío his non-American character, but it also made him definitely the poet of the swan. "If we should be asked for the animate being that should symbolize the *familiar genius* of his poetry, it would be necessary for us to cite,—not the lion or the eagle that obsess Victor Hugo's imagination, nor even the nightingale beloved of Heine,—but the swan, the Wagnerian bird; the white and delicate bird that surges at each instant upon the foamy wave of his poetry, summoned by his insistent evocation, and whose image might be engraved, on that day when poets have coats of arms, in one of the quarters of his escutcheon, even as upon Poe's escutcheon there would be engraved the raven, and on Baudelaire's the pensive and hieratic cat." True, of *Prosas Profanas*; perhaps of Darío as a whole; but the later Darío knew the flights of the condor as well as the placid elegance of the swan.

Rodó saw clearly that Darío's Parnassianism was not mental. "It is not Parnassianism extended to the internal world, in which ideas and feelings play the rôle of canvas and bronze." He recognized that there was a broader significance to the modernist movement, for toward the close of his famous essay he confesses that "I, too, am a *modernista;* I belong with all my soul to the great reaction that imparts character and meaning to the evolution of thought in the final years of this century; to the reaction which, originating in literary naturalism and philosophic positivism, leads them, without a loss of their fecund elements, to dissolve in higher conceptions. And there is no doubt that the work of Rubén Darío responds to this higher meaning; it is in art one of the personal forms of our contemporary idealistic anarchism. . . ."

There is in *Prosas Profanas* a variety, a melody, a suppleness, that was not evident in the poetry of *Azul.* . . . *Prosas Profanas*, indeed, has been recognized as having accomplished for poetry that same innovatory purpose worked by the prose of *Azul.* . . . The six intervening years have been active ones for the poet; through the maze of sorrows,

travels and studies he has found himself. His spirit has
become even more cosmopolitan, and at the same time more
Gallicized. His art has become deep as well as broad,
and tinged with that symbolist-decadentism that he transplanted to Castilian soil.

If I choose for comment certain of the poems, it is not so
much that they reveal superiority to the rest, as that the
chosen examples illustrate important attitudes.

Thus, in *Era Un Aire Suave*, the poet feels the universal
and eternal power of love, with its cruel golden laughter.
His *Eulalia* is of yesterday, of today, of tomorrow, of all
climes, but ever in the same attitude:

> Fué acaso en el Norte ó en el Mediodia?
> Yo el tiempo y el día y el país ignoro,
> pero sé que Eulalia ríe todavia,
> Y es cruel y eterna su risa de oro!

Divagación states plainly Darío's conception of Hellenism.
"More than the Greece of the Greeks I love the Greece of
France, for in France to the echo of laughter and play
Venus pours her sweetest drink. . . . Verlaine is more
than Socrates; and Arsène Houssaye surpasses old Ana-
creon. Love and Genius reign in Paris. . . ." Once
again it is universal love that absorbs the poet:

> Amor, en fin, que todo diga y cante;
> amor que encante y deje sorprendida
> á la serpiente de ojos de diamante
> que está enroscada al arbol de la vida.
>
> Ámame así, fatal, cosmopolitana,
> universal, inmensa, unica, sola

y todos; misteriosa y erudita:
ámame, mar y nube, espuma y ola.

In *El Reino Interior,* which first reveals what has been
termed the mystic phase of Darío, there shines through the
beautiful symbolism a sense of the inner unity between good
and evil.   The poet's soul gazes through the window of the
tower in which she has dwelt for thirty years.   First appear
seven white maidens, seven princesses,—the seven virtues.
The seven white princesses give way to seven red youths,—
the seven potent capital sins.   And now the youths gaze
upon the maidens and the retreating rout is lost in the distance.   Which would his soul follow?   But his soul makes
no reply.   Pensively she leaves the window, falling asleep
in the tower where for thirty years she has dreamed.   And
what does she dream?   Perhaps we may guess, for she
speaks in her sleep and cries

—Princesses, enfold me in your veils of white!
—Princes, embrace with your arms of red!

It is easy, of course, to over-interpret such poems as
these.   Why interpret at all?   Yet as one reads and re-
reads *El Reino Interior* he feels without even seeking any
esoteric meaning, that there is far more beauty than meets
the eye.   If a most rigid choice were made of Darío's
lyrics, I should not hesitate to select this as one of the
representative pieces that combines beauty of diction, varied artistry of metre and beauty of thought.   This aspect
of the collection appeals far more to me than the pictorial,
vocalic effects of such a piece as the *Sinfonía en Gris
Mayor.*   There is astonishing verbal skill, rare technical

facility, but it is the stuff of which poetry is made rather than poetry itself,—or, lest that sound too preceptive and imply a cramped definition of poetry, it is impersonally brilliant, and once its technique has been marvelled at, does not linger in the memory like other poems in the book. Not so, for instance, the beautiful sonnet *Margarita*, with its tender metaphor of the maiden who was plucked by Death even as she plucked the petals of the daisy, to find whether her lover loved her or not.

It is in the *Coloquio de los Centauros* that the book reaches its highest point.   For the Colloquy of the Centaurs is the essence of the poet's personality as it was developed up to that date; it embodies and harmonizes the varied elements of the collection.   It is classic in background, yet modern in feeling; it betrays an impeccably refined taste, yet throbs with something deeper than formal perfection; it is rich in imagery as in meaning; it blends the old and the new in the eternal.   What is the meaning of the poem?   That is for every reader to decide for himself. It has many meanings, because there centaurs gather to discuss our whole existence.   They voice the poet's own queries before the enigma, and suggest his own inadequate reply which is but another question.   "Death is the inseparable companion of Life," says Arneo.   "Death is the victory of the human race," asserts Quirón.   "Death," exclaims Medón,

> No es demacrada y mustia
> ni ase corva guadaña, ni tiene faz de angustia.
> Es semejante a Diana, casta y virgen como ella;
> en su rostro hay la gracia de la nubil doncella
> y lleve una guirnalda de rosas siderales.
> En su siniestra tiene verdes palmas triunfales,

Y en su diestra una copa con agua del olvido.
A sus pies, como un perro, yace un amor dormido.

AMICO

Los mismos dioses buscan la dulce paz que vierte.

QUIRÓN

La pena de los dioses es no alcanzar la Muerte.

"The grief of the gods is their inability to die." Is this colloquy the voice of nature pronouncing the vanity of all creation? Is it the poet's attempt to reconcile himself to the inevitable,—a vain struggle that consumed his whole existence? Whatever the poem may suggest to its many readers, one thing I believe it worth while to insist upon,— that Darío is there, listening to the centaurs and quite disappointed when they vanish as suddenly as they came, leaving the air still tremulous with the query they brought.

Note the beauty of the opening image:

"On the island at which the argonaut of immortal Dreams stops his shallop. . . ." Note, too, a suggestion of that same inner unity of good and evil in Quirón's statement that

Ni es la torcaz benigna, ni es el cuervo protervo:
son formas del Enigma la paloma y el cuervo.

Neither is the dove benign, nor the raven perverse.
Both the dove and the raven are forms of the Enigma.

Among the technical innovations of *Prosas Profanas* have been noted the following: a new musicality of verse,—new strophic forms, such as the single-rhymed tercet,—the met-

rical interruption of the grammatical connection,—free
movement of the cæsura, considered independently of the
pauses in meaning. "It should be noted," says M. E.
Ureña, "that the monorhymed tercet had already been employed by Julián del Casal in his *En El Campo*, although
not in dodecasyllables, as in Rubén Darío's *El Faisán*.
Nevertheless, Rubén Darío communicates to this strophic
combination a singular animation and flexibility. Moreover, although the anapestic hendecasyllable, employed by
Rubén Darío in the *Pórtico* [8] to the book *En Tropel*, by Salvador Rueda, is not an invention, it possesses all the character of a most valuable resurrection; and although a
young modernist, Carlos Albert Becu was, as Darío himself
declares in his autobiography, the first to employ free metre
in Castilian, and although before Darío, the Bolivian Ricardo Jaimes Freyre used this new form, the tendency to
free metre is already evident in *La Página Blanca*. The
metrical combination of the *Responso á Verlaine*, derived
from an analogous French metre, had the character of a
genuine novelty in Castilian." [9]

It is now a platitude of Spanish criticism that Darío's
metrical innovations were in reality renovations. We have
seen from his autobiography that this purpose of expand-
ing the expressional powers of Castilian prose and poetry
became early a conscious program, and was founded upon
a thorough knowledge of the past. It is equally instructive to recall that, much as the Symbolists and Decadents

[8] It is this poem which is looked upon as having introduced modernism
into Spain.

[9] Darío's autobiographical references to *Prosas Profanas* may be found
in his *Vida*, pages 177 to 186. Unbelievable as it may seem, the poems
were for the most part written in haste.

contributed with their deep sensitivity to musical stimulus, they did not often lead Darío's auto-critical nature into the absurdities of the Rambauds and the Ghils.

The years that passed between *Azul* . . . and *Prosas Profanas* had produced such a crop of "pseudo-modernistas" that Darío, in his preliminary words to the latter book, found it necessary to protest against the insincere, merely and incapably imitative poetasters who, like all parasites of the new, were bringing ridicule upon the movement. He deplored the general ignorance not only of the aspiring artists, but of the great mass of professors, academists, journalists, poets, legal lights and *rastaquoueurs* whom, using an expression of Rémy de Gourmont's, he named *Celui-qui-ne-comprend pas:* He-who-does-not-understand.[10] And there is another type of ignorance or misunderstanding that is particularly liable to interfere with the study of poets like Darío,—an excessive attention to innovations at the cost of the poet behind them. As a matter of record I indicate the innovations, but let us not deceive ourselves; they belong to history, not to literature, and the poet himself later protested that his poems were born whole, not first the skeleton of form and then the flesh of

[10] After *Azul* . . . after *Los Raros,*" says Darío in his Preliminary Words to the *Prosas Profanas,* insinuating voices, good and bad intention, sonorous enthusiasm and subterranean envy—an excellent harvest, solicited that which, in all conscience, I believed neither fruitful nor opportune: a manifesto." This he refused because of the lack of an adequate audience, because of general ignorance even among creators, and most important of all, because "proclaiming, as I proclaim, an acratic esthetics, the imposition of a model or a code would imply a contradiction. . . . My literature is mine *in me;* whoever follows my footsteps slavishly will lose his personal treasure and, page or slave, will be unable to hide his seal or livery. One day Wagner said to Augusta Holmes, his disciple, 'First of all, imitate nobody, and least of all, me.' A great utterance." This, too, was Ibsen's attitude toward the pullulating "Ibsenites," was it not?

thought. There is, of course, a natural explanation of Spanish preoccupation with Darío's technical aspect; he brought freedom, amplitude, and blazed new paths. But within that freedom he spoke of his age; over those paths he drew new vehicles of beauty. And after all, mankind feeds upon feelings and thoughts, not hexameters and heptasyllables. I would not be understood as underestimating the technical aspect of art. The temple of technique is an imposing edifice, but a god must dwell within. By all means let the temple be beautiful, but do not leave it empty. . . .

Among the poet's personal observations regarding *Prosas Profanas* are his relating of *Era Un Aire Suave* to Verlaine's musical theory, and to the music, not of Wagner (as has been written) but of Rameau and Lulli. *Divagación* he describes as "a course in erotic geography." The *Sonatina*, the most rhythmical and musical of all the poems in the collection, proved most popular in Spain and in Spanish America. In *El Reino Interior* he points out the influence of Dante Gabriel Rossetti and some of the French Symbolist leaders.

Azul . . . had been a rosy dawn after a night of uncertain wandering and doubt. *Prosas Profanas*, a dazzling noon of brilliant, yet cold classic sunlight. The swan sails placidly over the lake, whose waters are now and then ruffled by an uneasy ripple. Over both the early books hovers now and then the shadow of the condor. The next volume, however, is deep afternoon; there is the sap of life, the soul of hope, power; there are, too, moments of melancholy introspection. If, in the previous volume, France had taught him much, here life is at once his slave and his master, his despair and his joy.

4. *Cantos de Vida y Esperanza* (1905)

The nine years that intervened between *Prosas Profanas* and the Songs of Life and Hope were fraught with many changes. The Spanish-American war had been fought and had induced in the younger generation of Spain a deep pessimism that turned it to foreign channels. Modernism, with *Prosas Profanas,* had made, too, a successful invasion of Spain. At the same time that the Spanish-American nations sympathized with Cuba, they felt a fear of the United States which has as yet by no means been entirely allayed. Darío, by the force of world events, was being drawn closer to his continental brethren, and out of himself. The days of the ivory tower were over; his muse, while retaining the grace and elegance of the previous volume, gains in vigor and power. The poet, at bottom always personal, becomes more plainly so; his inspiration is more mature, his hand surer, his outlook broader. Quite futilely Darío, in his *Prosas Profanas,* had expressed dissatisfaction with the age into which he was born. He would have been a poet in any age; he was rich in response to the most varied stimuli. This book, in which there is more of life than hope, in which the intensity of the melancholy is more impressive than the exultant optimism, should prove, even without the collection which followed, that Darío was not merely the poet of grace, delicacy and subtle charm, but a modern personality with more than one chord to his lyre. There is a surprising continuity of growth in the man, as is shown by a reading of his works in chronological order. We have already noted his remarkable faculty of assimilation; add to this that the assimilation was complete; wherever the impulse came from, it had been transformed into Darío's own before it issued from his pen.

In *Cantos de Vida y Esperanza*, then, we are to expect a poet of the multiform early twentieth century, afloat upon the turbulent waters of a very real and agitated life. It is just possible, too, that Darío was affected by Rodó's criticism of *Prosas Profanas*, particularly in its statement (made without reproach) of Darío's non-Americanism, as well as by the rising note of Chocano. At any rate the poet himself is deeply conscious of the inner change, which, with greater concision and beauty than any critic could state it, he confesses in the affecting opening poem of the collection.[11]

[11] The various verses here quoted from this important poem may be read entire in Thomas Walsh's fairly adequate rendering of them in *Eleven Poems of Rubén Darío*, G. P. Putnam's Sons, New York and London, 1916, from which I take the following stanzas, corresponding, in order, to those given above in the original:

> I am the singer who of late put by
> The verse azulean and the chant profane,
> Across whose night a rossignol would cry
> And prove himself a lark at morn again.
>
> .   .   .   .
>
> Within my garden stood a statue fair,
> Of marble seeming, yet of flesh and bone;
> A gentle spirit was incarnate there
> Of sensitive and sentimental tone
>
> So timid of the world, it fain would hide
> And from the walls of silence issue not,
> Save when the Spring released upon its tide
> The hour of melody it had begot—
>
> .   .   .   .

Yo soy aquel que ayer no más decía
el verso azul y la canción profana,
en cuya noche un risueñor había
que era alondra de luz por la manaña.

The very first lines announce a change; the poet of yesterday's blue and yesterday's profane proses prepares us for
a new orientation in his verse; there are lines of sincere
self-revelation and certain overtones of repentance or apol-
ogy for previous divagations.   There is, too, I believe, a
protest against the narrow conception of his previous work
which looks upon it as beautiful Parnassianism without
any essentially human implications.

The poet realizes the various epochs of his progress as
keenly as any biographer; this is but another indication of
the self-consciousness with which the man proceeded in his
labors,—perhaps not only self-consciousness but that morbid introspection so characteristic of neurotic natures.   He
knows that he has been dwelling in a dream garden, companioned by roses and swans; that he has been very much
of the eighteenth century and very modern; audacious, cos-

All longing and all ardor, the mere sense
And natural vigor; and without a sign
Of stage effect or literature's pretence—
If there is ever a soul sincere—'tis mine.

.   .   .   .

As with the sponge that salt sea saturates
Below the oozing wave, so was my heart,—
Tender and soft,—bedrenched with bitter fates
That world and flesh and devil here impart.

But through the grace of God my conscience
Elected unto good its better part;
If there were hardness left in any sense
It melted soft beneath the touch of Art.

mopolitan; "with Hugo strong and ambiguous with Verlaine, and thirst of infinite illusions." He has known
grief from childhood, and his youth—"was mine youth?"
—still sheds a fragrancy of melancholy from its roses.   He
recognizes the element of chance in his success and then
comes to a series of quatrains that is exceedingly important
to the man's critics and admirers:

> En mi jardín se vió una estatua bella;
> se juzgó marmol y era carne viva;
> un alma jóven habitaba en ella,
> sentimental, sensible, sensitiva.

> Y tímida ante el mundo, de manera
> que encerrada en silencio no salía,
> Sino cuando en la dulce primavera
> era la hora de la melodía. . . .

Does not this read very much like a protest against having been classed as a poet of swans, of marmoreal Parnassianism, of unfeeling quest of beauty?   Does not this seem
to proclaim the powerfully human impulses that were concealed behind a mask of aloofness?   If any further proof
be needed, it is furnished by a later quatrain:

> todo ansia, todo ardor, sensación pura
> y vigor natural; y sin falsía,
> y sin comedia y sin literatura. . . .;
> si hay un alma sincera, esa es la mía.

From the knowledge of the man that has come to us through
his autobiography and through his friends' comments, I
believe we are justified in taking these words literally;
more than a touch of imitation there may have been in the

early work, but it was untainted by merely literary display;
"if there is a sincere soul, that soul is mine." And is there
not a silent reproach in Darío's assertion that his labors
were "without a sign of stage effect or literature's pretence"? He himself could perhaps never understand why
literature and sincerity should dwell apart, yet is here
forced to make a distinction, suggested, most likely, by the
famous line in Verlaine's *Art Poétique:* "Et tout le reste
est littérature."

The poet's desire for escape from the world is plainly revealed in his confession that he was tempted to climb into
the tower of ivory; but once there he found the atmosphere
depressing; he was seized with hunger for space, with
thirst for the heavens as he peered out of the shadows of
his own abyss.

> Como la esponja que la sal satura
> en el jugo de la mar, fué el dulce y tierno
> corazón mío henchido de amargura
> por el mundo, la carne y el infierno.
>
> Mas, por gracia de Dios, en mi conciencia
> el bien supo elegir la mejor parte;
> y si hubo áspera hiel en mi existencia,
> melificó toda acritud el Arte.

Again I choose to take these words quite literally; the
poet's heart was in reality a sponge that absorbed all outward influences and returned them to the world purified and
unified by the healing power of Art. It is just this sensitivity that made of Darío the universal poet he is; that
kept him from becoming a mere absorber of foreign
models; that rendered him responsive to conflicting cur-

rents of modern thought.   Yet through it all he seems to
have preserved not only a certain pantheistic faith (a faith
with which his early religious teachings often mingled
quite harmoniously) but a veneration for art that amounted
almost to a religion,—that perhaps formed part of his
faith.   And when he seeks for a symbol that shall best
express his conception of Art, the name of Christ occurs
to him, and he writes:

> el Arte puro como Cristo exclama:
> *Ego sum lux et veritas et vita!*
>
> Pure Art, like Christ himself, exclaims,
> I am light and truth and life!

Sincerity is power, he proclaims; to this power must be
added tranquillity.   And for that tranquillity there must
be, too, that faith without which Darío could not have
done.   "On to Bethlehem . . ." concludes the poem.
"The caravan passes!"   Yet it is a halting caravan; his
later poetry reveals the pauses.   Much of his anguish
during life, much of that duality of his nature, was
caused by the struggle between such opposing attitudes as
Christianity and Paganism.   Some element of that struggle which we noticed in Gutiérrez Nájera was undoubtedly
present in the poet; mingled with his religious feelings was
more than a tithe of childish superstition, neurotic fear,
need for solace.   And this feeling, as the years went on,
grew more intense rather than less, if the evidence of his
poetry is to be credited.   His optimism, to me at least,
seems as often as not to be the clamorous assertion of a
wish to believe rather than the exultant cry of the genuine
believer.

We have seen that the poet had been classed as non-American; to some this implied an unjust reproach, and Justo Sierra, in his *Prologo* to Darío's *Peregrinaciones*, written a few years before the publication of the present volume, wrote a sort of reply to Rodó. "Yes," he asserted, addressing the author of the book, "you are American, pan-American, for in your verses, when they are attentively listened to, sound oceanic waves, the murmurs of forests and the roar of Andine cataracts; and if the swan, which is your heraldic bird, floats incessantly over your Hellenic lakes in search of Leda, the condor is wont to descend in winged flight, soaring from crest to crest in your epic strophes; you are American because of the tropical exuberance of your temperament, through which you feel the beautiful; and you are from all parts, as we Americans are wont to be, because of the facility with which on your polychord lyre there sounds all the human lyre, converted into your own music. . . . You desire to belong to nobody; the only words of prose that I found in the *Prosas Profanas* are 'I raise my bridge and enclose myself within my tower of ivory,' and these words clutch at the heart. Return to humanity, return to the People, to your father, despite your citizenship papers in the republic of Aspasia and Pericles. Poets should employ their lyres in civilizing, in dominating monsters, to draw them along to the summit of the sacred mount on which the Ideal is worshipped."

Whether it was Rodó or Sierra (or, what amounts to the same thing, the opinion they represented), that brought Darío back to the People, the note is loud in *Cantos de Vida y Esperanza*. The poet seems to have abandoned his ivory tower and to have emerged into the hurly burly of life.

He has now become undoubtedly American in the sense that Sierra gives to the term, and signalizes not only his Americanism, but a certain type of Hispanism, in poems that are as remarkable for their metrical innovations as for the indication of a new orientation of the poet's thought.

Chief among these is the *Salutación del Optimista*, with its sonorous hexameters that sounded so new to Spanish ears, and much less acceptable than Longfellow's similar experiment in *Evangeline* to his English audience.[12]

Inclitas razas ubérrimas, sangre de Hispania fecunda,
espíritus fraternos, luminosas almas, salve!
Porque llega el momento en que habrán de cantar nuevos himnos
lenguas de gloria.   Un vasto rumor llena los ámbitos;
ondas de vida van renaciendo de pronto;
retrocede el olvido, retrocede engañada la muerte;
Se anuncia un reino nuevo, feliz sibila suena,
y en la caja pandórica de que tantas desgracias surgieron
encontramos de subito, talismanica, pura, riente,
cual pudiera decirla en su verso Virgilio divino,
la divina reina de luz, la celeste Esperanza!

The poem is a ringing call to all of Spanish blood; away

[12] In his *Prefacio* to the *Cantos de Vida y Esperanza* Darío sends an arrow in the direction of the academists.   Referring to his use of the hexameter, he writes: "In all the cultured countries of Europe the absolutely classic hexameter has been employed without causing any astonishment among the lettered majority and least of all among the well read minority.   In Italy, for a long time, not to quote old writers, Carducci has authorized hexameters; in English, I should scarcely dare indicate, through respect for my readers' culture, that Longfellow's *Evangeline* is in the same verses that Horace used to express his best thoughts.   As far as concerns modern free verse . . . is it not truly singular that in this land of Quevedos and of Góngoras the only innovators of the lyric instrument, the only liberators of rhythm, have been the poets of the *Madrid Cómico* and the librettists of the género chico? . . . I make this observation because it is form that first appeals to the crowd.   I am not a poet for the crowd.   But I know that indefectibly I must go to it."

with sloth, diffidence and apathy; there is a renaissance
of the ancient virtues that distinguished Hispania; it
breathes in the two continents wherein repose the glorious
bones of the great dead.   The poet seems to have foreseen
the cataclysm of 1914; he speaks clearly, and without the
haze of prophecy, of muffled roars heard in the entrails of
the world, and the imminence of fatal days; amid this universal upheaval it is no time for the Spanish race to remain dormant; let the blood of Spain unite and yield glory
as of yore.

The same stirring note resounds from *Al Rey Oscar:*

> Mientras el mundo aliente, mientras la esfira gire,
> mientras la onda cordial alimente un ensueño;
> mientras haya una viva pasión, un noble empeño;
> un buscado imposible, una imposible hazaña,
> una America oculta que hallar, vivirá España!

Darío's faith in the Spain that will discover hidden Americas as long as they exist to be discovered is a faith justified by history and by contemporary events.   Whence derives the inexhaustive fecundity of that wonderful nation?
Now in the field of enterprise and discovery, now in the
realm of creative art, the Spanish nation, despite obvious
drawbacks, despite obvious retrogressive influences, burns
with an inextinguishable flame.   Retarded by illiteracy, by
reactionary thought, it yet produces, in our own day, novels,
dramas and poetry that are the delight and the wonder of
all lovers of the beautiful.

It is in this collection that Darío voiced a fear of the
United States which he later modified.   The early sentiments occur in his much-quoted ode *A Roosevelt.*

It is with the voice of the Bible, or the verse of Walt Whitman,
that one should approach you, hunter!
Primitive and modern, simple yet complex,
With somewhat of Washington and more of Nimrod!
You are the United States,
you are the future invader
of that ingenuous America in whom glows indigenous blood,
and which still prays to Jesus Christ and speaks Spanish.

You are a proud and powerful exemplar of your race;
You are cultured, skilful; you oppose Tolstoi.
And dominating horses, or assassinating tigers,
You are an Alexander-Nebuchadnezzar.
(You are a professor of energy
as today's madmen declare.)
You believe that life is a conflagration,
that progress is an eruption;
that wherever you send the bullet,
You implant the future.
No.

The United States are powerful and great.
When they shudder there is a deep trembling
That passes along the enormous vetebræ of the Andes.
When you cry there comes the roar of the lion.
Hugo told it to Grant: "The stars are yours."
(There scarcely shines, as it rises, the Argentine sun,
and the star of Chile surges forth. . . .)   You are rich.
To the cult of Hercules you join the cult of Mammon;
and lighting the way of facile conquest,
Liberty raises its torch before New York.

And against this conception of Northern America he places
the fragrant America of Columbus, Catholic America,
Spanish America, the America in which the noble Guatemoc
said "I am in no bed of roses."

That America
Which trembles with hurricanes and lives on love;

And with a final warning to Roosevelt, the personification
(to him) of North American aggression, he places his ulti-
mate faith in God.[13]

Is it too great a fondness for the Darío of personal revelation and of the inner struggle that makes us see, in such
poems as the *Salutación* and *A Roosevelt*, more of the in-
dignant recipient of outward suggestion than the pure poet?
I do not mean to question the genuineness of the writer's
views, nor to deny the moments of intense poetry that he
achieves in the expression of them. They are poetic, however, only at moments; they are, if I may so express it, the
poeticization of views rather than poetry itself. They are
more important as revealing the man's reaction to the times
than for that intrinsic merit which all art should retain
after the circumstances of its origin have disappeared.
It may be said that despite Justo Sierra, despite González-
Blanco, despite some brilliant poems like the *Canto á la
Argentina*, Darío is not the poet of America, and that America,—Darío's own America—gains by it. On the other
hand a good case may be made out for Darío not only as
the poet of America, but as a poet who, in a few notable
poetic works, voices a Pan-Americanism that is less ambiguous than Chocano's. The more one reads the later
Darío, the more one feels that this is the true man in all
his expansion,—that he is in a very true sense universal,

[13] Compare the similar spirit of the first poem in the group called Los
Cisnes (The Swans) in *Cantos de Vida y Esperanza*. "Will so many millions of us speak English?" Recall, however, the later change in Darío's
attitude. (See section on *El Canto Errante*.)

not merely in the statement of that universality (as in Chocano), but in the evidences of it as presented by poems of
intensity and depth that are, in the words of Pedro Henríquez Ureña, "beyond art." [14]

There are indications in the volume under consideration
that for all Darío's emergence from the ivory tower, he felt
a nostalgia for it,—that his regret at having been born
into his age had a root of genuineness,—that his evocations
of the past are but another proof of his attempt to escape
the multifarious life about him.   That longing is evident
in such poems as the *Letanía De Nuestro Señor Don Quijote*
and the beautiful sonnet to Cervantes.   "Pray for us who
are hungry for life, our souls groping and our faith lost
. . . for we are without soul, without life, without Quijote,
with neither feet nor wings, with neither Sancho nor God."
And then comes a strange denial of his previous studies in
foreign letters and the lore of contemporary science.

> De tantas tristezas, de dolores tantos,
> de los superhombres de Nietzsche, de cantos
> afonos, recetas que firma un doctor,
> de las epidemias de horribles blasfemías
> de las Academias,
> líbranos, señor!

What is the poem but the cry of an agitated soul for a peace
that it will never know,—for a peace which at bottom it
may not even desire?

Cervantes it is who, like a good friend, sweetens his bitter moments:

[14] In a letter to the author.

Though heavy hours I pass and mournful days
In solitude, Cervantes is to me
A faithful friend.   He lightens gloom with glee;
A restful hand upon my head he lays.
Life in the hues of nature he portrays;
A golden helmet jewelled brilliantly,
He gives my dreams, that wander far and free.
It is for me he sighs, he laughs, he prays.

The Christian and the lover and the knight
Speaks like a streamlet clear and crystalline.
I love and marvel at his spirit bright,
Beholding how, by mystic Fate's design
The whole world now drinks mirth and rich delight
From deathless sadness of a life divine!

Something of that "tristeza inmortal de ser divino" attaches to Darío's own labors.

I am most impressed by the autumnal spirit of the volume.   The poet realizes that youth is fast departing and sings it his sad farewell in a poem (*Canción de Otoño en Primavera*) that has been called the finest Spanish poem since the sixteenth century.   That praise is not needed for the appreciation of its haunting beauty; it is instructive, too, that the poet refers to that varied quality of his works which has not yet been generally recognized.

Juventud, divino tesoro,
ya te vas para no volver!
Cuando quiero llorar, no lloro. . . .
y a veces lloro sin querer. . . .

Plural ha sido la celeste
historia de mi corazón.

Programa Matinal preaches an epicurean, yet utilitarian
creed; *Melancolia* presents an auto-diagnosis, in which the
poet attributes his ailment to dreaming.   Poetry becomes
to him the iron shirt of the thousand points that he wears
next his soul.   *Lo Fatal* is another outburst of the age-long
query   addressed   to   the   Sphinx   of   Life.   Whence?
Whither?   Why?   In his anguish he envies the tree that
is scarcely sensitive, and even more the utterly insensitive
rock,

> for there is no grief greater than that of living,
> nor more grievous woe than conscious life.

> To be and yet know nothing, to have no certain goal,
> and the fear of having existed, and a further terror. . . .
> and the certain horror of being tomorrow dead,
> and to suffer because of life and because of the shadows,

> And for that which we know not and scarcely suspect,
> and the flesh that tempts with its fresh clusters,
> and the tomb that waits with its funeral branches,
> and not know whither we go,
> nor whence we came . . .!

So, in the *Dulzura del Angelus,* he reveals the search for a
faith that he cannot feel, and in *Otras Poemas XIII,* the
conflict between the Pagan and the Christian ideal.   Was
Darío one or the other, or was he both?   I am inclined to
the paradoxical solution.   If ever an artist displayed an
oscillation between opposing tendencies, Darío did.

The poet's pessimism at times reaches such depths that
he doubts whether life itself be worth while (*A Phocas El
Campesino*); yet he is capable of swinging to the other
extreme and glorifying woman in a most passionate, dar-

ing, aphrodisiac hymn to the flesh. (*Otras Poemas;*
XVII.)   Here one is more inclined to agree with González-Blanco when he terms it the "most original thought,
woven into the most vibrating lyric hymn that may be
culled from Spanish poetry since the epoch of Romanticism."   How far are we now from the juvenile misogynist
of *Abrojos!*   With mastery of self-expression has come a
deep sincerity.

But not all is ardent passion, profound melancholy, sincere confession, in *Cantos de Vida y Esperanza.*   There is
something of the pure joy of creation, the joy of the artist
in the domination of his tools, such as rises with orchestral
clangor from the *Marcha Triunfal:* [15]

> The cortège is coming!
> The cortège is coming!   Now we hear the clarions shrill
>   and clear!
> The sword-blades announcing themselves in vivid reflections!
> Now it comes, steel and gold, the cortège of warriors vic-
>   torious!
> Now it passes under the arches adorned with the white
>   statues of Minerva and Mars—
> The arches of triumph where the figures of Fame stand with
>   their trumpets long and erect.
> The solemn glory of the banners
> Borne by the robust hands of athletic heroes.
> We list to the sound of the arms of the cavaliers,
> The rattle of harness masking the sturdy war-horses,
> Their trappings scarring the ground;
> And the timbals
> That accent the steps with their martial rhythm.
> Thus pass the fierce warriors
> Under the arches of triumph!

[15] Version by Sylvester Baxter.

In clearness the clarions are lifting their voices:
Their chanting sonorous,
Their calid chorus
Which enfolds in its thunder of gold
The flags with their august superbness.
It speaks of the combat, of vengeance that's wounded,
Of manes roughly flowing,
Of plumes rudely tossing, the darts and the lances,
The blood that in heroic crimson
Has been laving the earth;
The black death-mastiffs that come with War.

The golden sounds
Announce the triumphant
Advance of glory;
Deserting the peaks that guard their nests,
Spreading their enormous wings to the wind,
The condors arrive,
And Victory has come!

The cortège is passing.
The grandsire points out the heroes
To the child by his side:—
Behold how like the old man's beard
The golden curls are surrounded by ermine—
Beautiful women bestow their garlands of flowers
And under the porticos their faces are showing like roses;
And the most beautiful one
Smiles on the fiercest of conquering heroes.
Honor to him who bears captive the enemy's banner!
Honor to the wounded and honor to the faithful
Soldiers who died at the hands of the foe;
Clarions!   Laurels!

The noble knights of glorious days
Salute from their panoplies the new wreaths and laurels:
The aged knights of the grenadiers, stronger than bears,

Brothers to the lancers who once were centaurs—
The trumpets of war resound,
Filling the air with their clamor—
To those ancient knights,
To those illustrious swordsmen
Who incarnate past glories,
And to the sun that today illumines new victories won,
And to the hero who leads his band of fiery youths,
To him who loves the emblem of his maternal soil,
To him who has struggled—rifle and sword in hand—
Through the heats of red summer,

The snows and the winds of frigid winter,
Through the night, the frost,
And hatred and death
That his country may live immortal.
They salute you with voices of brass,
The trumpets of war that are sounding
The March of Triumph.

There is a lofty hope, not unmingled with that uncertainty which flecks all virile optimism. Deeply expressive of this aspect is the *Song of Hope*, which I present in the original Spanish and in Miss Blackwell's faithful version:

Un gran vuelo de cuervos mancha el azul celeste.
Un soplo milenario trae amago de peste.
Se asesinan los hombres en el extremo Este.

¿Ha nacido el apocalíptico Anticristo?
Se han sabido presagios y prodigios se han visto
y parece inminente el retorno de Cristo.

La tierra está preñada de dolor tan profundo
que el soñador imperial, meditabundo,
sufre con las angustias del corazón del mundo.

Verdugos de ideales afligieron la tierra,
en un pozo de sombra la humanidad se encierra
con los rudos molosos del odio y de la guerra.

¡Oh, Señor Jesucristo!   ¿Por qué tardas, qué esperas
para tender tu mano de luz sobre las fieras
y hacer brillar al sol tus divinas banderas?

Surge de pronto y vierte la esencia de la vida
sobre tanta alma loca, triste o empedernida
que amante de tinieblas tu dulce aurora olvida.

Ven, Señor, para hacer la gloria de ti mismo.
Ven con temblor de estrellas y horror de cataclismo,
ven a traer amor y paz sobre el abismo.

Y tu caballo blanco, que miró el visionario,
pase.   Y suene el divino clarín extraordinario.
Mi corazón será brasa de tu incensario.

The blue is stained with a vast raven-flight;
A wind blows, threatening pestilence's blight;
In the far east, men slay in deadly fight.

Has anti-Christ been born within the land?
Portents are seen, and marvels dire and grand.
Christ's second coming seems to be at hand.

The Earth is pregnant with so deep a smart,
The royal dreamer, musing sad apart,
Grieves with the anguish of the world's great heart.

Slaughtered ideals have brought sorrows great;
Humanity is prisoned now by fate
In a dark pit, with hounds of war and hate.

Lord Christ, why dost thou wait to show thy might,
To stretch o'er these wild beasts thy hand of light,
And in the sun display thy banners bright?

Swiftly arise, and poor life's essence free
On souls that crazed or sad or hardened be,
Loving the dark, forgetting dawn and thee!

Come then, O Lord, thine own true glory show!
Come with stars' trembling and with earthquake's throe;
Bring love and peace from out the gulf below!

Let thy white horse the prophet saw, pass by,
Thy wondrous clarion sound from heaven on high!
My burning heart shall in thy censer lie.

As a collection, the *Cantos de Vida y Esperanza* is the
keystone of Darío's poetical arch. It most exemplifies the
man that wrote it; it most reveals his dual nature, his inner sincerity, his complete psychology; it is the artist at
maturity. There is a wider sweep, a subtler music, a
closer approach to universal amplitude of expression and
linguistic sonority. In the *Prosas Profanas,* says Gon-
záles-Blanco, the poet's æsthetic was at its highest; in the
Cantos de Vida y Esperanza it is his technique that triumphs. Yet how much more than technique it contains in
its pages!

In his *History of My Books* Darío, considering this collection, gives ample evidence of its source in a fuller life,
of his struggle between Catholicism and Paganism, of an
optimism that was, it seems, more a manifestation of will
than of conviction. He proclaims himself a "Spaniard of
America and an American of Spain," with an admiration

for the race's past that cries out "Hispania forever!" Prayer has always rescued him, he confesses, yet he acknowledges hours of doubt and rage. "Certainly there exists in me, from the beginning of my life, the profound preoccupation with the end of existence, the terror of the unknown, the fear of the tomb, or rather, of that moment in which the heart ceases its uninterrupted task and life disappears from our body. In my desolation I have rushed to God as a refuge, I seized upon prayer as upon a parachute. I have been filled with anguish when I sounded the depths of my faith and found it insufficiently sturdy and rooted, when the conflict of ideas has caused me to waver and I have felt that I had no constant and certain support. All philosophies have appeared impotent to me, and some abominable and the work of madmen and malefactors. On the other hand, from Marcus Aurelius to Bergson, I have greeted with gratitude those who bring wings, tranquillity and pleasurable flights, and teach us to understand in the best way possible the enigma of our earthly existence. . . . And the principal merit of my work, if it possess any, is that of a great sincerity. . . ."

Among the metrical innovations that have been noted are: free metre, both with and without a rhythmic basis; hexameters; the revival of the hendecasyllable without accent on the sixth syllable. With regard to the hexameter, Darío believed, despite authorities, that long and short syllables exist in Spanish.[16]

---

[16] Readers especially interested in Darío's technique will find in Cejador y Frauca, op. cit., pages 113 and 114, a detailed summary (quoted from Lauxar) of the poet's innovations in metre and metrical combination.

5. *El Canto Errante* (1907)
And Other Poems

Before approaching Darío's final notable collection, let
us pause for a moment upon the *Oda á Mitre* (1906) to
express the opinion that it is on the whole, despite its lofty
sentiments, but equal to the much earlier Ode to Hugo.
Darío is more the poet than the statesman.   The later ode
seems labored, "d'occasion," and lacking in the enthusiasm
of the poem to the great poet.   The very first lines, with
their quotation from Whitman's "Oh, Captain; oh, my captain!" as well as the epigraph, from Ovid, seem to reveal a
groping inspiration.   Darío the poet, however, will out,
and it is the poet in Mitre that he most admires.

> Y para mí, Maestro, tu vasta gloria es esa;
> amar los hechos fugaces de la hora,
> sobra la ciencia á ciegas, sobre la historia espesa,
> la eterna Poesía mas clara que la aurora.

And when he recites his litany of glory to the master, whose
name comes to his lips as the summit of human fame?
Victor Hugo's.

> Gloria a tí que, provecto como el destino plugo,
> la ancianidad tuviste más límpida y más bella;
> tu enorme catafalco fuera el de Victor Hugo,
> si hubiera en Buenos Aires un Arco de la Estrella!

The finale is a noble piece of writing and reveals Darío as
a thinker whose vision could see beyond even continental
frontiers.   "Rest in peace! . . . But no; rest not.   Let
your soul continue its labor of light unto eternity, and let

your inspiration guide our peoples, friend of the beautiful and the just, of the good and the true. Your presence is gone; may your memory grow . . . and may your labor, your name, your prestige, your glory, be like America, for all Humanity!"

The poet of *El Canto Errante* continues the varied manner of the preceding volume. He is outspokenly opposed to any narrowing conception of art, which he considers "not a combination of rules, but a harmony of caprices." He has no use for such terminology as old and new. "My verse has always been born with its body and its soul, and I have applied to it no manner of orthopedics. Yes, I have sung old airs, and I have attempted to march toward the future, always under the divine rule of music: music of idea, music of verse." *El Canto Errante* secures Darío's reputation as a universal poet and emphasizes, perhaps, the pantheistic element in that universality. How far we are from the ivory tower of the *Prosas Profanas!* As the poet says in his Ballad to Martínez Sierra, the exquisite stylist and translator of Maeterlinck, the best muse is of flesh and blood. Darío has now become a wandering Jew of poesy. He is the singer who journeys over all the world, "reaping smiles and thoughts, amid white peace and red war." Upon the elephant's back, through vast India, in palanquin through China, over the pampas of South America,—everywhere he received the inspiration of his universal chant; Harmony and Eternity is his device. Here we may see why Darío is not the poet of America; his mission, like that which he discerns in the soul of Mitre, is to reach humanity; he feels himself, it is true, American in spirit and in origin, but his patriotism does not blind him to the larger im-

portance of the human unit. His travels, perhaps, have
taught him his own multiplicity as well as the essential
similarity that underlies human diversity. That is why he
is Majorcan as well as Oriental, Greek as well as Spanish.

SLINGS

I dreamed a slinger bold was I,
Born 'neath Majorca's limpid sky.
With stones I gathered by the sea
I hunted eagles flying free,
And wolves; and when a war arose,
I went against a thousand foes.

A pebble of pure gold one day
Up to the zenith sped its way,
When mid the heavens blue and wide
A huge jerfalcon I espied,
Attacking in the fields of air
A strange, bright bird, of plumage rare
A wondrous bird; its course on high
With ruby streaked the sapphire sky.

My stone returned not; but to me
The Cherub-bird flew fearlessly.
Straight to my side it came, and said:
"Wounded, Goliath's soul has fled.
I come to thee from out the sky:
Lo, David's radiant soul am I!"

Apply this universality of humanity to the sphere of nature and a modern pantheism is the result. Measured by
the totality of his work, which forms a rarely ordered rising curve, Darío is nothing less than cosmogonic; he identi-

fies himself with all times, all moods, all animate nature, all peoples.

It is this sense of his multiplicity that assails him in poems like *Eheu.*

> Here by the Latin sea,
> I speak the truth:
>
> In rock, in oil and wine
> I feel my antiquity.
>
> Oh, how old I am, good God!
> Oh, how ancient I am! . . .
> Whence comes my song?
> And I, wither am I going?
>
> The knowledge of myself
> Is costing me
> Many abysmal moments,
> and the how and the when . . .

Nor was this mood a new one to Darío, in whom from the very first, as a collation of his poems with his autobiography may show, existed the germs of all his later moods and manners.   It seems that his frequent questioning of self led to a deeper knowledge of humanity.   It has been said that all genius is neurotic.   Without pressing that point, it is quite safe to assert that certain types of neuroticism enlarge appreciably the sufferer's view of himself as well as of mankind.   As early as 1893, in *Metempsicosis,* Darío had imagined himself the soldier lover of capricious Cleopatra, and had evoked the past through the mouth of the dead.   This is but one of the examples, by the way, of the poet's early control over that interior rhythm which he mentioned in *Prosas Profanas.* And what a haunting effect is achieved by the refrain: "Eso fué todo,"—That was all!

There is a most beautiful return to the autochthonous theme in such an evocation of rare pictorial charm as *Tutecotzimi,* in which the beauty of the thought is by no means the least of the beauties. His poem to the pines reveals him in an attractive mood of self-revelatory tree worship:

SONG OF THE PINES

O pines, O brothers of the earth and air,
I love you! Sweet, good, grave are all your words.
You are a tree that seems to think and feel,
Caressed by dawns, by poets and by birds.

The wingèd sandal touched your lofty brows;
You have been mast, and stage, and judge's chair,
O sunny pines, O pines of Italy,
All bathed in charm, in glory, in blue air!

Mute, sombre, knowing not the sunlight's gold,
Growing 'mid icy vapors gray and dull,
On dreamy mountains vast—pines of the night,
Pines of the North, ye too are beautiful!

Like statues or like actors in your mien,
Outreaching towards the kisses of the sea,
O pines of Naples, girt about with flowers,
O pines divine, ye haunt my memory!

When in my wanderings the Golden Isle
Gave me a place of refuge on her shore
To dream my dreams, there too I met the pines—
The pines my heart holds dear forevermore.

Dear for their sadness, beauty, gentleness,
Their monkish look, their hair spread wide above,
Their fragrance, as of one enormous flower,
Their sap, their voices, and their nests of love.

O ancient pines, which by the epics' wind
Were swayed, of which the glowing sun was fain!
O lyric pine trees of the Renaissance,
And of the gardens in the land of Spain!

Their arms æolian by the winds are stirred,
Tossed by the gusts that wake there, as they roam,
Sounds of soft plumage, sounds of satin robes,
Sounds of the water and the ocean foam.

O night on which the hand of Destiny
Brought me the grief that still my heart's depths hold!
On a dark pine the moon her silver shed,
And by a nightingale I was consoled.

We are romantic.   Who that lives is not?
He that feels neither grief nor love divine,
He that knows naught of kisses nor of song,
Let him go hang himself upon a pine!

Not I.   I persevere.   The past confirms
My eagerness, my life that onward flows.
A lover I of dreams and forms, who comes
From far away, and towards the future goes.

In *A Colón* the native note momentarily becomes one of pessimism at sight of the internecine strife amid the Spanish-American peoples; the poet recalls the memory of the indigenous chiefs and compares them most favorably with the colonizing whites; he is sorry that the continent was ever discovered by the latter:

Pluguiera á Dios las aguas, antes intactas
no reflejaran nunca las blancas velas;
ni vieran las estrellas stupefactas
arribar a la orilla tus carabelas!

Cristóforo Colombo, pobre Almirante,
ruega á Dios por el mundo que descubriste!

"Christopher Columbus, poor Admiral, pray to God for the
world that you discovered!" The image of Columbus, as
of Hugo, accompanies him in all his thoughts, and when
he salutes the volcano Momotombo he sees in it a symbol of
the two great men:

Your voice was one day heard by Christopher Columbus;
Hugo sang your legendary geste. The two
Were, like you, colossal, Momotombo,
mountains inhabited by the fire of God.

Darío's attitude toward the United States did not remain
that which he so forcefully expressed in his address to
Roosevelt. In his *Salutación al Aguila,* in hexameters that
some of his countrymen have found superior to those of
the *Salutación del Optimista,* he intones a view expressive
of greater confidence in the United States, as well as of its
possibility as a model for the Spanish Americans in certain respects. From the Yankees, he feels, the dreamy
youth of the southern continent, with so marked a weakness
for rhetoric and ostentation, may learn constancy, strength,
character. The Condor is not the Eagle's rival, but its
brother. "May Latin America receive your influence, and
may a new Olympus be reborn, peopled with gods and
with heroes." The poem, while important because of re-

vealing Darío's altered attitude, does not strike that echoing note which rises from so much of his other work. The eagle is not Darío's heraldic bird; his swan is more sure, as is his condor. His Pan-Americanism at times seems an utterance made in compliance with outward circumstances rather than an impulsive, spontaneous cry from within. Yet, at other times it strikes me as being of a powerful, resonant sincerity.

The *Canto á la Argentina* (1910) is an inspiring, polyphonic, vast hymn,—the longest of Darío's poems, in forty-five stanzas of a length varying from eight lines to seventy-six, with lines of from six to twelve syllables,—sung as much to liberty as to Argentina. The longer Darío lived the closer he drew to that crowd which he thought he despised, and the more Pan-American, as well as universal, he became. He acquired, too, a certain noble magniloquence that one might scarcely have suspected in the poet of an *Azul* . . . or of *Prosas Profanas*. As a celebration of the centenary of Argentina's independence, the *Canto* is fully matched to its lofty theme. There is an epic sweep to the sonorous stanzas, which scatter upon the air a proclamation of freedom; there is a biblical fervor that welcomes the exiles of all nations to this new Promised Land.

"Here is the region of El Dorado, here is the terrestrial paradise, here the longed-for good fortune, here the Golden Fleece, here the pregnant Canaan, here the resuscitated Atlantis. . . ." Here, too, is the land "of the visionary poets who on their Olympuses or Calvaries loved all the people," the land where "is reared the Babel wherein all may understand one another."

In strophes that seize with rare skill upon salient traits,
epitomizing a national character in each, he calls upon the
Russian, the Jew, the Italian, the Spaniard, the Swiss, the
Frenchman, the German,—all the disinherited of the earth
—to come to the arms of this mother nation. To the Jews
Argentina becomes Zion; to the Spaniard it becomes a new
Spain; the Plata's shores are a mystic Eden on which new
Adams shall arise; here all religions shall be free.

> All hail, Fatherland, for thou art mine, too,
> Since thou belongest to humanity;
> All hail, in the name of Poesy,
> All hail, in the name of Liberty!

The Argentina that Darío sings offers "homes and rights
to the citizens of the world"—*Ave, Argentina, vita plena!*
It is a nation of peace, arming itself only for defence:

> Be a sentinel over Life,
> Not an adjutant of Death.

As the glorious song continues the harmonies swell. A
beautiful bit of imagery visions the northern and southern
Americas as the huge plates of a continental balance having the isthmus of Panama as the needle; into these plates
each continent places its wealth of hope, all in the cause of
liberty; this Pan-Americanism of imagery is in the same
long stanza explicitly stated in terms of a fraternal union
of the "Anglo-Saxon race with the Latin-American." The
poet's aspiration rises higher in another long stanza devoted to universal peace: "War, then, only against war!
Peace, so that thought may rule the sphere, and sweep, like
the biblical chariot of fire, from firmament to firmament.

Peace, for the creators, the discoverers, inventors, seekers after truth. . . ."

The finale is a quotation from the national hymn,—at once the source and the goal of the stirring *Canto:*

> Oíd, mortales, el grito sagrado:
> Libertad!   Libertad!   Libertad!

> Hearken, mortals, to the sacred cry:
> Liberty!   Liberty!   Liberty!

The poem is in more than one way remarkable. First, for its sustained flight and the genuine inspiration. It produces upon the reader the effect of having been written (even declaimed) in a single outburst. Then there is a human outlook which contrasts markedly with the early aristocracy of the singer. To me, at least, the international sentiments ring more genuinely from these lines than from earlier ones. The Darío who began as a Romantic, then ranging through Parnassianism and Symbolism, here seems to revel in the pure, untrammeled, uncatalogued joy of creation. *El Canto á la Argentina* is a logical development of the two collections that preceded it.

Later poems, as well as the various posthumous collections issued, add little to the poet's fame. The master was capable of writing some most pedestrian verse, such as the poem to *La Gran Metropolis,* in which New York's contrast of wealth and misery is sung in limping verses of lustreless facture; of such pretty conceits as *Dama,* in which we encounter the startling metaphor

> The smile of the Gioconda
> Made by the Virgin Mary;

he can become most unpoetic in his political utterances, as
witness the verses of farewell written to the actress María
Guerrero shortly after the publication of *Prosas Profanas*.
On the other hand, in his marvellous *Poema del Otoño* he
intones a hymn to love that pulses with the passion of even-
tide; for beneath its bacchanalian rhythm is the slackening
gait of resignation.   In two lines of luminous beauty he
seems to sum up the mystery and the enchantment of life:

> The dove of Venus flies
> Above the Sphinx.

Is so much often compressed in as many words?   And in
the final stanza of a poem that tempts one to complete
transcription, he expresses what may be taken as the essence of his poetic career:

> En nosotros la Vida vierte
> Fuerza y calor.
> Vamos al reino de la Muerte
> Por el camino de Amor!

> We journey to the realms of Death
> Over the pathway of Love!

6. *Prose Works*

With the exception of the prose section of *Azul . . .*
Darío's prose labors were the outgrowth of his journalistic
career.

In that characteristic tissue of paradoxes which Oscar
Wilde has called *The Critic As Artist*, Ernest asks, "What
is the difference between literature and journalism?"   To

which Gilbert facetiously replies, "Oh, journalism is unreadable and literature is not read. That is all." Which explanation, if it be forgiven on the Wildean principle that an artistic untruth is preferable to an uninteresting verity, omits the consideration that literature and journalism sometimes become interchangeable terms. How different the attitude of another English paradoxical spirit, Bernard Shaw, who has told us in his *Sanity of Art* that

> I am also a journalist, proud of it, deliberately cutting out of my works all that is not journalism, convinced that nothing that is not journalism will live long as literature, or be of any use whilst it does live. I deal with all periods; but I never study any period but the present, which I have not yet mastered and never shall; and as a dramatist I have no clue to any historical or other personage save that part of him which is also myself, and which may be nine-tenths of him or ninety-nine hundredths, as the case may be (if, indeed, I do not transcend the creature), but which, anyhow, is all that can ever come within my knowledge of his soul. The man who writes about himself and his own time is the only man who writes about all people and all time. The other sort of man, who believes that he and his period are so distinct from all other men and periods that it would be immodest and irrelevant to allude to them or assume that they could interest any one but himself and his contemporaries, is the most infatuated of all egotists, and consequently the most unreadable and negligible of all the authors. And so, let others cultivate what they call literature; journalism for me!

Not that Shaw has said anything really new in this gay paragraph. He has merely taken what most of us always called good literature and labelled it "Journalism" in order to emphasize the proposition that posterity can be interested only in those traits of man's writings which are always contemporary because always human.   But there is virtue in the paradox.

It was journalism of the Shavian sort that was produced by such reformers of prose as Gutiérrez Nájera, Martí and Darío.   How remarkably little of what Darío wrote as the result of his various travels and studies is unworthy of preservation between covers!   And how much our own journalists and magazine writers could learn from his pages in the way of enthusiasm, patience, human insight and a sincerity that makes few sacrifices upon the altar of cleverness and mere glitter.

There is little necessity here for an extended consideration of the poet's prose works.   Everywhere may be discerned the mind of the poet which never quite lost its aristocratic cast, however much it recognized the value of the crowd as a background of art.   If I mention *Los Raros* as my favorite, it is because in that book Darío the poet and Darío the extremely sensitive human being are most evident in Darío the writer of prose.   It is questionable whether such a prose would prove acceptable to the majority of English readers; the non-Spanish element in it, of course, would not bother them.   What might, however, seem not fully acceptable, is the quasipoetic glow that shines from every page.[17]   It was of this book that William

---

[17] "He has done more damage with his prose than with his verse among the young writers, especially the Spanish-Americans."—*Cejador y Frauca*, op. cit., page 84.   Of all prose, so-called poetic prose, which so easily degenerates into airy nothing, is most difficult to manage.   How much harm has Maeterlinck worked, for example, even among our young United States writers, especially in the domain of the one-act play!   And has not the influence of Dunsany led to what has most properly been dubbed "Dunsanity"?   But "youth, of course, must have its fling" and will cling to its prerogative, whatever the influence to which, parasitically, it attaches itself in quest of a personality.

Archer said that from what he could half make of the work he would learn Spanish, to read it.

7. *Summary*

Such is the remarkable figure who so dominated an epoch that his very name serves to characterize it. Can Darío really be pinned down in the critic's sample case like the entomologist's butterfly? Perhaps, by some refinement of the critic's art an appearance of inner unity may be imparted to the man, his life and his labors. To me, however, he is most human in his questionings, his fears, his vacillations, his wavering, his unresolved doubt. From the very first he reveals these dominant characteristics. He is of the past, of the present, of the future. From the very nature of poetry and its incapability of being transferred into another tongue it is inevitable that he will never be to other peoples what he will remain to Spaniards; that is one of the disadvantages under which the poet, more than any other creative artist, labors.

He crystallized an epoch; he transformed a language; he infused new life into the Castilian muse; he retained his own personality while absorbing all the currents that appeared during his career; he became, as we have seen, a legendary figure even during his own life. He belongs

Darío's chief prose works, outside of the prose section which forms the greater part of *Azul* . . . and the pamphlet *A de Gilbert*, 1889 (written on the death of his friend Pedro Balmaceda, the Chilean poet) are:

Los Raros, 1893	*Parisiana*, 1908
España Contemporánea, 1901	*El Viaje á Nicaragua*, 1909
Peregrinaciones, 1901	*Letras*, 1911
La Caravana Pasa, 1903	*Todo al Vuelo*, 1912
Tierras Solares, 1904	*La Vida de Rubén Darío, escrita*
Opiniones, 1906	*por el mismo*, 1912.

not only with the greatest poets that have written in the Spanish tongue, but with the masters of universal poesy. For above the early Parnassianism, the later Symbolism and the final complex humanism, is the eternally human of a poet who was peculiarly of his day and, by that same token, of all ages.

CHAPTER III

JOSÉ ENRIQUE RODÓ

(1872–1917)

In many respects the life and labors of José Enrique
Rodó, the noted Uruguayan philosopher and litterateur,
present a marked contrast to those of Rubén Darío. The
Nicaraguan poet was himself a human lyre upon which the
passing winds and events played their own subtle songs; he
responded in remarkable degree to the varying influences
of his time, presenting, in that response, an organic, mental
and spiritual growth. Rodó, no less responsive, was of a
more Olympian nature; indeed, if we are to use a phraseology that Nietzsche made popular, Darío is the Dionysian
spirit, Rodó the Apollonian. Yet they are both men of
their age; both represent, in varying degree and in most
diverse manifestation, the self-expansion that characterizes
the times.

Despite his static life (which was altered only toward
the end by a voyage to Europe during which he died, at
Palermo), and his classical serenity, Rodó was one of the
most dynamic spirits of his day. More than any other he
realized the fluidity of modern thought, the resurgent self
that lay at the bottom of the modernist movement and the
general overturn in the world of ideas. In his famous
study of Darío's *Prosas Profanas* he proclaimed, as we saw,

his own modernism, not in the sense of the word that connotes a prurient curiosity for the new, but in that larger significance which aligns a man with the spirit of the advancing age. Rodó's entire philosophy of unending self-renewal is, indeed, one of the most striking aspects of the search for self which, in latter days, has often assumed such ludicrous forms. He is the philosopher not only of modernism, but of eternal youth in the realm of thought. His work reveals how complex is that inner self which once seemed so simple to fathom; complex not only in its modernity, but in the heritage of the past and the previsions of the future which lie dormant in every personality, however humble and seemingly sterile. And here we approach Rodó's great service not only to the youth of Spanish America, but to the youth of the world. He realized in most intense degree, as we shall see from a study of his chief works, the infinite possibilities of the human species; while others were, properly and laudably enough, seeking self-expansion from within outward, he delved from without inward and revealed the immense store of riches there. In such a sense his philosophy (and I dislike to use a word that seems too static for Rodó's dynamic method), is centripetal. "Know thyself," he said, with Socrates; but what a revelation of our inner selves he afforded us! And he was himself the best example of his method. Not until the close of his life did this man, who had preached the necessity of travel as one of the methods of self-renewal, stir from his beloved Montevideo; yet his life was infinitely richer than that of many a globe-trotter. It was a continuous expansion in both directions; it was, both in its daily manifestations and in the thoughts that grew out of

it, a splendid example of what I have called creative eclecticism,—a harmonious structure of the present built upon
solid foundations of the past,—perhaps the only method
possible in these days of growing complexity. The only
method, because it is in reality no method, but a flexible
view that permits of personal variations and continuous
change in accordance with new knowledge. There is nothing essentially novel in Rodó's protean philosophy; novelty long ceased to bask in the solar rays. What is refreshing, vitalizing and stimulating in the thoughts of the
great Uruguayan, whose intellectual ancestry dates from
Plato and in our own day from Taine, Renan and
Bergson, is the emphasis upon the necessity of constant
self-renewal. "O rinnovarsi ó morire," d'Annunzio had
written,—Self-renewal or Death—and the flaming line was
taken up by the modern spirits in all the Spanish nations.
Characteristically enough, however, Rodó, whose thoughts
are upon life rather than death, recasts the phrase and
transforms it into "Reformarse es vivir"—Self-renewal is
Life." That is the idea at the bottom of everything Rodó
wrote; that is his great contribution to the Spanish-American
renaissance of the previous century in its later phases.
That is the spirit which informs his essays upon representative Spanish Americans, his criticism of Hispano-
American writers, his writings upon a fuller and broader
life. Rodó was among the great essayists of his generation; he was, speaking for Hispanic America, the philosopher par excellence of his time, called into being (as are
most great men) by the necessity of the epoch. And although his specific ideas may be altered, subtracted from
and added to, the basic element of his philosophy, from the

very nature of its call for continuous readjustment to a changing environment, will itself long remain unchanged. He erected, not a system that attempted to include all psychological phenomena within the bounds of a rigid dogma—and dogma is all the more distasteful and harmful for being philosophic or scientific—but a strangely adaptable structure that from the very pliability of its nature may better resist those social changes that spell the downfall of more rigid systems.

I

Modern Uruguay presents, in its intellectual development, a spectacle far out of proportion to the diminutive size of the republic. Out of years of strife has emerged a nation which, in the last half of the nineteenth century, produced such a galaxy of important figures as Samuel Blixen and Victor Pérez Petit (representative of the naturalistic theatre), Carlos Reyles (influential in the field of the naturalistic novel) and Julio Herrera y Reissig, a modernist poet with an involved style quite his own. Rodó is of their generation,—a generation as rich in intellectual struggles as the previous years of the nation had been in the bloodier contest of the battlefield. Everywhere wages hot discussion of literature, politics and philosophy. In the very year of Rodó's birth was founded the University Club, later called the *Ateneo* (Atheneum) of Uruguay, in which the spirit of free investigation waged combat against cramping mental restrictions.

Rodó was born in Montevideo of an old and well-established house. It is significant that he received his education in the first lay school that was established in the country.   At home, however, he was brought up in that Catholic faith which is the common emotional and religious background of all Spanish-American youth.   It was, as Rodó's friend Barbagelata points out,[1] an undogmatic, non-clerical Catholicism that young Rodó imbibed from his mother.

The future philosopher, however, early abandoned his visits to the church.   His college days were so well spent in serious study that he was accounted a prodigy at the age of twenty-one, and unlike prodigies at that age, an unpedantic one.

Like most of us, he consumed not a few of his youthful hours in the composition of verse.   One of the sonnets of these early days gives us a hint as to his early readings, and as to something more which, strangely enough, his numerous commentators seem to have overlooked.   Let us first read the sonnet:

> De la dichosa edad en los albores
> Amó a Perrault mi ingénua fantasía,
> Mago que en torno de mi sien tendía
> Gasas de luz y flecos de colores.
>
> Del sol de adolescencia en los ardores
> Fué Lamartine mi cariñoso guía
> *Jocelyn* propició, bajo la umbría
> Fronda vernal, mis ocios soñadores.
>
> Luego el bronce hugoiano arma y escuda
> Al corazón, que austeridad entraña.
> Cuando avanzaba en mi heredad el frío,

---

[1] *Prologo* to *Cinco Ensayos*, by José Enrique Rodó.   Madrid.

Amé a Cervantes—sensación mas ruda
Busqué luego en Balzac . . .y hoy, cosa extraña!
Vuelvo a Perrault, me reconcentro y río! . . .

There are several noteworthy things about the sonnet,—
not as a piece of poetry, but as a bit of self-revelation.
Notice that most of the authors named by Rodó are French.
Notice, too, the implication of the literary circle that brings
him back to Perrault.　Charles Perrault, it will be recalled,
besides having been the match that ignited the famous quarrel between the Moderns and the Ancients in seventeenth-
century France, was the author of charming fairy-tale
adaptations that have been the delight of childhood for
many generations.　Is not this return of Rodó to the author
of childhood days symbolic of Rodó's own eternal youth?
And may he not have received something of the fairy
character that informs his beautiful parables from the delight of his early days and his later ones?

Rodó, in the sonnet quoted above, speaks of laughing.
His friend Barbegelata is thereby led to remark that the
philosopher rarely laughed, and when he did, it was a soft,
almost noiseless phenomenon.　"Those who were his
students at the time he gave his most absorbing lectures in
literature at the University of Montevideo, never saw him
laugh in the professorial chair, and all admired the gravity,
untainted by petulancy, of that twenty-six-year-old master. . . ."

In 1901 Rodó abandoned teaching for politics.　It was
for the *Revista Nacional de Literature y Ciencias Sociales*
(founded in collaboration with the brothers Martinez Vigil
and Victor Pérez Petit), that he wrote much of his work,
which is reproduced in his collection, *El Mirador de*

Próspero. It is with this review that Rodó's fame began to grow, and his home on la calle Cerrito in the old section of Montevideo soon became a literary shrine whither journeyed countless publications and letters from all parts of the continent.

"The correspondence of the creator of *Ariel*," wrote Barbegelata shortly before Rodó's death, "is numerous, and he attends to it personally, without a secretary, leaving no interesting letter unanswered, no printed matter without its due attention, no manuscript without its place in his files. . . ."

Rodó, like Darío, had a powerful effect upon Spanish prose. Indeed, Andrés González-Blanco, one of the few Spanish critics who has made a serious and thorough study of Spanish-American letters, and who is apt to wax most enthusiastic over his literary predilections, publicly places him upon the loftiest pedestal he can erect in the gallery of masters of style. "I have called him," says González-Blanco," [2] and I will repeat it once more, "the magician of Spanish prose, the publicist who writes the best Spanish in all the globe, he who has best known to play the instrument of our language in all its mastery, surpassing Valera in flexibility, Pérez Galdós in elegance, Pardo Bazán in modernity, Valle-Inclán in erudition, Azorín in critical spirit. . . . He lacks certain qualities and subtleties of one and the other: Galdós's creative art, Valera's bland, aristocratic skepticism, Pardo Bazán's spirit of observation, Valle-Inclán's dazzling poetry, Azorín's assiduous application . . . but who could have imagined that beyond the sea

[2] Andrés González-Blanco: *Escritores Representativos de America.* Madrid. Page 3.

there was to flourish, at the very end of the nineteenth century, the greatest prose writer of the Castilian language? . . ."

As with Vargas Vila's glorification of Darío as the Unique, so we need not accept this fulsome praise of Rodó in its entirety. But it is, like all such laudation, significant, and here doubly so since it comes from Old Spain, which has even now much to forget of prejudice against Spanish-American letters, and much to learn of their excellencies. More important than the superlativity of the praise is the fact that Rodó's contribution to the renovation of Spanish prose was, on his part, a conscious program which, in his own words, tried to return to Castilian prose color, relief and melody, to infuse it with new blood, give it stronger muscles. For such a purpose he felt that syntactic and lexical changes were necessary, and it may be said that his final result was superior to that of Darío himself.

It is not, then, surprising, that the fetters of journalism should have chafed him. But that same necessity which forced so many other gifted Spanish Americans into the arms of literature's sister Cinderella, constrained him, too. And there was another feeling,—one similar to that which brought him from naturally contemplative life for a while into the arena of politics. "To be a writer, and not to have been, if only accidentally, a journalist in a country like ours," he said, "would confer, more than a title of superiority or selection, a patent of egotism; it would mean that one had never felt within him that imperious voice with which the popular conscience calls those who wield the pen to the defense of common interests and common rights in hours of tumult and agitation." This passage alone should, together with essays like *Jacobinismo y Liberalismo* and *Trabajo Obrero en el Uruguay,* show that the writer was no mere tower philosopher (for philosophers, too, have their ivory towers), but a man who realized that life is not only thought, but lived. When all is said and done, however, his gifts were those that are born of meditation. The man who rarely laughed, who (as far as is known) never loved, delighted little in idle talk and was fond chiefly of reading. From intimate acquaintances, however, we learn that like Martí he was a fascinating conversationalist. His writing seems to have required little polishing; it sprang mature from a mind that had done all the editing within.

The great war came to tear Rodó from his beloved city and sent him to Europe as the representative of the well-known Buenos Aires magazine, *Caras y Caretas.* He went directly to Spain, remaining there almost incognito for but a few hours. Thence he proceeded to Italy, where he was overtaken by death on May 1, 1917, at Palermo. He had intended, while abroad, to issue a complete edition of his works, and did not to the very last lose the same optimism that characterized him and leaped from him into the bosoms of all with whom he came into intellectual contact through word or book. Rising above the débris of the conflagration he could behold new literary ideals, new artistic forms, and a new Spanish America at last achieving a definite intellectual and economic personality.

II

The man Rodó is clearly visible in his literary labors, as is eminently fitting in an apostle of the fullest expansion of personality. A thorough examination of the few but precious volumes he left will yield not only a fuller understanding of him, but of ourselves. Is not that one of the great tests of an artist? Let us consider, chiefly, *Ariel,* the clarion call to Hispano-American youth which contains the germ of the master's greatest work, *Motives de Proteo;* after a study of that treasure-house of counsel and suggestion, we will turn to the *Mirador de Próspero,* wherein are gathered much of the author's journalistic labors. Nor shall we pass over the great essays upon Darío, Bolívar, and Montalvo, which teem with ardent apostrophes to that freedom, tolerance and expansion to which Rodó consecrated his career.[3]

In one of his first writings,—*El Que Vendrá* (He Who Will Come)—Rodó, in whom the literary apostle was born very early, reveals a deep sense of optimism for the future. "When the impress of ideas or of present affairs inclines my soul to abomination," he declares to the new prophet whom his lines invoke, "you appear before my eyes in the guise of a sublime, wrathful avenger. In your right hand will shine the Archangel's sword. The purifying flame will descend from your mind. The symbol of your soul will be contained in the cloud, which at the same time

[3] The essays on Bolívar and Montalvo belong originally in *El Mirador de Próspero;* they are more easily accessible now, together with Ariel, Darío, and Jacobinismo y Liberalismo, in the *Cinco Ensayos* published in Madrid by the Editorial-America, of which the directing head is the author Rufino Blanco-Fombona.

weeps and fulminates. The iamb that flays and the elegy composed of a constellation of tears will find in your thought the somber bed of their union.

"At times I imagine you as a sweet, affectionate apostle. In your evangelical accent there will resound the note of love, the note of hope. Upon your brow will glitter the colors of the rainbow. Guided by the Bethlehem star of your word, we shall be present at the new dawn, at the rebirth of the Ideal—of the lost Ideal that we goalless travelers seek in the depths of the glacial night, through which we are journeying,—the Ideal that will reappear through you, to summon souls today chilled and scattered, to a life of love, peace, harmony. And at your feet the waves of our tempests will be hushed, as if a divine oil were cast upon the waters. And your word will resound in our spirits like the tolling of the Easter bell in the ear of the doctor bent over his draught of poison.[4]

"I behold only a hazy, mysterious vision of you, such as the soul intent upon rending the starry veil of mystery may picture to itself, in its ecstasies, the glory of the Divine Being. But I know that you will come. . . ."

Was it not natural for many Spanish Americans to behold in Rodó the selfsame literary Messiah of which he spoke in this youthful invocation? For he, too, brought a renaissance of the Ideal; his word, too, rose like a star of Bethlehem upon a new dawn.

Between *El Que Vendrá* and *Ariel* intervened but three years; yet in *Ariel* we almost feel that "he who will come" has already arrived.

[4] An allusion to *Faust*.

1. Ariel

The purpose of the classic essay *Ariel* is at once apparent from its symbolistic title. It is a manifesto of Ariel against Caliban, of beauty against ugliness, of the spirit against a myopic utilitarianism. I have said manifesto, yet the word should be purged of its propagandistic, partisan flavor. Rodó is deeply, though not dogmatically or denominationally religious. Like so many of his continental brethren, he broke away from the intellectual fetters of the epoch, but most unlike them, he acquired a serenity, a tranquillity, a spiritual harmony, that rescued him from the excesses and the morbidity of so many modernist poets. He reveals himself in *Ariel* that which he asks his youthful audience to become,—a glowing idealist, mindful of the utilitarian element in life, yet considering it only the basis of a higher expansion. *Ariel* has been called the intellectual breviary of Spanish-American youth. That is a beautiful phrase, indicative of the unobtrusively religious element in the master's injunctions; and if the youth of Spanish America, which is more or less naturally given to an aversion for the purely material considerations of life, is in need of the counsel, what shall we say of our own, to whom *Ariel,* with little change, might become no less an intellectual breviary?

The thought of the United States, indeed, occurs powerfully to Rodó in the present essay as elsewhere, and he comments upon our country in a manner that reveals him as a keen student of modern civilization. He recognizes our power of carrying through all projects of a practical nature, in which the will is the dominant force. He recognizes, too, our lack, as a nation, of spiritual cultivation and refinement. "The will is the chisel that has sculptured this people out of solid rock. Its salient characteristics are two manifestations of the power of the will: originality and audacity. Its entire history is the manifestation of a virile activity. Its representative personage is named *I will*, like the superman of Nietzsche. If anything rescues it collectively from vulgarity, it is that extraordinary exemplification of energy which carries it everywhere and with which it imprints a certain character of epic grandeur even upon the struggle of interests and material life. . . . And this supreme energy . . . is discoverable even in those individuals who present themselves to us as exceptional in and divergent from that civilization. None will deny that Edgar Poe is an anomalous and rebellious individuality within his people. His select soul represents an inassimilable particle of the national soul, which not without reason stirred among the others with the sensation of an infinite solitude. And nevertheless, as Baudelaire has deeply revealed, the fundamental note in the character of Poe's heroes is the superhuman temper, the indomitable resistance of the will. When he conceived Ligeia, the most mysterious and adorable of his creations, Poe symbolized in the inextinguishable light of her eyes the Will's hymn of triumph over Death."

Yet for all his admiration of our characteristics, Rodó feels a certain singular impression of insufficiency and emptiness about our life. Do not mistake his attitude for the carping and harsh, if, doubtless genuine, dislike of a Blanco-Fombona. Rodó holds up our life in general as an example of a people without any deep traditions to orientate

it,—a people that has not been able to substitute for the
inspired idealism of the past a disinterested conception
of the future. "It lives for the immediate reality, and
through it subordinates all its activity to the egotism of
personal and collective well-being.—Of the sum of the elements of its riches and its powers, one might say what the
author of *Mensonges* said of the intelligence of the Marquis
de Nobert, who figures in one of his books: it is a heap of
wood which it has been impossible to ignite." The spark
has been missing. To him we lack the poetic instinct; even
the North American religion becomes nothing more than
"an auxiliary force of penal legislation which would
abandon its past on the day when it would be possible to
give to utilitarian morals that religious power which Stuart
Mill was so desirous of endowing it with." [5]

From what we have read it is easy to see that it is not the
United States that Rodó will point to as the inspiration of
Spanish-American youth. He frankly considers us, for all
our enormous development, as yet the embodiment of a will
and a utility that, he hopes, will some day become intelligence, feeling, idealism as well. The reproach is a common one, often levelled at this country through a sense of
envy, if not from more practical motives not entirely dis-
sociated from propaganda in its worst diplomatic meaning,
but is there not some truth,—however much or little,—at
the bottom? Is there not something about rapid material
progress and the sense of power it confers which produces
the illusion of intellectual superiority? I am no believer
in chauvinism or narrow nationalism, yet I cannot share

[5] Rodó's acquaintance with the currents of our national thought is so
intimate that he quotes with disapproval the utilitarian moral of the once
popular *Pushing to the Front*, by Orison Swett Marden.

Rodó's thoughts as to our future. We are a young nation, a nation which, to make use of a paraphrase, is living its Odyssey before writing it, yet which contains every posibility of a vast continental culture, to which it will eventually attain, either despite, or because of, its proud materialism. Rodó himself would be the first to recognize that it is after all an unhealthy, anæmic spiritualism that does not rest upon a material foundation. However much mistaken he may have been in his views as to our immediate future, his objection to this country as a model for Spanish-American youth had firmer foundations. There is, first of all, the racial difference, which naturally accounts for a good deal of the South-American preference for France as an intellectual leader; with that racial difference is bound up the cultural one which blossoms from it. Without agreeing then, to Rodó's details, we may lend a most respectful ear to his general proposition, and yet not slight our own nation. As Darío and Chocano have realized, Spanish and English America may, as a union of complementary forces, accomplish great things.

Just as readily may we assent to his views upon democracy without thereby slighting the so-called common people. Rodó is no believer in the quantitative democracy of the politicians. He desires that genuine democracy which is inspired by a true appreciation of human superiorities,—a democracy in which intelligence and virtue receive their authority from prestige and liberty. And with the syncretistic method that is so characteristic of his eclecticism, he roots that democracy in both Christian and Pagan characteristics. "From the spirit of Christianity is born, in effect, the feeling of equality, vitiated by a certain as-

cetic scorn for spiritual selection and culture. From the
heritage of the classic civilizations is born the feeling for
order, for hierarchy, and religious respect for genius, vitiated by a certain aristocratic disdain for the humble and
the weak." It is these two elements, shorn of their vitiat-
ing factors, that will be harmonized by the future civilization.

It is that future civilization which concerns Rodó in
Ariel. It is because he beholds the future in the youth before him that he counsels them, in words that have reechoed
over the continent, to consecrate part of their lives to the
non-material. "There were, in antiquity, altars for the
'unknown gods.' Consecrate part of your soul to the unknown future. In proportion as societies advance, the
thought of the future enters in greater measure as one of
the factors of its evolution and one of the inspirations of its
labors. . . ."

To Rodó's optimistic vision there is ever present the
sight of an immortal Ariel triumphing over the temporary
victories of Caliban. Ariel is eternal youth, which, as a
nation, is symbolized by Greece. Yet is there not a subtler
symbolism in Rodó's address,—something he himself may
not have caught? He imagines himself as Prospero in
this speech, even as his collected journalistic articles have
been sponsored by that same spirit of Shakespeare's *Tempest*. The title of the famous address is likewise Shake-
sperian. In the same breath with which he expresses dis-
trust of one Anglo-Saxon people he extols the greatest genius
who has written in their language! This is, of course, indicative of many things,—his broad culture, his high idealism; but it indicates far more. The race that produced a

Shakespeare has a worthy tradition; the people out of whose midst grew the creator of Prospero and Ariel to furnish Rodó with a personality and a symbol, may look with confidence toward the future. If these digressions serve to suggest anything, it should be that no nation, no people, has a monopoly upon idealism, the manifestations of which are various and the results no less so.

We have said that *Ariel* contained in germ the distinguishing characteristics of Rodó's personality. What are these?   A deep sense of life's uninterrupted continuity with the flame of its enthusiasm and its vigor. It is this sense that lies at the bottom of Rodó's eclecticism and enables him to attempt a harmonization of Pagan and Christian virtues,—for pagans have their virtues as Christians their vices. Out of this sense, indeed, may grow all those other qualities we discern in the man,—his fine tolerance, his aristodemocracy, his cosmopolitan culture, his anxiety to effect a constant readjustment of the inner self with the outer world. Here there appear, too, the chief elements of that style which has so enchanted two continents,—a flowing, glowing prose that verges upon the poetic without dissolving into sentimentality, illumined by similes and metaphors organically related to the text. What a beautiful, placid close is that of *Ariel* in which the master, taking leave of his audience, hears the youngest of his disciples exclaim, as he points to the stirrings of the human multitude and then to the radiant beauty of the night:

"While the crowd passes, I observe that, although it does not gaze at the sky, the sky gazes down upon it. And into its obscure, indifferent bulk, like the furrows of the land, something falls from high. The vibration of the stars seems like the movement of a sower's hands."

Such a sower, in *Ariel* and in his other labors, Rodó sought to be. Is it a deeper trust of the human flock and its instinctive impulse to justice and truth, that makes me see in Rodó's manner, if not in some of his actual admonitions, a residue of that aristocratic blood which he inherited from his pure Spanish ancestry? Is there not a world of truth in the perspicacious statement of the discerning poet-critic, Max Henríquez Ureña, that "if in America the ignorant mass needs instruction, the directing class needs ideals"? [6] And although by America the author meant only Spanish America, I for one am willing to add the northern continent and make the statement unanimous.

There is more in *Ariel*: that consciousness of Spanish America's vast potentialities which informed everything that sprang from Rodó's pen. For Rodó, remember, was a partisan of the Magna Patria, the continental dream of Bolívar. That vision inspired some of his noblest pages, even as it led him to interpret its spiritual parent. It is that spirit, too, which must have been present when he said that Darío was not the poet of America. One of the very last things, indeed, that Rodó wrote, in the city of Rome, was an article entitled *The Spiritual Union of America*, in which he called for the formation of the Hispano-American spirit, to sow in the consciousness of the peoples that idea of "our America as a common force, as an indivisible power, as a sole fatherland (patria única). The entire future lies virtually in that work."

[6] *Rodó y Rubén Darío.* Page 43.

We have already noted the literary aspect of this American-icanism.   Let us for the present see how its broader implications shine out of a series of notable essays in which Rodó, interpreting the great spirits of Spanish America that appealed to him, interpreted himself as well,—his opinions upon tolerance, democracy, liberty and justice.

Pick up the essay on *Montalvo* or *Bolívar* and you realize almost at once that you have made a literary discovery. This writer, you tell yourself, has well merited comparison with Emerson, Macaulay or Carlyle.   In his essay upon the beloved Liberator, as in that upon the great Ecuadorian, there glows Rodó's own ardent belief in the destinies of a Spanish America joined by the bonds of an enlightened solidarity.   In revealing the nobility of Bolívar he reveals his own as a firm priest of the higher democracy in which (as he explicitly states in *Ariel*), the people will rise above the mere fascination of their own numbers.

Professor J. D. M. Ford of Harvard University, whose influence has been as potent as it has been silent and unostentatious in cultivating the study of Spanish and Spanish-American letters in this country, has, in his *Main Currents of Spanish Literature*,[7] registered an interesting contrast between the literary fates of Bolívar and Washington. "Fate has shown herself far more kind to Bolívar than to Washington," he writes, . . . "for she raised up for the southern military genius a poet worthy to chronicle the success of his arms, while Washington, though first in the hearts of his countrymen, has yet to be commemorated in song, in a manner befitting his proportions."   Rodó's essay upon Bolívar, whom many believe greater than Washing-

[7] New York, 1919.   Page 256.

ton, and who was certainly more versatile, is one of Fate's kindnesses to the great Spanish American. It reveals him as "great in thought, great in action, great in glory, great in misfortune, . . . great because he endures, in abandonment and in death, the tragic expiation of greatness. There are many human lives that are characterized by a more perfect harmony, a purer moral or æsthetic order; few offer so constant a character of greatness or power; few subject the sympathies of the heroic imagination to so dominating a rule." Is not that a superbly, yet simply, orchestrated introduction to a study that amplifies upon the opening theme with illuminating virtuosity of thought and language? "The tragic expiation of greatness." Is not that a memorable phrase, and does it not sum up the isolation of superiority? For Bolívar's life, multiple as it was, reveals at the close the tragedy of greatness and the irony of it. To the great Liberator, indeed, might have been inscribed the haunting lines that Darío wrote to another Liberator who built better than he knew:

> Cristóforo Colombo, pobre Almirante,
> ruega á Diós por el mundo que descubriste!

"When ten centuries have passed," concludes this remarkable essay, "when the patina of a legendary antiquity extends from the Anahuac to the Plata, there where today Nature glows or civilization sinks its roots; when one hundred human generations will have mingled, in the mass of earth the dust of their bones with the dust of the forests that will have been a thousand times bereft of their leaves, and of the cities that will have been twenty times reconstructed, and cause to reverberate in the memory of men who would frighten us with their strangeness if we could imagine what they will look like, myriads of glorious names in virtue of deeds and victories of which we can form no conception; even then, if the collective sentiment of a free and united America has not lost its essential power, these men . . . will behold that in the extension of their records of glory there is none greater than Bolívar."

No less sympathetic and laudatory is the essay on Montalvo, in whom Rodó sees the representative writer of his continent, a combination of Sarmiento's inspiration and Bello's art. With a skill all the more surprising because he had never visited the scene, Rodó reconstructs the complete environment into which the author of the *Siete Tratados* was born and reveals himself eminently fair to historical characters embodying principles repugnant to him. García Moreno is thus not merely a tyrant to be declaimed against, but a religious fanatic in whom obsession is to blame for his tyranny, rather than any innate perversity or distortion of human attributes. And when, in the midst of a most perspicacious criticism of Montalvo's literary productions we come upon the following paragraph, we are quite ready to transcribe Rodó's estimate of Montalvo and use it as our own of Rodó:

"Another essential feature of his literature, because it was also one of his person and his life, is the tone of nobility and superiority. This perennial agitator against false and petty authorities, had a deep feeling for the great and the true. He was liberal in the noble sense of the word; demagogue or plebeian, never. In quality of ideas, as in temper of spirit, as in taste of style, a caballero from head to foot. He loved liberty with the love of a heart that turned to justice and of intelligence subjected to order; never with the livid, loathsome passion of him who suffers hunger for that which nature or fortune conceded to others."

And in one of the finest passages in all of Rodó's works, which illustrates his gift for producing comparisons doubly beautiful for their intrinsic linguistic skill and their aptness of thought, the great Uruguayan suggests that it was the sight of Cotopaxi that first induced in Montalvo his love of order and beauty.

The essay on Rubén Darío is no less revelatory of Rodó's remarkable gift of reaching the heart of his subject and casting upon it, from every angle, the light of a deep learning and a sympathy no less deep. Be not led astray by the paragraph I have quoted from the essay on Bolívar. Rodó is not given to superlatives. If anything, there is most of the time about his work a certain classic repose, an unruffled equanimity, that makes one long for an occasional outburst of passion.

It was Rodó, as we have seen, that once and for all stamped the attribute of grace upon Darío's poetry. His analysis, limited to the *Prosas Profanas,* does not reveal the whole poet (nor, to my own way of thinking, the essential poet), but within the limits of the single collection which it treats it has already become a classic and has, as we have remarked, literally rendered further analysis of *Prosas Profanas* superfluous.

It is in *Liberalismo y Jacobinismo* that Rodó's fine tolerance displays itself most fully. An order from the Comisión de Caridad y Beneficencia Pública of Montevideo had decreed that all the crucifixes of the city hospital be cast out.   Whereupon a controversy ensued in which our author took up the cudgels for the crucifix against one Emilio Bossi.   It is by no means impossible (adopting a mite of Rodó's own syncretism), to assent to the general theses of both men.   A liberation from the dogmas of all religions is by no means incompatible with a recognition of the need felt by many for religion's healing and soothing power.   There is a fanaticism of atheism as well as of religion, and fanaticism, wherever encountered, is to be deplored.   In arguing for the retention of the crucifixes Rodó revealed his deeply human understanding and his overflowing sympathy.   For all his equanimity he was a man of feeling, who realized that none has a monopoly of truth; he had no use for a liberalism that could itself become sectarian and intolerant.   What is gained by a swapping of one intolerance for another?   And what is gained by the imposition of an idea?

The Rodó of *Ariel* and of the essays is a perspicacious, patient thinker, moderate in judgment, moderate in counsel, tolerant in attitude, glowing with a constant, rather than a volcanic, passion for justice and freedom.   His style is eminently matched to his subject.   Nowhere better than in such contrary temperaments as Rodó and Blanco-Fombona, united only by the same aspiration for a glorious continental future, is illustrated the oft-repeated yet little understood dictum that the style is the man.   Rodó's rare laughter might have been discerned from his prose, in which that element of humor which so brightens the pages of Gutiérrez Nájera is absent.   His deeply meditative nature blossoms in a thousand metaphors that illumine his meaning and not, as in so much fine writing, befog it.   He is

not, like Blanco-Fombona, a volcano; not, like Darío, a
flame; not, like Chocano, a trumpet; he is a glow,—an intense, radiant, many-colored glow in the heart of things.
He is no more of the crowd than Darío, yet he loves it more
despite his stern interpretation of democracy; he is a disciple, let us say, of nature's nobility, a leader of leaders.
His influence will perhaps penetrate not directly, but
through its effect upon Hispano-American thinkers who will
in turn communicate that influence, slowly but surely, to
the thinking crowd.

2. *Motivos de Proteo*

It is in the *Motivos de Proteo* that Rodó's philosophy is
developed to the point of a dynamic system. I do not know
how deeply Rodó was acquainted with the methods of
psycho-analysis, but his plumbing of our undreamed-of potentialities is not a little related, in both premises and conclusions, to the methods, if not the aims, of Freudian psy-
chologists. He deals, of course, with the normal mind
(which, like the normal eyesight of which Bernard Shaw
speaks in one of his logorrheic prefaces, is so rare), but
his realization of the possibilities of the average man and
of the paramount importance of the unconscious in every-
day life ranges him with the foremost contemporary psy-
chologists. He gives us a new realization of self; he discovers, even to the most introspective natures among us, a
veritable universe of new worlds within. He exhibits us
to ourselves not as a single being, but as the sum total of
our entire past, worked upon by influences we know not of,
yet in a measure able to direct those forces. Self-knowl-

edge, self-adaptation in the light of that knowledge, continuous re-adjustment in the light of newer knowledge,—self-renewal is Life.

And why Proteus as the symbolic speaker?   Here again, as in *Ariel*, in a single symbol the author concentrates his entire philosophy.   *Ariel* is eternal youth; *Proteus* is eternal change guided by the essential unity of a dominant personality.   For was it not Proteus who could at will assume new forms?   "A form of the sea, a spirit of the sea, from whose restless bosom antiquity drew a fecund generation of myths, Proteus was he who guarded Poseidon's flocks of seals.   In the *Odyssey* and in the *Georgics* is sung his venerable ancientness, his passage over the waves in the swift marine coach.   Like all the divinities of the waters he possessed the prophetic gift and complete knowledge, fled all consultation, and in order to elude human curiosity resorted to his marvellous faculty of transforming himself into a thousand divers forms.   It was this faculty by which he was characterized in mythology, and it determines . . . his ideal significance.

"When the Homeric Menelaus desires to learn through him what course his vessels shall follow; when the Aristæus of Vergil goes to ask him the secret of the evil which consumes his bees, Proteus has recourse to that mysterious virtue with which he disorientated those who surprised him. Now he would change into a wild lion, now into a wriggling, scaly serpent; now, converted into fire, he would rise like a tremulous flame; now he was the tree that lifted its crest to the vicinity of the heavens, now the brook that rippled rapidly along.   Ever elusive, ever new, he ran through the infinity of appearances without fixing his most subtle essence in any of them. And because of this infinite plasticity, being a divinity of the sea, he personified one of the aspects of the sea: he was the multifarious wave, intractible, incapable of concretion or repose; the wave, which now rebels and now caresses; which at times lulls to rest, and at others thunders; which possesses all the volubilities of impulse, all the nuances of color, all the modulations of sound; which never rises or falls in the same way, and which, taking from and returning to the ocean the liquid which it gathers, impresses upon inert equality form, movement and change."

Such is the invocatory foreword to the *Motivos*. By a masterful choice of a single word, as it were, Rodó symbolizes to us the Protean personality that we conceal within, —that personality of which most of us learn to know only a single form, and which is yet as latently multiform as the Greek divinity of the waters himself.

Max Henríquez Ureña, in his excellent study of the inspiring Uruguayan, has rather ingeniously (yet following a similar cue in such an essay as Rodó's own masterly one upon Montalvo) suggested that it was the ocean itself that helped to originate Rodó's philosophy of eternal change. For, ever before the scholar's sight, facing the city through which the noted figure (tall and recalling to many the swooping condor of the Andes) was wont to stroll, was the restless, ever-changing yet eternal ocean.

"How often the immense sea changes color!" Rodó has written. "Who spoke of the monotony of the sea? The firm earth varies only in space; the sea changes and transforms itself in time. . . . This immensity is a perpetual *becoming* [Rodó here employs the French word *devenir*]. . . .

What scale like the scale of its sounds?   What palette like
that which supplies its hues?   What imagination richer in
forms than the wave, never resembling itself?"

Once again I may recall the pregnant saying of La Roche-
foucauld, which surely deserves to stand as one of the
epigraphs of the *Motivos:* "We differ mostly from ourselves." A most *protean* saying in the light of Rodo's
inner delvings, and one most rich in suggestions to the
man who seeks self-knowledge. For, from the very fact
that we are ourselves, we are all men. Must not such a
notion have underlain Rodó's exemplary tolerance?

To return for a moment to Henríquez Ureña's suggestion.
"After knowing this page," he writes[8] (he has just quoted
the passage from which I translated the above excerpts),
"would it be rash to affirm that the constant vision of the sea
served as inspiration and guide to Rodó's philosophic
thought, by the sole process of transmuting the material observation into a spiritual conception?" Such was Rodó's
habit, as he himself has told us: "My imagination is of
such cast that every material appearance tends to translate
itself into an idea. Nature always speaks to me the language of the spirit." Surely enough, as we have seen, it
is a divinity of the sea that Rodó invokes at the beginning
of his masterwork. And was not Ariel himself somewhat
of a sea sprite?

Let us now follow, in outline, the rich content of the
work in which the Uruguayan scholar entraps the elusive
spirit of Proteus and compels him to yield a tithe of his
fascinating lore.

The great motto, as we have seen, is *Reformarse es vivir,*

[8] *Op. cit.* Page 15.

—Self-renewal is Life.   None more than Rodó realizes
the compelling need for continual change; none more than
he feels that life is not a definite, inalterable result, but a
becoming.   Is not this the negation of all that is static and
reactionary?   Does not this principle, so easy to accept in
theory and so difficult to countenance in practice, underly
all progress?   To Rodó, time is the greatest innovator,
and by that same token the ally of all change, which,
whether we will or not, is ever going on within us.   We may
not heed ourselves, one might phrase it, but our selves heed
us.   Each one of us is, successively, not *one,* but *many.*
And these successive personalities, which emerge one from
the other, offer themselves the rarest and most astonishing
contrasts.   And within us, nothing happens without a result; everything leaves its trace.   Our personalities are,
then, in this constant flux, a "death whose sum is death;
resurrections whose persistency is life. . . . We are the
wake of the vessel whose material entity does not remain
the same for two successive moments, because incessantly
it dies and is reborn amid the waves; the wake, which is,
not a persisting reality, but a progressive form, a succession
of rhythmic impulses which act upon a constantly renewed
object."

We are, as it were, a vortex of incessant inner changes
in an ocean of outer ones.   And "he who lives rationally is
he who, aware of the incessant activity of change, tries each
day to obtain a clear notion of his internal state and of the
transformations that have occurred in the objects that surround him, and in accordance with this knowledge . . .
directs his thoughts and his acts."   And here, at the very
outset, the author comes upon a most important applica-

tion of his fecund principle to modern education, pointing out that one of our worst errors is the view that existence is divided into two consecutive and naturally separated parts, —that in which we learn and that in which we use the results of the accumulated knowledge.   If life is a perpetual *becoming*, it follows that knowledge is a constant acquiring. "As long as we live, our personality is upon the anvil. . . . We must try, in the intellectual field, never to diminish or lose completely our interest, the child's curiosity,—that alertness of fresh ingenuous attention and the stimulus which is born of knowing oneself ignorant since we are always that. . . ." That eternal youth which Rodó preached, and which he so well exemplified, is attained by the constant self-renewal without which life becomes worse than vegetative, sinking to the level of the mineral kingdom.

Renovation, transformation, reintegration.   "Is not this all the philosophy of action and life?   Is this not life itself, if by life we are to understand in the human sphere something other than the somnambulism of the animal and the vegetation of the plant?"

Rodó is an optimist, though not of the type represented by Dr. Pangloss and his great-great-grandaughter Pollyanna.   He sees, from the very multiplicity of our inner selves, the possibility of changing apparent failure or misfortune into a new orientation of our lives, the chance to obtain good out of evil.   Nor is he content with cold counsel; patiently and with a readiness that attests his vast reading and retentive memory, he adduces example after example to sustain.his point, not to speak of secular parables that have passed into the anthologies for their illuminative beauty.   There are so many latent powers within us, there is such a wealth of spiritual reserves, that the frustration of any one power is compensated for by the discovery of another. Men cheated of a life of action (like Vauvenargues) turn to fruitful contemplation; spirits opposed in their desire for diplomatic preferment (like Ronsard) develop poetic powers; a Prescott forced by illness to abandon the Forum becomes a glorious historian. Our *self* is an inexhaustible fund of potentialities. "Man of little faith, what do you know of that which dwells within you? . . ." Herein lies the fascination of our self-discovery,—the enchantment of becoming our own Columbus. "Is there anything that interests you more than the discovery of what is within you and nowhere else: a land that was created for you alone; an America whose only possible discoverer is you yourself, without the need of fearing, in your gigantic design, either rivals to dispute your glory or conquerors to usurp your gain?" By this, however, Rodó does not mean sterile, morbid introspection, but fruitful contemplation,—he prefers Marcus Aurelius to Amiel. Thus we are aided to realize how many of our supposed personal beliefs are but the imposition of society; we are to strive, however, for the assertion of our true selves, without forgetting that originality, so-called, is but a returning of ideas to society, rather than a gift. The point is well worth dwelling upon. We call that liberty, that originality, *genius*, when it reaches a certain degree. But how often is "the contribution with which individual thought seems to bring new elements to the common horde in reality a restitution of ideas that have been slowly and silently absorbed! Even as one would be apt to judge, from outward appearances, that it is the rivers which supply the ocean with water, since they pour into it, while it is the sea whence comes the water in which the rivers rise." A beautiful comparison and a true, which should make our "leaders" more humble and the flock more confident.

In this philosophy of ego-culture there is little egotism; it is self, not selfishness, that Rodó is concerned with. The realization of our internal cosmos confronts him at every turn. "By a general law, a human soul may give of itself more than its consciousness believes and perceives, and much more than its will transforms into deed." In *Peer Gynt* the philosopher beholds the highest expression of the remorse that overtakes the spendthrift of personality. "Peer Gynt! Peer Gynt! You are a legion of legions!"

The fluidity of self must form the basic principle of education, declares Rodó. "Any philosophy of the human spirit; any investigation into the history of man and peoples, any judgment upon a character, an attitude or a morality; any proposal for education or reform, which does not take into account . . . this complexity of the moral person, may not flatter itself with the hope of truth or certainty." Hence our contradictory natures (so well depicted, says Rodó, in Shakespeare's characters); hence Rodó's own splendid tolerance in the vast, human sense of the word.

Rodó realizes deeply that the soul of each of us is the sum of the souls of all our predecessors, back to countless generations. "All those who have passed from the reality of the world persist in you. . . . What is the mysterious mandate of the instinct that works in you without the intervention of your will and your consciousness, but a voice which . . . rises from the depths of an immemorial past and compels you to perform an act preordained by the customs of your ancestors?" It is out of these elements that we construct our personality; the changes are often forecasted by signs that we little heed or recognize at the time they first occur. No psychiatrist was ever more aware of the importance of the apparently least significant mental phenomena; our impulsiveness (so-called) possesses deep roots. No real understanding of our conscious selves is thus possible without some acquaintance with the submerged element. To Rodó there is no such thing as events great and small; all are potentially great. Did not the flight of birds (and what more poetically innocent than this?) determine the discovery of the North American continent? And every act of ours, every thought, may be just such a flight. . . .

A considerable part of the first half is devoted to the absorbing subject of human vocation, which the Uruguayan philosopher terms "the consciousness of a determined aptitude." Human aptitude is indeed an unfathomable well, as is shown by the Titans of the Renaissance. Yet if we may not all be Leonardos, how little of our garden do we cultivate! And in the matter of human potentialities Rodó is glowingly optimistic; we are all, so to speak, latent supermen,—not quite in the sense commonly attributed to Nietzsche's blond beast, but in the significance of a broadly developed, many-faceted personality.

Rodó's lengthy argument on vocation should be studied not only by our so-styled vocational trainers (who, too often in practice, serve to stifle non-utilitarian gifts in favor of materialistic development) but by all teachers and parents. What a mine of suggestion there is in his anecdote about

Pestalozzi, whose instructor could make no progress with him, "not suspecting surely that the bad pupil was destined to invent new and better" methods. Hence the need for fostering natural inclinations.

It is difficult to believe the assertion of his friends that Rodó never loved; for section LIV of the *Motivos* is devoted to an admirable exposition of Love as the motive power of art. "Love is the pole and the quintessence of sensibility, and the artist is sensibility incarnate." And further on: "He who loves is, in the intimate recesses of his imagination, a poet and artist, although he may lack the gift of forming into a real and palpable work the divine spirit that possesses him."

We have seen that Rodó has an intense and abiding faith in human capabilities,—that he does not tire of studying the methods of their cultivation and the reasons for their aberration; he has, too, a deep realization of how much talent, and even genius, is stifled by the harsh conditions of modern life. "How many forces capable of a lofty dynamism remain unknown, and are lost forever in the obscure depths of human society!" he exclaims, in lines that recall, at once, the imperishable beauty in which our own Gray has framed the same idea. "Is there a thought more worthy than this of deep, serious attention? . . ." And in the chaotic, opaque mass of the common people's spirit he thus sees, potentially, an excellent literature and a high art, a science impregnated with clarity, and thousands of heroic battles, in such a manner that, according to the superb image of Tyndall, even the dramas of Shakespeare existed, like all things else, potentially in the nebulous haze of the world's beginnings. Is it not significant that every age

summons forth the heroes that it needs?   Not that they
arrive in steady numbers, for "many more are the seeds
that the earth allows to go to waste than those it receives."
And then this notable excerpt in which the philosopher is
at once humanist, scientist, commoner and inspirer: "In
the eternal conflict which determines which shall be the
chosen from the number that are *called,* since there is not
room for all, the greater fitness or power prevails; superiority triumphs and imposes its will; but this alone does not
satisfy justice, for we still have to reckon with those who
are among neither the *chosen* nor the *called;* those who
may not even arrive at the arena of the contest, since they
live in such conditions that they are unaware of their own
selves or it is forbidden them to bring forth the gold from
their own mine.   And among these, ah! who knows whether
there are not the first and the best?" . . .

Consider the deep human sympathy this memorable passage connotes.   See how Rodó applies his philosophy of
self-culture not alone to individuals but to society.   Just as
human personality is vibrant with countless potentialities,
so is the social personality aquiver with innumerable latent
gifts that never come to light.   Much of this loss is inevitable; much, however, is a direct effect of social and economic maladjustment.

The cogent thinker carries his ideas into the realm of
letters, with the result that he perceives the folly of writers
and personalities grouping themselves solely by "schools"
and thus achieving a false uniformity.   Not for him the
preceptive attitude of the taskmaster critic who seeks to
teach the creative artist what to think and how to express it;
he recognizes most explicitly the psychological root of such

"isms" as bristle in our forest of classification so densely that we cannot see the authors for the terminology.   Provided that the realism or the idealism, the subjectivity or impersonality of the author is a sincere, unforced, spontaneous product, he would foster it most sympathetically.   The mere imitator he with justice deplores, for such imitation is the very negation of personality.   Such imitation should not be confused, however, with the natural attraction of kindred spirits to one another.

It is surprising how, as Rodó develops his great theme, he manages to extract new meanings, new aspects, new orientations, from a simple statement that, when uttered, seems to demand little further elucidation.   The fecundity of his central thought that self-reformation is life, thus mirrors the very fecundity of that self whose cultivation he preaches,—not the superficial self-culture of rapid correspondence courses, but a daily discovery of a new world within us.   In the beauty of his diction and thought is a reflection of the author's own beauty; his was a life that discovered riches where others had seen only monotony. He was himself the best example of that "perfect and typical exemplar of progressive life" which he mentions in section LXXXII, for "his philosophy is like the light of each dawn, a new thing, because it is born, not of a logical formalism, but from the living, seething bosom of a soul." Rodó was rightly the enemy of "schools" and "systems"; his dynamic philosophy is inconsistent with anything that attempts to place a seal upon human knowledge and activity, saying "Thus only is it, and this is all of truth"; he was that *protean* mentality of which he became the great exponent.   Nor is his method an abstract one, dealing in *a pri-oris*.   The *Motivos* are in a very vital sense a history of human personality,—of the world's representative men.   It is from the knowledge (and an intimate knowledge) of many lives in all ages that he evolved these notable thoughts. His *Proteism*, as the expression of man's unboundedly wealthy inner life, is nothing new; indeed, I am not certain that it is possible to place a finger on any specific passage in the *Motivos* and say "This is new."   Is it even desirable? What *is* fresh, however, in Rodó, is the constant, patient delving into the personality, his examination of it from a hundred different angles, his renovation of ancient example, his transformation of the material into a self-revelation.

His anxiety for self-renewal led him to consider the importance of travel.   If self-reformation is life, travel is self-reformation.   It serves to break us away from the roots that we naturally sink into our environment (and how the protean master fears the immobility connoted in roots!) and to enrich our views.   "The expatriation of voy-ages is therefore the supreme antidote for routine thought, for fanatic passion, for all manner of rigidity and blind-ness."   Travelling, like solitude, is a method of with-drawal, which is so necessary for a summary of our inner state.   Travel, too, (and this I consider a most important element in the protean philosophy of Rodó) leads to intel-lectual internationalism.   Nations, like individuals, must know themselves to know each other; man is, at bottom, as Rodó asserts, "a citizen of the world."   Is not the study of foreign literatures, too, a sort of mental travelling?   The author is rich in examples of men whose travels have wrought profound influence not only upon themselves but upon their generation,—Goethe, Gautier, Cervantes, Gibbon, Irving. . . .

Is it surprising, then, that Rodó should possess a *protean* conception of Truth?   For truth itself, like life, is not a concrete entity, but a *becoming;* not a static measure but a dynamic force.   Significantly enough, it was not truth, but love of truth, that Rodó sought to bring to his fellow man. In asserting the utility of a conviction or a belief as the guide of our will and our thought, he is characteristically careful to recall that such convictions or beliefs are not always present in some personalities, whereupon he adds, in italics, *or a diligent and disinterested desire for truth that may guide our mind upon the road to acquiring them* (i. e., conviction or belief.)   There have been creative artists who have asserted that their very aimlessness is their goal; I am not sure that the paradox is an altogether futile one, but in all probability the Uruguayan would call such an "aim" the "sterile fatigue of a purposeless motion."

Just as our ideas and acquisitions tend to crystallize about a certain conviction or belief (which should be the resultant and not the dictator of those ideas), so human aptitudes, though multiform within the same personality, are usually subordinated to a dominant gift.   Alfonse the Learned, Dante, Raymond Lully and Leonardo da Vinci were all very versatile men, but it was the legislator who predominated in the first, the poet in the second, the philosopher in the third, and the painter in the last.   Often one vocation suggests another; even hostile personal forces may be harmonized within the same individual or race; Rodó points out that primitive Christianity was thus born of a

race in which the most fervent religious spirit was united
to the finest economic tact.   As usual, Rodó, whose interest
is centered with untiring steadiness upon human beings
and not upon abstract principles, is plentiful in examples.
There is Wagner, in whom the literary faculty aided the
musical; there is Boito, poet and musician in one; there are
Beethoven and Mozart, skilled alike as creators and inter-
preters; Plautus, Shakespeare, Molière, who could act as
well as create.   And Rodó is quite right when he flies in the
face of not only popular, but "intellectual" opinion, with
the assertion that "it is a common error to imagine that the
gift and energy of practice . . . inhibit or take away
power from the aptitude for theory."   Here again he is
rich in personal example of men gifted with both the creative and the critical powers.

Does not all creation imply a form of criticism,—if not
unconscious self-criticism?   And is not criticism a form of
creation?   Indeed, do not many of our unsuspected powers
go to waste, or rather, never rise to consciousness because
circumstances have never summoned them?   I believe the
Spanish people on both sides of the Atlantic furnish a
striking proof of versatility called into being by necessity.
How relatively often do we encounter, in one man, the poet,
the statesman, the playwright, the journalist!   May not
this be due, in part, to the great percentage of illiteracy,
and to the resulting fact that the various functions of the
intellectual life must be performed by the same few who
have received the advantages of an education?   There are
such things as special gifts, of course; but there are infinitely more gifts, special and general, that are submerged
beneath the waters of social and economic maladjustment.

Rodó insists upon the potent influence of the unconscious, even when it never rises to the surface of the individual's consciousness.   And returning to his theme of the directing idea,—even, indeed, when that direction is vague,—he asks, in almost Tennysonian phraseology, whether, as a directive power in life, the absence of love is of more value than love devoted to one who is unworthy of inspiring it.[9] "Let me gaze into the depths of your soul and see in what direction your love points, and I will tell you . . . whither you are going over life's paths, and what is to be expected of you in your thoughts and your works."   He recognizes, too, the great releasing power of love as a liberator of ideas and acts, and that frequently it "triumphs over the inferiority of the object."   Such a lover, then, is really in love with an ideal rather than with the real object, and it is the ideal that is his compass.

The philosopher insists, then, upon the crystallization of thoughts around a central idea, whether that be love, a conviction, or a belief.   "How many a fecund thought, how many a happy invention, how many a new truth or new beauty, a victory for good, an amelioration in the condition of man has not Humanity lost in this manner!" (i. e. through lack of adhesion to a central thought-power). Even bootless search may prove fruitful in by-products, so to speak, so long as the guiding impulse is there.

We must subject our ideas to a continual test in the light of our new knowledge; if they do not survive that test they

[9] Far be it from me to intrude psycho-analysis into these studies. But, since Rodó's friends have noted that he never had a love affair, may not some of his lines, as here summarized, indicate that he had suffered a disappointment, whence he had sought to draw consolation? For one who has never loved, Rodó ascribes far too much potency to the passion.

must disappear. Unwillingness to change is, in reality, alienation of personality. Nor does Rodó fear the cry of "Apostate! Traitor!" For well he knows that "there is no human creed that has not originated in an inconsistency, an infidelity. The dogma that is today a sacred tradition was at its birth a heretic piece of daring. In abandoning it to attain to *your* truth, you do but follow the example of the master who, in order to found it, broke the authority of the idea which in his day was dogma. . . ." Here we have not only one of the noblest passages from a writer rich in such nobility, but one of the pivotal principles of his entire philosophy. Is not this eternal heterodoxy (which, none the less, may not be termed extremism because of its deep sense of evolution) the fruit of Rodó's intense belief in the necessity of self-renewal? Is it not a natural corollary of his conception of truth, no less than life, as a *becoming?* From his beautiful parable of *La Despedida de Gorgas* (Gorgas's Farewell; section CXXVII of the *Motivos de Proteo*) we may transcribe that master's words and make them Rodó's own: "I was to you a master of love; I have tried to impart to you the love of truth; not truth, which is infinite." Like the psychologist he was, Rodó knew that beliefs may be abandoned, yet they leave something of themselves behind. We are what we were, as well as what we are. And when we are assailed by doubt—if we are strong—that doubt is neither "epicurean idleness nor affliction or dejection,—it is the forerunner of a reintegration"—the germ of a new truth.

But the new truth must proceed farther than sterile cerebration; it must be translated into action. "It is not the truth or the error that convinces you which reforms your

soul; it is the truth and the error that impassion you."
And more succinctly: "Reality is not a cold tablet upon
which are inscribed sentences, but a live, palpitant engen-
dering of feeling and action."

Rodó's philosophy, of course, implies the utter negation
of a false consistency, which many mistake for firmness of
character.   He would see no knighthood in the knight of
whom it was written that "faith unfaithful kept him falsely
true."   He knows, too, the frequent intervention of accident
in what we call virtue and vice.   Paraphrasing a noted
figure in English theology, he might well have said upon
beholding a criminal led to the scaffold, "There, but for
the grace of God, goes José Enrique Rodó."

For this reason Rodó has no sympathy with the "uplift"
nature of so much social education; herein, too, lies the inspirational character of his teachings,—or rather his suggestions.   If Hope is his compass, Will (with the renewed
consciousness of our manifold possibilities) is the vessel
that carries us to the goal, and the first object upon which
this will is applied is our own personality.   Our wills, as
our aptitude, may be dormant.

Self-renewal unceasingly,—self-renewal of personality
and of that group of personalities called a nation; therein
lies the essence of the Uruguayan's philosophy, which, when
carried to its logical conclusion (conclusion is too definite
a word for so dynamic a conception) must inevitably lead
to that international mind which corresponds to a full development of personality.   Rodó hinted at such a mind, but
did not develop the thought.

The Uruguayan philosopher has been compared to Emerson.   Is not Rodó's masterpiece in a sense a vast amplifi-

cation of the essay upon Self-Reliance?   Is not the great
New Englander equally jealous of the seal of personality?
"It is easy in the world to live after the world's opinion;
it is easy in solitude to live after our own; but the great
man is he who in the midst of the crowd keeps with perfect
sweetness the independence of solitude."   Have we not
here the essence of purpose that actuated Rodó's words
about solitude and travel and the harmony of their teachings
in the man of true originality?   Is there not in Self-Reliance that same scorn of a false consistency?   Has not
Emerson in six words written what might well serve as the
motto of the *Motivos?*   "Live ever in a new day."   Does
he not likewise declaim against the worship of the past?
"The centuries are conspirators against the sanity and majesty of the soul."   And nearer still to the essence of Rodó's
entire system, long before that Bergson from whom Rodó
is said to have received his suggestion: "This one fact the
world hates, that the soul *becomes* (the italics are Emerson's) ; for that forever degrades the past, turns all riches to
poverty; all reputation to a shame; confounds the saint
with the rogue; shoves Jesus and Judas equally aside."
Allowing for differences of style and Rodó's lack of the
Emersonian vehemency, the resemblance is, to say the least,
most striking.   "Every new mind is a new classification."
. . . "Insist on yourself; never imitate."

Of course such resemblance by no means implies identity of thought or purpose.   The resemblance may even
be merely verbal.   Yet Rodó's implications are far-reach-
ing.   He gives us, in that masterwork, not so much a fund
of thought as a well of inspiration; not so much a goal as a
direction; not so much a body as a spirit.   This he achieves

not by preaching but by furnishing abundant example; he fertilizes our personalities, so to speak, with the rich soil of others. The *Motivos de Proteo* should be known in every language and should form part of every educational system.

3. El Mirador De Próspero

The collection of articles that goes under the title *Through Prospero's Window* is valuable as casting light upon Rodó's application of his personality to the matters of the intellectual as well as to the political world. There has been some word of censure, I believe, about Rodó's having inserted a political essay in the collection; such political activity, which arose from the master's sense of duty to his nation, was in conformity with his own call for something more than pure thinking,—for the translation of action into thought. There are so many retrogressive or stagnant spirits in contemporary life who can tolerate or even applaud the dynamic conceptions which a man expresses in his poetry or his other creative literature, but who, when they find him intent upon bringing them about in reality, are seized with concern or dismay. Rodó was not what we could call a conservative; on the other hand, he was by no means an extremist; is was not in his nature to be extreme. His political views, aptly stated in a notable essay upon labor conditions in Uruguay, show his tendency to be a progressive one,—not so much socialistic (like Chocano's poetic internationalism and Blanco-Fombona's active socialism) as patient reform. Yet, as we shall soon note from an examination of the speech—which forms, in *El Mirador de Próspero*, an illuminative exception amid the more purely literary discussions—it is as much a matter of patience, or time, as anything else, that separates Rodó from his confrères. Besides, he was thinking in terms of Uruguay. For the rest, we have noted in him a continental aspiration that is a logical step toward the international spirit. Had he lived to complete his *New Motives of Proteus*,[10] who knows what changes he would have brought back from his trip to Europe at a time when an old world and an old economic system were crumbling in the fires of a vast crucible?

The sights that Prospero beholds through his window comprise a varied yet unified panorama. The advantage of such a collection (organic only in the sense that it is composed of views as seen by a singularly composed and ordered spirit) is that the window may be closed at will, and our looking resumed whenever we please. Or, to quote the epigraph, from Taine: "J'aime, je l'avoue, ces sortes de livres. D'abord on peut jeter le volume au bout de vingt pages, commencer par la fin, ou au milieu; vous n'y êtes pas serviteur, mais maître; vous pouvez le traiter comme journal; en effet, c'est le journal d'un esprit."

And in fact, these selections from Rodó's journalistic labors are in the best sense a "journal of a spirit." There are such sterling essays as that on Bolívar, on Juan Carlos Gómez, on Juan María Gutiérrez and his epoch (an account that is indispensable to all who would understand the origins of "literary Americanism" as well as the native contribution of Spanish America to Castilian letters,) on Samuel

[10] Incomplete, and not yet published. A collection of articles written in Europe, under the title *El Camino de Paros*, was published in 1918 in Valencia, by the *Editorial Valencia*.

Blixen, and other important literary figures of the continent; there are inimitable cameos expressive of his attitude
toward art,—its inspiration and its problems; there are reviews of novels and dramas that embody valuable statements; there are impressionistic gems, sheer poetry of
thought, such as the piece on the sea which was quoted at the
beginning.   And wafting through every paragraph is the
spirit of an Ariel, a Proteus, a Prospero.   It is not only the
beauty of language and thought that attracts one to Rodó,
it is the beauty of his attitude; as much as what he says,
as much as how he says it, is his outlook upon the world of
thought and action, so truly symbolized in the ever-changing yet constant sea.

It is not necessary to analyze the book in detail.   I shall
choose just enough to complete an adequate knowledge of
the harmonious personality,—his political views, his attitude toward the continental dream of Bolívar (a more than
political question, implying all the spiritual outgrowths of
an economic substructure), his beautiful cameos that seem
the embodiment of a lyric intellect.

Rodo's *Del Trabajo Obrero en el Uruguay* reveals him
as a deep student of practical, world-wide problems.   He is
too well versed in economics to accept the shallow notion,
promulgated by many politicians for purposes best known
to themselves, that the struggle between capital and labor
is a product of this age; he sees that our age intensified
rather than originated that antagonism.   He is also suffi-
ciently cognizant of environmental influences to shun fiat
legislation in favor of laws that take into account specified
national conditions as well as general revolutionary aims.
Speaking for Uruguay, in which the acute problems of

capitalism and the proletariat had not yet appeared, he favored a social prophylaxis,—measures destined to anticipate future contingencies. Although his view of capital is, to many contemporary thinkers, conservative, none was more aware that the interests of society are deeply bound up with justice to the laborer,—a justice that has all too often been largely verbal or promissory. Students of our labor problems, especially of the length of the working day, will find excellent data in Rodó's speech, from which they may draw conclusions not entirely in consonance with those of the speaker.

Rodó scores a good point when he indicates that terms like individualism and socialism, rather than antagonistic, are harmonious and complementary, just like authority and liberty, right and duty. He is very sensitive to the harm being worked by the exploitation of the toiler,—and insists that his moral as well as physical interests must be rigorously guarded. He is alive to the fallacy of the so-called "freedom of contract"—a fallacy into which many of our own workingmen have been led by some of our highest officials, themselves deceived or deceiving. "The oppressed laborer to whom is granted the right to liberate himself (i. e., from his work) is not a slave; but if that flight or liberation which is conceded to him as a right is to him equivalent to hunger and death, what difference is there between his condition and that of a slave, unless it be the emptiness of a name?" And it might have been expected from the author of *Ariel* that his views upon child labor would be more enlightening than those which characterize our own ostensibly civilized mill-owners. Nor is Rodó's argument a "sentimental" one (have we really done with sentimentality?) ; he regards the matter in the light of the nation's vital energies. Is not, after all, every victory for the ideal a practical victory as well, when viewed in the broad light of universal welfare? Rodó wastes no time, similarly, with "woman's place is the home,"—a slogan that sounds with such ill grace from the lips of so many of our own employers who, because of cheaper labor, have done their share to draw woman from that hypothetical hearth of domestic felicity. He knows that woman is in industry and that, like the child, she is being exploited physically, mentally, economically; with his ever-present sense of the future, he realizes the dangers to the race arising from maltreatment of woman in industry; he pleads (to think that it should be necessary in the twentieth century!) for the official recognition of maternity among industrial workers, with compensatory privileges of adequate rest.

Finally, as one would have foreseen from a study of *Motivos de Proteo*, he reminds us—and how often we need the reminder, who enact laws that enslave us in their perpetuity, though they are but the creatures of our own very fallible selves—that "laws are rectifiable," and that they may be changed in the light of new knowledge.

Rodó's speech is a thorough, sincere study of an all-important topic. He shows evidence of deep delving, and presents his opinions with a clarity and directness remarkable for a politico-economic essay. There are the same even style, broad humanity, fairness, tolerance that distinguish everything he wrote. Before such a master as this, economics ceases to be the "dismal science" that abysmal stylists have made it; it acquires, in fact, something of "la

gaie science" itself!   One need by no means assent to
Rodó's premises or to all of his conclusions to see that his
method of approach and his attitude are eminently preferable to the insincere "radicalism" of the present day so frequently encountered in "labor leaders" and large employers alike.   Wherever he went, Rodó shed a soft, warm
glow.   In life, in speech, in thought, his was the golden
medium; and if, at times, he did not advance far enough to
please some of us, we should recognize that his medium was
none the less golden.

For evidence of his intense Hispano-Americanism one
need but open the works of Rodó almost at random.   *El
Mirador de Prospero* teems with an ardent Spanish-Amer-
icanism,—there is now and then evident (see the paper on
La España Niña) a certain Pan-Hispanism such as has been
current in recent literature.

In a speech delivered in Chile on October 8, 1905, upon
the occasion of the return to the country of Juan Carlós
Gomez's remains, he concluded with the significant declaration that "the idea of the fatherland is a lofty one; but
among the peoples of Latin America, amid this living harmony of nations bound by all the ties of tradition, race,
institutions and language, such as were never presented by
the history of the world in such union and comprising so
vast an extent, we may well say that there is something
loftier than the idea of nation, and that is, the idea of
America; the idea of America conceived as a great and
imperishable unity, as a glorious, vast fatherland, with its
heroes, its educators, its tribunes; from the gulf of Mexico
to the sempiternal ice of the South.

"Sarmiento, Bilbao, Martí, Bello and Montalvo are not

the writers of one or another part of America, but they are rather the citizens of (Spanish) American intellectuality."

Is this not a species of super-patriotism? Is this not, if not internationalism, at least internationism? And by a lofty and logical expansion of the patriotic conception, is it not possible to reach an allegiance that embraces the world of humanity?

To return, however, to Rodó: in *Magna Patria* he declares succinctly that "the fatherland of Spanish Americans is Spanish America. Within the feeling for one's nation resides the not less natural and indestructible sense of allegiance to one's province, region, district; and provinces, regions or districts of that great Patria of ours are the nations into which it is divided politically. For my part, I have always so understood it, or rather, I have always so felt it. The political unity which this moral unity consecrates and incarnates—Bolívar's dream—is still a dream the realization of which, perhaps, today's generations will not witness. What does that matter! Italy was not merely Metternich's 'geographical expression' before Garibaldi's sword and Mazzini's apostolate constituted it into a political expression. It was the idea, the *numen* of the fatherland, the fatherland itself consecrated by all the holy oil of tradition, justice and glory. United, personal Italy already existed; less corporeal, but not less real; less tangible, but not less vibrant and intense than when it assumed color and outline upon the map of the nations."

And in *La España Niña:* "I have never felt a doubt as to the future of this America born of Spain. I have ever believed that in (Spanish) America, the genius of Spain,

and the most subtle essence of its genius, which is its language, possesses the firm bridge over which it will cross
the streams of the centuries. . . ." . . . "My American
pride—which is pride of land, and is, moreover, pride of
race—is satisfied with nothing less than the assurance that
the distant house, whence comes the escutcheon chiselled
out upon the door to my own, will remain ever standing,
very firm, very beautiful and highly revered." . . . "I
have thus habituated myself to effacing from my imagination the common image of an old, decrepit Spain, and to
associate, with the idea of Spain, ideas of childhood, future,
hope." Nor is Rodó's optimism strained. The current
idea that old Spain is decrepit becomes ridiculous in the
light of its unceasing intellectual foment. Economically,
—that is another question; but Cervantes wrote *Don Quixote* in poverty. . . .

The short article upon *Ibero-América* is important not
only for its hint of a Portuguese-American and Spanish-
American entente (beautifully symbolized in the Amazon
and the La Plata rivers) but also for its contribution to a
question of terminology that has only lately caused discussion in Spain and in America. It will be noticed, in
the excerpt quoted above from Rodó's speech on Juan
Carlos Gómez, that he employed the term "Latin America";
the term, it seems, is a new one, and not at all to the liking
of many Hispanophiles. The outlines of the arguments
against the name "Latin America" and in favor of some
such term as "Hispanic" or "Spanish" or even "Ibero-
America" may be summed up as follows:

1. The adjective Latin as used in the objectionable term
properly applies to the group of tongues and peoples de-

rived from ancient Latium. In such a sense the word embraces not only Spain and Portugal, who were chiefly responsible for the colonization, civilization and Christianization of South America and Central America, but also France, Italy and Rumania,—countries which had little or nothing to do with the republics that have sprung up from the Spanish and Portuguese roots in the Western hemisphere. The use of the adjective Latin, then, works an injustice upon the mother countries by implying credit to France and Italy as well, and sinking Spanish and Portuguese identity in the common term Latin. If it be argued that the linguistic basis surely is Latin, the opponents come back, quite properly, with the answer that proceeding on linguistic lines, the United States and Canada might be spoken of as Teutonic America—a term the falsity of which is at once evident.

2. The terms Spanish America and Spanish-American have been used for the past four centuries; historically they are correct; they have been sanctified by usage. Why substitute an intruder like Latin America which has come to life only during the past ten years, partly through the desire of certain Latin countries to receive credit where it is not due them?

3. If it be objected that Spanish America seems to leave out Brazil, where the language spoken is Portuguese, the proponents reply that the term Spanish or Hispanic has long been recognized as including both Spanish and Portuguese; that so notable a Portuguese as Almeida Garrett has argued in its favor, and that Rodó has shown that the word Spanish is a geographical name originally, not one of nationality or political import. Rodó, too, asserts, in

the same paragraphs upon *Ibero-América*, that Almeida
Garrett, the great national poet of Portugal, believed that
the Portuguese, without prejudice to their independent
spirit, could call themselves Spaniards.

It will be seen, then, that Rodó suggested the corrective
to his own use of the objectionable term. But has a really
satisfactory term ben reached? Does "Hispanic America" really fill the bill? Or "Spanish America?" Or
even "Ibero-America"?

The proponents of the new terms (and we may agree
at once that the old term is somewhat of a misnomer) must
recognize that there is certain to be confusion; Professor
Espinosa, the editor of *Hispania*, suggests that when Brazil
is meant to be included the general term Hispanic America
be used, while for the Spanish republics, Spanish America
be employed. In support of his stand for "Hispanic" he
points to the use of the word in its Spanish-Portuguese
meaning as a name for historical reviews, school series, the
Hispanic Society of America, and so on. It will be noted
that all these cases are closely allied to scholarship rather
than to popular usage.

It is at this point that Espinosa and those who side with
him will encounter trouble, if not opposition. There is no
doubt that a good case is made out against the use of the
adjective Latin in the designation. The characterization
is too broad, too inclusive; this holds true whether any nations are trying to belittle the part played by Spain and
Portugal or not. But the very reason for the growing
prominence of this inadequate, misleading and unjust adjective is also the reason why, in all probability, Espinosa's
substitution or restitution of Hispanic or Spanish America,

will not find favor with the man in the street. And the man and woman in the street are to be considered if scholarship is to be anything more than a close intellectual corporation. After all, no scholar would be for a moment in doubt as to what Latin America stood for, any more than a silver expert would imagine that German silver was actually pure silver from Germany. The use of "Latin America" originated through a desire to distinguish between Brazil and the Spanish-speaking republics, and at the same time have a designation to cover them as a whole. "South America" is inadequate because inexact; it leaves out Central America. Spanish America will not do, except for the scholar, who does not need it in the first place. To the average man and woman, regardless of four centuries of usage and of the historical connotations imbedded in the word, Spanish will mean pertaining to Spain. The same, in less degree, holds true for Hispanic, which, though more clearly inclusive of both Spain and Portugal, and used so by scholars, signifies Spanish to the average person, if it is ever used by that average person. "Ibero-America" might do, even if it does seem at first "high-brow"; etymologically it is fully as good as Hispanic. And in regard to the term Spanish, as applied to both Brazil and the Spanish-speaking countries, it does not seem to have occurred to its defenders that, despite Almeida Garrett, to more than one Portuguese it might sound just as exclusive of Portuguese rights as the term Latin seems to the aforementioned defenders inappreciative of the efforts of Spain and Portugal together.

For our present purpose, however, it is of greater importance to point out that Rodó's admirable little essay is more than an argument about terminology; it is another aspect of his continental thought,—thought becoming truly continental in its embracing of a sister language and a sister civilization.[11]

Of Pan-Americanism, as we understand it, there is little or none in Rodó. He does not underestimate us, but he feels strongly that imitation of us would run counter to traditional inheritances. Indeed, he is the avowed enemy of imitation in every field, for as we may have divined from the lips of Proteus, mere imitation is the negation of personality, national as well as individual. A better mutual understanding there well could be,—an understanding in which imitation need play no part, and one of the results of which should be an advantageous cross-fertilization.

Of the charmingly beautiful literary cameos in which

[11] There is an easy way out of the matter. Why not be content to speak of Spanish America and Portuguese America? These designations mean exactly what they say; they are readily seized by the scholar and the average person alike; they require no knowledge of etymology, history, or national jealousies. They are ideal terminologies, because they explain at the same time as they name. And while we are waiting for an ideal term that shall include, at the same time, both the Spanish and the Portuguese elements of this hemisphere, will not someone arise and call to our attention the complacent use we of the North make of the word American? For the rest of the continent, as well as all of the land south of the Isthmus of Panama, is filled with Americans—of the South, to be sure, but Americans none the less. The same state of affairs, reversed, might be called to the attention of the other Americans, by whom the word "Americano" is rarely meant, of course, to include us.

Philology, too, it would seem, has its irredentists in the land of words. For that reason it may be worth while, in most friendly spirit, to call to the attention of Professor Espinosa that the quarterly which he edits—a fine magazine that deserves to grow rapidly—is called *Hispania: A Quarterly Journal Devoted to the Interests of Teachers of Spanish*, etc. Not teachers of Spanish and Portuguese, you will notice. Now, when intellectual journals use the word Hispania in their titles to denote something exclusively Spanish, how can one reasonably expect its Spanish-Portuguese meaning to become current among teachers, let alone the average man and woman?

Rodó is so rich, I shall translate two in full.   The first reveals Rodó as a lover of formal beauty; the second initiates
us into one of the most peculiar qualities of his style,—a
certain religious hush that comes over lonely landscapes
at twilight.   From the *Geste of Form* we may easily gather
an adequate notion of Rodó's verbal punctiliousness that
would seem to modify the statement of some of his friends
that his writings leaped·full-grown from the forehead of the
great Uruguayan.   Struggle there certainly was, though it
may not have been visible in the scrawls and scratches of
the agonizing sheets that make the author's labor such a
joy—and such a torture.

THE GESTE OF FORM

"What a prodigious transformation is that undergone by
words meek and inert in the flock of common style, when
they are convoked and commanded by the genius of an
artist. . . . From the very moment in which you desire to
make an art,—a plastic and musical art—of expression,
you sink into it a spur that arouses all its rebellious impulses.   The word, a living, wilful being, looks at you then
from the nib of the pen, which pricks it in an attempt to
subject it; it disputes with you, compels you to meet it;
it possesses a soul and a physiognomy.   Revealing to you,
in its rebellion, all its innermost content, it often obliges
you to return to it the freedom of which you desired to
deprive it, and to summon another, which comes, coyly
and sullenly, to the yoke of steel.   And there are times
in which the battle of these diminutive monsters exalts and
exhausts you like a desperate struggle for fortune and

honor. All the voluptuousness of heroism is contained in this unknown contest. You feel alternately the intoxication of the conqueror, the qualms of the timorous, the wrathful exaltation of the wounded. You understand, before the docility of a phrase that falls conquered at your feet, the savage cry of triumph. You learn, when the scarcely grasped form escapes you, how it is that the anguish of failure enters the heart. Your whole organism vibrates like the earth atremble with the crashing palpitation of battle. As upon the field where the struggle took place, there remain afterward the signs of the fire that has passed, in your imagination and in your nerves. Upon the blackened pages you leave something of your being and of your life.—What, besides this, is worth the complacent spontaneity of him who opposes no personal resistance to the affluence of the colorless, unexpressixe phrase, no proud intractibility to the rebellion of the word which refuses to give up its soul and its color? . . . For the struggle with style should not be confused with the cold pertinacity of rhetoric, which adjusts painstakingly, in the mosaic of its conventional correctness, words that have not been moistened by the warm breath of the soul. This would be to compare a game of chess with a combat in which blood flows and an empire is at stake. The struggle for style is an epic which has as its field of action our innermost nature, the deepest profundities of our being. The poems of war do not speak to you of strength more superb, of carnage more cruel, nor, in victory, of jubilation more lofty or divine. . . . Oh, formidable, beautiful Iliad! Iliad of the heart of artists, from whose unknown combats are born into the world joy, enthusiasm and light as from the heroism and

the blood of the true epics!   You should some time have
been written, so that, narrated by one of those who bore you
within him, there would endure in you the testimony of
one of the most moving human emotions.   And your
Homer might have been Gustave Flaubert."

Is that not a page which Flaubert himself would have
enjoyed?

It was such external beauty (and is it really external
when made, as in the case of Rodó, an organic part of
thought?) that our author cast about the beauty of his ideas.
By no means is this an idle dallying with style in its restricted sense.   It is the worship of a silent prayer.   And
just as Rodó's verbal battles were a mute Iliad, so was his
deep apprecation a speechless wonder.   How eloquently
has has expressed this silence in *Los Que Callan!*

THOSE WHO ARE SILENT

"One of the deepest feelings of respect I have ever experienced in the world, is that which is produced upon me
by a certain lineage of spirits,—certainly very rare, and
difficult to recognize without having been received into
their most chosen intimacy; a certain lineage of spirits who
unite to an infallible, perfect, aristocratic sense of beauty
in matters of Art, the absolute disinterestedness with which
they silently profess their cult, immune to all stimulus of
vanity, all purposes of criticism or creation, all simoniac
greed for fame.   They understand the work of art in its
most delicate shades, with that fulness of intelligence and
sympathy which is a second creation; they are the ideal
reader or spectator of which the artist has dreamed; they

offer up their entire soul in the religious sacrifice of the
artistic emotion, in that absolute immolation of the personality whence the mysticism of Art takes its origin.   They
retain within them the perennial echo in which is prolonged
the true, original accent of the poet and which the crowd
perceives only in disturbed and incomplete fashion,—the
crystal clear reflection in which is reproduced, with the
matutinal freshness of creative inspiration, the image of
the painting or the statue.   They compensate for triumphant, noisy vulgarity; for inferior boasts; for abominable
snobism.   They cherish, in the calm and sheltered recess of
their devoted memory, names and works which the injustice and the indolence of an epoch have condemned to
common oblivion.   For them the lie stamped upon the false
coin of renown and glory has no currency.   Within their
secret disdain, animated by a serene and terrible certainty,
they bear the hell whence those will not be able to escape
who attain success by committing crimes against beauty,
against taste, against noble pride.   And they keep silent.
. . . And they pass through the world with an indifferent,
almost common appearance.   And as in the chapel of a
mysterious, proscribed cult, they conceal, within their deepest self, the tabernacle of this ideal love, which beautifies
the mystery like the modesty of a sweetheart.

"Do you doubt that such souls exist? . . . I have come
to know some, after having known only the opaque film
that veiled them from my sight.   And ever since I have
discovered them their presence dominates me, subjects me
with the sense of a superiority that I do not recognize, so
imperious and of such high character is it, either in the
creative artist whom I most admire or in the magisterial

wisdom that inspires me with most respect. For these souls of celestial silence are the only ones who have given me the complete intuition of how much there is that is vulgar and petty in all this struggle for notoriety, this sensualism of admiration and applause,—the coarse alloy that we of the literary comedy compound with the gold of our ideality of love and beauty. Only they know how to love you, Beauty, as you, oh Goddess, deserve to be loved! In the company of these souls I am overwhelmed by I do not know what noble shame of being an author, a professional writer. And when I return to this task, they comprise the unknown and unknowable public that most exalts and most tortures me. To this public I commend myself, with an austere and melancholy hope, as one who commends himself to the justice of a posterity that he will never behold, whenever I believe that a word of mine has not been understood in all its virtue and beauty; when a creature of my imagination has not found the loving bosom to receive it. And it is of this public that I think, filled with an innermost disquietude,—as if anguished with the impossible desire of learning the truth from the lips of a marble god,—when applause and praises wish to persuade me that something good and beautiful has blossomed from my soul.

"Ah, how many of these self-denying monks of beauty pass you by without your recognizing them; perhaps scorned by you. . . . Perhaps there is one of them in that indeterminate, colorless spectator who occupies his chair in the theatre, not far from yours, applauding as much as the rest, assenting with trivial remarks to his neighbor's comments, being lost in the crowd as it leaves. Perhaps another is hidden behind the mask of that traveler who, with the

appearance of a merchant, reads, opposite your seat in the
train, a book that may be a Baedeker guide as well as a
poem by Wilde or a novel by d'Annunzio.   Perhaps you
will discover still another in that fellow whom popular
opinion—cruel irony!—judges as an unsuccessful poet,
feeling deep disdain for his impotence; for it does not know
his premature renunciation was spontaneous and most lofty
religiosity,[12] and that in his aversion toward speaking of
art with those who were his rivals and friends there is only
the delicacy of a transfigured sensibility and the consciousness of a stranger's solitude. . . . In one or another dis-
guise, they pass in their irrevocable silence.   And this silence is neither humility nor pride.   It is simply the complete possession of a boon that carries its end and its recom-
pense within itself, and for this reason contains itself within
ts own amplitude, without aspiring to break its bonds im-
petuously; like the wine which, when it has matured, forgets
the restlessness and the seethings of fermentation, or like the
splendor of the serene night which, ecstatic in the soft glory
of its lights does not publish it with the flashes of the lightning or the music of the sun."

This is one of the fundamental passages in Rodó; it gives
us to behold in him just such a silent potent figure as he
speaks of,—just such a hushed worshipper of beauty as he
describes.   It is, in the original at least, an excellent example of a musical, suggestive, luminous prose that produced, in the words of one of his chief commentators,[13]
"pages of so radiant a serenity that they inspire the same
melancholy as days that are too beautiful."

[12] May this contain a hint as to Rodó's own early renunciation of poetry?
[13] Gonzalo Zaldumbide, in *Mercure de France*, July 16, 1917.

The ethical aspect of Rodó's work has been succinctly treated by Pedro Henríquez Ureña in a lecture given before the Ateneo de México on August 22, 1910, and since reprinted in several Spanish publications. Señor Henríquez Ureña considers that Rodó's great originality consists "in having joined the cosmological principle of creative evolution to the ideal of a standard of action for life." Much of Rodó is in Bergson, as it is in Goethe and many before him. This lay mystic is "of the family of Epictetus, and of Plutarch, of Seneca and Marcus Aurelius, Luis de León, Raimonde Sebonde, Emerson, Ruskin,—the family over which, sheltering it with one of his archangel's wings, the divine Plato presides."

The most searching critique of Rodó's achievement is from the pen of Gonzalo Zaldumbide, in the *Revue Hispanique*, (XLIII, 103, June, 1918, pp. 205–307). Señor Zaldumbide's discussion is a wholesome corrective for the excessive praise that has been heaped upon the great Uruguayan, although the critic's anxiety not to overestimate Rodó leads him, I believe, to underestimate such a capital work as the *Motivos de Proteo*. When he says that Rodó brought no new thoughts, and that his work will endure chiefly because of its language, he is on the whole right. But did Rodó aim to bring new *thoughts?* Was it not the *love of truth*, not *truth*, that Rodó aimed to instil? And is not Rodó's insistence upon continuous change new in its implications, and of necessity so? "The book (i.e., *Motivos de Proteo*) to which he desired to impart above all a dynamic virtue, a guiding impulse, becomes a static book, motionless in its perfection," writes Zaldumbide. But this is little more than a play on words. Rodó's book *is* dynamic, by virtue of the sense of necessity for continuous growth which it instils. Nor is there any greater value to the critic's objection that only those who do not need that sense in the first place, will be benefited by the dynamic view. For Rodó will penetrate to those who need his dynamic ethics through those others whose sense of the necessity for change has been quickened, if not inculcated, by the *Motivos*. Rodó was in a very true sense an inspirer, not a dogmatist. "If he proved the necessity and the poetry of an ideal, he imposed no ideal as the true one, to the exclusion of others," objects Zaldumbide. But this would have been opposed to Rodó's cardinal tenet of the self-determination of personality, so to speak. There is more force to Zaldumbide's objection that Rodó "limited the drama of our destiny to the immediate problem of vocation." Yet the *Motivos* contain the corrective to their own limitations, because of their indubitably dynamic effect. No one who wishes to know the complete Rodó may do without Zaldumbide's deeply penetrative study.

Radiance, serenity, an insight that is none the less clear for its depth, classic repose combined with a dynamic conception of modernity, eternal intellectual youth—these are the distinguishing attributes of a power whose influence should not be confined to the Spanish tongue.

CHAPTER IV

JOSÉ SANTOS CHOCANO

(1875–)

DURING the lifetime of Darío, José Santos Chocano was looked upon by many as his rival; after the death of the great Nicaraguan, the Peruvian was proclaimed his successor, although that distinction is by no means an undisputed one. We may well afford to leave that particular matter to the politics of art. The two men were not rivals; it is enough to read Darío's generous poetic introduction to Santos Chocano's *Alma América* to dispel that notion. They were, in a great measure, complementary personalities, although one need not go so far (as has been done) as to pronounce Darío the feminine element and Chocano the masculine. In Chocano we find but a trace of the doubt that constantly assailed Darío during his agitated, neurotic career; in him we find nothing at all of the morbidity that consumed the author of *Cantos de Vida y Esperanza*. In this respect the Peruvian more resembles Martí and Blanco-Fombona; it would seem that a life of action in rebellion against political and economic institutions did not leave these spirits time for morbid introspection.

We shall find in Chocano, too, a certain change of attitude toward the United States, although it is not untempered by fear and veiled threat. He possessed, from the very first, an international outlook that was not limited to mere book readings, and that did not confine itself to artistic channels. If Darío was a vibrant lyre, Chocano is a ringing bell, a blasting trumpet; look over his writings from his earliest protests, which landed him in the regulation fashion behind the prison bars of an unfeeling tyrant, through to the very latest, and you will find a singular predominance of the exclamation point; the fact is symbolic of a large part of his proud, sonorous, arrogant, polyphonic utterances. He is as much bard as poet,—as much epic as lyric,—as much universal as more restrictedly American in the Spanish sense. And through all his labors, early and late, is evident a strange duality of mood, outlook and expression. He is at once, as we have seen, epic and lyric; he seeks to reconcile the old Spain with its former colonies; to bring about a certain Pan-Americanism that includes the United States (although it is easy to exaggerate this part of his labors, as I believe it has been exaggerated); he is classic and romantic, most sensibly denying adherence to any artistic creed; he is savage and aristocratic; he is the man of nature, in Rousseau's meaning, and the man of refinement; he is at once the past, the present and the future; he combines power with delicacy; he is pantheistic, yet devoutly and publicly a modern believer. The list of attributes might be extended indefinitely; beneath the apparent contradictions lies a contemporaneity no less universal than Darío's, yet expressing itself through an entirely different personality. Like Darío, he feels that he has been born out of his age, yet one feels the plaint more genuine in the case of the former, for Chocano is very much a man of the times; indeed, he came a little too early rather than, as he has complained, much too late; this

it was that brought him to the prison cell at the age of
eighteen in his native Callao. To paraphrase Patrick
Henry's memorable sentence, Blanco-Fombona had his
Gómez, Montalvo had his García Moreno, José Marmol
had his Rosas, and so, too, did Chocano wage battle against
the entire social system.

1. *Earliest Productions*

The earliest productions from Chocano's pen were *Iras
Santas* (1895); *En La Aldea* (published later in the same
year, although the poems were written two years earlier)
and *Azahares* (1896). There is much in these youthful
efforts that the author himself has since, with good judgment, repudiated; a study of the verses, however, repays us
for the insight they afford into the poet's thoughts and personality, and for the further proof they offer that the poet-
child is father to the man-poet.

Iras Santas quivers with the holy rage of a passionate,
ideally-minded youth against the maladjustments of contemporary society. The youngster had evidently read a
great deal; he was familiar with the same Hugo that inspired so much of Darío's earlier efforts; he must, as even
the work of his middle period shows, have literally swal-
lowed not a few volumes of socialistic and anarchistic doctrine. His conception of the poet is that of the proud
spirit who must break yokes and sing the redemption, for

> Siempre al cantar Victor Hugo
> tembló Napoleón tercero.

The poet bids Lazarus arise and Justice be born anew. Not

the ivory of the meditative tower, but the iron of labor and struggle is his symbol; nor is our juvenile redeemer, who knows his Bible well and possesses more than a smattering of the classics, very modest in his pretensions. "If another Christ be necessary to succumb, here am I!" he proclaims in his *A Lázaro;* beneath the quasi-blasphemy of the utterance, however, flames a sincere purpose that lights up all the verses in the collection of "sacred wraths." If life is a struggle, the poet must perform his share; by a universal law all roses have thorns, and "verses without thorns are not roses"! If verse-thorns could make verse-roses, *Iras Santas* would be a veritable conservatory.

It should be emphasized, however, that beneath all the bombast of language and thought lies a redeeming sincerity. The youngster was a child of his age. Was it not the hey-day of colors? Then what more natural for his ardent spirit than to print these verses in red? Nor has the mania subsided; for some reason unknown to the public a certain Parisian composer of today prints his music in the same color. The singer of vengeance in *Iras Santas* is an enemy, not to organized society, but to society as at present organized; he is a fearless Samson who (in *Excelsior!*) warns Delila that it will be useless to shear his locks:

> Vano, vano será que una Dalila
> recorte mi melena de poeta. . . .

He demands (*Para Todos*) universal equality, and demands it in picturesque metaphors that cast an undeniably poetic glamor over communism.

> Yo quiero la igualdad, ya que la suerte
> es común en punto de partida:

> si todos son iguales en la muerte,
> todos sean iguales en la vida!

"If all are equal in death, let all be equal in life!"   The people is great, and if it be ignorant, that is the fault of the masters; we are all "the verses of a single poem." Such, then, is the mission of the poet, the mission of youth; for such an ideal would young Chocano borrow the lute of Hugo and the lash of Christ.

His *El Sermon de la Montaña* (Sermon on the Mount) characteristically blends his own beliefs with those of Christ.   It has been noted that the Savior of the poem speaks more like Bakounin and Réclus than the figure of the New Testament,—that He embodies the radical readings of an ardent young spirit; the coupling of the holy name with the doctrine so unholy to many, however, once more attests what we must henceforth accept as unquestioned fact, —the sincerity of a forceful personality born into a world that he is intent upon bettering.   Out of such a purpose grew, quite naturally, the early utilitarian beliefs as to the poet's function.   When the Christ of the poem proclaims

> Crucificadme; ¿y bien?   ¿Yo hablo al presente?
> No: yo hablo al porvenir. La igualdad sacra
> será el ideal de la futura gente. . .

he speaks through the writer's mouth; nor is his spirit so far removed from that of the Redeemer.

> ¡Oh, la igualdad!   ¿Hermanos, no habéis visto
> al sol vertiendo rayos sobre todos?
> Asi alumbra también el Dios del Cristo;
> por eso nivelados en grandeza,

tenéis, ante este mundo, igual derecho
de recibir el Sol sobre la frente
que de tener á Dios bajo del pecho! . . .

Many a famous poet well above his twentieth year has
written far worse poetry than young Chocano produced in
this *Sermon,* which was dedicated to Rubén Darío.

There is an occasional softer note in the collection, such
as rises from *La Alondra* (The Lark), dedicated to Enrique
Gómez Carillo; it reveals the poet in a symbolistic mood
that was later developed in some of his best poetry, and has
been well rendered into English by Miss Alice Stone Blackwell, who has translated a large number of Chocano's poems
into our tongue, as well as a notable series from his
brother poets:

"O Romeo, go not yet away!" with love
Thus Juliet murmurs, 'mid the thinning dark,
And adds to that sweet call the tender words,
" 'Tis not the lark!"

Lo, I have visited the heavenly nests,
Struck the bright harps to which the angels hark,
And pierced into the fair dream's horoscope—
 'Tis not the lark.

I face to face have seen the golden star,
The prelude sweet I note by note could mark;
I journeyed through the heavens inch by inch—
 'Tis not the lark.

The sacred chalice I have quaffed, and shared
The Host, that wipes away earth's care and cark;
Beneath its golden dish I placed my soul—
 'Tis not the lark.

And I have plucked the young bird from the egg,
The beauteous almond from its covering dark,
And from the lukewarm word the golden thought—
  'Tis not the lark.

And I at last have flung free words abroad
Above the crowds, already hoarse with song,
That go forth following the new Ideals,
The virgin Longings, eager, deep, and strong—

With all the flags of triumph now unfurled
Of Dawn Eternal, which dispels the dark;
Go, Romeo, go forth; there still is time.
  It is the lark!

I have said that Chocano displays none of the morbidity
that characterizes so many of the modernists; yet in his
El Primer Adiós (First Farewell) he speaks of Werther's
ailment coursing through his veins; if it really did, it had
little ill effect upon his tropical nature; in the very same
poem, indeed, he gives ample evidence of a virility and an
aggressiveness sadly lacked by Goethe's romantic hero.
The century appears in the light of a battle and the poet
hastens with prophetic fervor to the strife intoning "the
Marseillaise of a yokeless love." There is a humorous
side to this long farewell of some fifty-four eight-lined
stanzas; just before setting out, the author was clapped into
prison. Little daunted, however, he wrote verses of more
than passing significance during his incarceration, and in
one of the sonnets from *En La Mazmorra* (the underground
dungeon of Casamatas, Callao) he sings his defiance in a
couple of metaphors that sum up, with that peculiar power
Chocano wields over rhetorical figures, his entire conception

of the poet as the enemy of the tyrant; as long as there remains a tyrant on the throne the poet will continue to sing his ire; he will sink his enemies into the dungeon of his verses, and his lyre shall form their prison bars!

The Chocano of the *Iras Santas* is a torrential, gushing, disordered, yet religiously ideal imagination, already giving ample evidence of his flashing metaphors and dazzling images; beside the influence of the ubiquitous Hugo, it is instructive to point out that of Díaz Mirón; read the Mexican's *A Gloria*, for example, and you will discover not only much of the Peruvian's indignation and arrogance, but not a little of his epigrammatic, arrow-like style. So libertarian a critic as Manuel González Prada sees in such a poem as *Juicio Final*, a genuine summary of Peruvian social and political life; this is important, for one of Chocano's early attributes was his attempt to poetize everything he read upon art, science and sociology; he lived up truly to his conception of the poet as a social redeemer. The epic spirit is already evidenced by the long-winded farewell; the tenderer strain is represented by the beautiful poem of the lark; there is a glimpse of love, which enters more fully, and more naturally, in the following collection.

Iras Santas had been printed in red ink; *En La Aldea* (In The Village) was printed in blue. The two colors symbolize most adequately the dominating spirits of the respective collections; *En La Aldea*, moreover, is furnished with a blue prelude. It is important to recall that these poems were written at about the same time as the more fiery ones; we thus have a further evidence of the poet's duality. "In *Iras Santas*," says González Prada quite vividly, "Chocano seizes poetry by the hair and gives it a rude tug";

the second collection takes us from prison walls and passionate harangue to the softer moods of nature and of man. The collection is subtitled *Poesías Americanas* and is a distinct precursor, in spirit, of *Alma América;* its blue tint, too, is not unmarred here and there by what Gonzáles Prada calls a greyish hue.   The cerulean prelude would serve to indicate also that young Chocano knew tyrants of a non-political nature, who wore petticoats.   For at the conclusion he addresses a maiden with the remark that she will note from his verses, filled with bitterness as they are, the enduring memory of his love for her.   "Now gentle, now violent my verses will sound to your ears; for within them the vulture and the dove possess the same nest!" (The ever-present duality, you will notice.)   And then, to show that our gallant is facile with the typically Spanish languishing simile:

> Lee mis pobres versos, ya que el yugo
> sé constante llevar de tus amores;
> devóralos y exprímeles el jugo;
> porque acaso el mayor de mis placeres
> está en verlos morir como esas flores
> que deshojan, jugando, las mujeres. . . .

The comparison of his poems to the flowers that women pull apart as they play with them is worthy of an anthology.

We must not imagine that because the poems are inspired by country life, they are utterly devoid of the poet's rebellious spirit.   For the village possesses former battle-fields as well as cemeteries, and the singer muses over them, beholding a day when the tool of the laborer that brings life will replace the instrument of the warrior that brought death.   The sight of the cemetery itself is not a

source of melancholy musings, but rather a mystic consolation, rare in youth. "How green the field seems,
stretched out there in the distance . . . !   And why does it
wear the color of hope?"   The sight of the mills recalls
the great Manchegan and inspires a symbolic sonnet.
Note, in passing, how rich in sonnets is Chocano; Spanish-
American modernists see little anachronistic in the use of
the form that our own young spirits are fast abandoning.

THE WIND MILLS

Yonder, borne onward by the strong wind's breath,
The village windmills' mocking sails are seen,
Circling with reckless haste and ardor keen,
With panting fury and impelling faith.
A music hovers o'er the sails, wind-caught;
They raise towards heaven the song divine and free
Of man triumphant over Destiny,
The wild wind harnessed by our human Thought.

When evening shades descend upon the earth,
And yonder there I see the windmills stand,
Kissed vainly by the great sun's glowing light,
Then from their sails I look to see come forth,
Upon his meagre steed, with lance in hand,
A spiritual type, La Mancha's knight!

For some reason or other it has pleased the poet, in his
later days, to insist upon his objectivity; from one who has
been so sensible in the matter of schools and terminology
the insistence comes with a little unpleasantness.   Chocano's conception of objectivity is quite his own; does he
mean that he is not subjective?   That is hard to believe.
Does he mean that he is, in a narrow sense, Parnassian?

That is equally hard to understand. No doubt the advancing years, as we shall see, have chastened his spirit and refined his art, but they have not effaced his personality, his subjectivity, his peculiarly dualistic view of man and the universe. In some of the poems of *En La Aldea,* indeed, he hits upon a symbolistic pantheism that he has never completely outgrown. Thus his *Arboles Viejos* looks upon the tree as possibly furnishing not only the cross for a Christ, but the branch upon which to hang a Judas.

OLD TREES

Even the old tree, fallen by the road,
That has no leaves, no fruit, no blossoms gay,
Can give a seat where shepherds may repose,
A staff to aid the pilgrim on his way.

So the old man, experienced and wise,
Gives maxims that ward off mishap and pain.
He, without perfume, sap, or colors bright,
Fulfills his law, and does not live in vain.

O workman, listen and give heed to me!
Thou shouldst oppose as steadfastly as I
Cutting off boughs, though they be bare of grace;
Because there may come forth from some old tree
Perchance the cross on which a Christ shall die,
Perchance the gallows for a Judas base.

Yet does the village bring him calm? No. He is the eternal fighter. He sees the beauty of love, of nature, of life, but there is something missing in that beauty if he is not engaged in the struggle for the amelioration of mankind's lot. He thinks of death (*Morir*), but it is not a death such as Gutiérrez Nájera and Casal longed for.

> I would wage battle with all my soul,
> With all my blood, with every nerve!

He would die at the height of the strife, with his lyre in
his hands. He knows, however, that while all may not be
right with the world, God's in His heaven and "all pro-
gresses toward the good." And just as all doubters have
their moments of faith, or an intense desire for it, so to this
optimist come his passing moments of doubt. In *Ante El
Abismo* he voices the eternal query and receives the eternal
reply: silence.

The poet of *En La Aldea*, far more than he of the sacred
wrath, reveals the singer of *Alma América*; the herald of
its fauna and its flora, the idyllic painter of its birds and
beasts, its landscapes and traditions; the familiar spirit of
its ambient. Chocano's pantheism endows his beloved
mountains not only with life, but with thought; it is as
much nature in contemplation of man as González Martínez's man in contemplation of nature.

Azahares (Orange Blossoms, 1896) is a lyric collection
in which the lover pays tribute to his beloved; woman is at
once his muse and his song; her very glance is a *Fiat Lux!*
The poet (*Ab Eterno*) reveals himself as a believer in the
life eternal for

> Traemos desde otros mundos,
> cual recuerdos de otros días,
> inefables simpatías,
> resentimientos profundos.
> ¿Los oleajes iracundos
> chocan sólo para chocar?
> ¿Amar es tan sólo amar?
> ¿Donde el punto de partida

> está para nuestra vida:
> en la playa ó en la mar?

Is not this the same as he who later feels himself of the past, present and future, all in one?

Note how the grandiose attitude (which becomes at times grandiloquent in the best sense of the word and more often, in the early poems, rhymed bombast) does not abandon him even in the moods of love. When he is thrust from the heaven of his Beatrice's eyes he falls like Lucifer himself, and dreams in hell of redemption through his sweetheart's protecting hand.

> debe de ser hermoso y eloquente,
> ver entrar á los cielos nuevamente
> á Satan redimido y perdonado.   (*Regreso*)

When she weeps, her tears are pure pearl; when he weeps, he weeps oceans; the very human heart possesses the form of a tear (*Rocío*). On the seventh day (*El Séptimo Día*) the Lord proclaims "Let there be Love!" and "there sounded a thunder like an immense kiss!" . . . "Let there be love!" cried the Lord again; "but let it be worthy of Me" . . . "And woman was created!"

> Entonces canté amor.   Quité los velos   5
> de encima de los génesis profundos;
> y abrí mi libro, como Dios sus celos;
> y ví mis versos, como Dios sus mundos. . .

The youth who would placidly liken himself to Christ would not hesitate to carry the similarity to the Lord himself; but when he opens his book, "as God his heavens," and

beholds his verses, "as God his worlds," the celestial imagery has gone too far!

The early collections by Chocano, then, reveal all the
attributes that distinguish his later work: an intense dualism of outlook, a radical conception of society, a gift for
illuminating figures, a soft touch that represents the giant
in repose, a communion with nature that endows it with his
own personality, a deep feeling for the indigenous flowers,
birds, beasts and trees, a religious spirit, a tendency to conceive things upon a grandiose scale and express them in a
bold manner commensurate with the conception. There is
as yet little sense of selection, although here and there appears a poem that proclaims the mature singer. There is
as yet little technical innovation, although we find a certain mastery of conventional forms that renders the verse
pliant to his thoughts. Yet the future Chocano is distinctly, if embryonically, present. The labors that follow
immediately upon those that we have scanned, leading
to *Alma América,* are in a sense intermediary; there is an
advance in technique and thought, a more ample sweep,
a firmer grasp. Maturity is rapid in the tropics, and Chocano is a tropical spirit.

2. *La Epopeya del Morro, El Canto del Siglo, Selva Virgen, El Derrumbe.*

In rapid succession, perhaps spurred on by the success
of *The Epic of the Morro,* Chocano wrote the pneumatic
Song of the Century, a finisecular poem, issued the collection *Virgin Forest* and at first fragmentarily, the romantic-
symbolic verse narrative, *The Landslide* or *The Collapse.*

La Epopeya del Morro (1899) celebrates, in quasi-epic style, the intense patriotism and heroism of the Peruvians as brought out by the war with Chile, which lasted from 1879 to 1883. Written when Chocano was but twenty years of age, it was awarded a prize by the National Congress of Peru; in his reprinting of it (in *Fiat Lux!*, which is in part an anthology of all his poetic works previous to *Alma América*) he tells us that he considers it the highest exponent of his first artistic stage. And without going into the raptures that González-Blanco feels for the youthful production, it is easy to consider it a remarkable work of combined patriotism and poesy. It would seem, too, that the youthful revolutionist was not so communistic in his fervors as to have lost all sense of nationality.

The *Epopeya*[1] in addition to the introduction and the

[1] I refer here to the revised form of the *Epopeya* as it appears in *Fiat Lux!* (1908). The earlier form is appreciably longer, consisting of ten parts in addition to the prologue. The revision has affected mainly the beginning. Thus, in the original first canto (called El Canto de Los Héroes) there is an irrelevant question whether progress is real or illusionary, and the firm belief that the memory of heroes will outlive that of all other human creatures.

> En medio de la noche, en que camina
> el mundo, hacia la aurora del mañana,
> cada héroe, coronando cada ruina,
> es como cada antorcha que ilumina
> las noches de Nerón. ¡Antorcha humana:
> llamarada infernal, lumbre divina! . . .

There is likewise a strong note of that internationalism whose more pronounced characteristics seem to have been abandoned later by the poet. Thus, in the early version, the author sings the internation before approaching the glorification of his nation's heroes. "Soon, soon, tomorrow, the idea of a fatherland that shall be the eternal union of the human species, will shine from the summits upon the sad and abject faces of the fettered multitudes. The old fatherland will change name; and the new name dreamed of in the mind will triumph at last in a fierce battle. . . .

epilogue, consists in its revised form, of six parts: In Wait-ing, the Last Cartridge, Before The Assault, The Assault, The Death of the Hero, The End of the Assault.   The epi-sode throbs with names that rouse a fierce pride in the heart of Peruvians, and the writer occasionally indicates the historical accuracy of the high deeds he celebrates. Uppermost in Chocano's mind seems to have been the tak-ing of the port of Arica, which occurred on June 7, 1880, —a sad date for Peru.

The piece is characteristic of the author, although it displays a surer hand and a firmer grasp upon technical detail than do the earlier poems.   It mingles classical with biblical allusion and at times falls into an exaggerated style that has never completely abandoned the Peruvian poet.   Yet its beauties far outweigh any occasional lapses. Did not even the good Homer nod?

The Hero, with his waning band of men, in a vain wait for reinforcements, is sadly disillusioned when he seems

Oh, Universal Fatherland! Fatherland of man, an entire century, dying, salutes thee!" But since the song is of a national hero, he ends the canto

> ¡Hoy canta al heroe de la patria vieja
> y al de la Patria Universal mañana!

> Sing, muse, today, the hero of the old fatherland,
> and him of the Universal Patria tomorrow!

Chocano's rather erratic method of publication, in which it is very diffi-cult to follow his artistic progress, is perfectly justifiable in the case of the man desirous of giving only his best to the public, but it is hard on the critic who is interested in the creator's development. Nor is it quite right to present the *Epopeya* as it appears in *Fiat Lux!* (where it is about half the size of the original form) without a note calling attention to the changes; Chocano (in *Fiat Lux!*) says that he regards the *Epopeya* as the highest point in his early poetry; very well, but the *Epopeya* as it appears there is not the original document, and hence misleads the reader and student as to just what degree of skill the poet had attained at the time the *Epopeya* was awarded national distinction.

to discern the long awaited succor arrive.   The newcomers
are not the longed for aid; they represent an added men-
ace from the enemy.   Soon a messenger is despatched
from the hostile lines, bearing the news that the small
force may escape with their lives if they will surrender
in the face of sure defeat.   The Hero's response is immediate; they will fight to the last cartridge; but before
giving that as a definite reply he leads the messenger
to the patriot chiefs and lets him hear the decision corro-
borated by the full council.   The messenger departs and
soon the attack begins.   Bravely the Peruvians wage combat, and as vainly, against superior forces.   A woman is
found fighting at her man's side, and in her death she
becomes, for the poet, the symbol of the slain Patria.
The Hero himself is at last slain, and the first night of
captivity falls over the fortress.   Thus was begun a war
which represents a decisive and disastrous moment in
Peruvian history, having set her back for many a year.

The poem literally flames with ardor; even the metaphors are drawn from the imagery of fire; time and again
we come upon the felicitous phrases and figures of which
Chocano alone, with all his tendency to overdo such things,
possesses the secret.

Thus, in the first canto, if we may call it such, the pa-
triots discover that the enemy is five times as great as was
believed; whereupon each Peruvian grows five times himself in bravery.

> Cinco veces mayor el acampado
> enemigo es al fin . . . Y cinco veces
> crece dentro de si cada soldado.

Thus the woman discovered fighting in the Peruvian

ranks becomes an eternal symbol of the unfortunate fatherland.

> ¡Y esa mujer, de carne desgarrada
> por infame puñal, con la mirada
> de un Sol de gloria en la pupila incierta;
> esa sobre el cañon sacrificada,
> esa . . . es la imagen de la Patria muerta!

And what a splendid climax is that of the Epilogue, in
which the nation is represented as making a pyre of the
branches lopped from its tree of life, from which, when
the flames have died, will rise the flag of the nation floating over the ruins "like a flame become a banner!"

> ¡y el patrio pabellón teñido en rojo,
> cuando se apague la gloriosa hoguera,
> floterá sobre el último despojo
> como una llamarada hecha bandera!

A single instance may suffice to illustrate the tendency
to exaggerated statement. Chocano is speaking of his
hero, whom he makes out as the synthesis of no less than
three Homeric heroes:

> porque el gran Bolognesi era el resumen
> de Agamenón, de Néstor y de Aquiles:
> así encarnaba el Héroe americano
> la majestad de Agamenón de Atreo
> la experiencia de Néstor el anciano
> y el arrojo del hijo de Peleo.

La Epopeya del Morro, says González-Blanco, "is an
epic song in the ancient manner, as resonant and virile as
the stamping hoofs of a war horse. Chocano's strophes

resound like lashes and cleave the air like arrows." Perhaps the Spanish critic, who is notable for his enthusiasm over things Spanish-American, has been infected by a little of Chocano's expansive spirit; yet his evaluation is indicative of the poem's high worth. The action moves swiftly, the language is luminous with imagery and occasional grandiloquence. *La Epopeya del Morro* went far to make Chocano the national poet of Peru,—the first step to his poetic conquest of the entire continent.

When we come to the *Song of the Century* (1900), however, we feel at once that we are in a different atmosphere, —a stifling ambient in which Pegasus kicks up so much dust that it is impossible to catch sight of him. The steed of poesy, possessing hoofs as well as wings, here elects to abandon his pinions and stick close to the earth; at times, being after all a steed, he runs at a mad gallop, but always he holds to the ground,—his wings lie idle.

Chocano's project in this now disowned *Canto del Siglo*, was nothing less than to epicize the century. The muse, as he tells us in his prologue, comes down from high heaven to sing in the dust of the earth all that it sees worthy of song. And she begins with Napoleon, "the great man of the century," even as Chocano himself begins with the inevitable biblical reminiscence:

At the beginning of the century was darkness.

Napoleon it was who rose from the depths to master the world. His labors were quite as great as the Lord's, "for God made his worlds out of chaos and out of the nothing you made yourself. . . ." Napoleon is thus greater than the Alexanders and the Cæsars, who shone with the re-

flected light of inherited glory and stimulus.   Yet young
Chocano knows Napoleon's faults as well as his virtues,
and has expressed the thoughts of many in two lines that
are far superior to most in the exhausting *Canto*.

> Podía ser la Libertad tu esposa;
> y solo llegó a ser tu concubina.

> Liberty might have been your wife;
> she became only your mistress.

Is there not a deal of history compressed into those two
lines?

But let us hasten through the "argument" of the finisecular epic before pausing for such analysis as helps us to
understand the mature artist.

Part I: Napoleon's career leads him from glory to ulti-
mate failure; Part II: the independence of Spanish America and the glorious names to which it gave birth; the former colonies express their spiritual allegiance to the mother
nation; Part III: the triumph of the sciences, which constitutes the greatest glory of the century.   Man launches
forth upon the quest of Truth, through the idealism of
Hegel and Krause, the positivism of Comte, the evolution-
ary doctrine of Darwin, the new discoveries of psychophy-
siology, the contributions of Pasteur, and so on; chemistry
makes new conquests; Fulton invents the steamboat, Steph-
enson perfects the locomotive, Lesseps initiates the era of
canals; the wireless telegraph astounds human thought;
Edison perpetuates the human voice in the phonograph;
X-rays, magnetism, the superman of science.   (Our youngster has been reading heavily, it seemeth, and fain would

rhyme all his data!) ; Part IV: The Final Vision; the great poet of the century, Victor Hugo; the great painter, Delacroix; the great sculptor, Rodin; the great composer, Wagner; the wonders of architecture, as represented in the Milan Cathedral, the Brooklyn Bridge, the Eiffel tower; the future path, universal peace, Socialism, Intellectuality, Mothers and Children, Science and Love.

One could easily imagine that Chocano had procured a set of the numerous sociological works published in Spanish versions by the radical firm over which Blasco Ibáñez presides, and for which the author of *The Four Horsemen of the Apocalypse* himself furnished so many of the translations, and had made up his mind to transform the prose of it all into poetic notes. As a whole, the *Canto del Siglo* possesses little, if any, artistic interest. It demonstrates an eager mind, a progressive spirit, a broad and all-embracing conception of humanity, a youthful fervor that all too frequently leaves little trace in the adult. It attests the author's cosmic interests; his identification of himself with all mankind; his eagerness to absorb a multitude of influences; an eclectic mind. Only in fragments, and these but few in number, is it of significance as anything like poetry. One would prefer to believe that it had been written before *La Epopeya del Morro*, which is so far superior in inspiration and expression.

As may be imagined from a knowledge of the poet's later work, it is the second part,—that dealing with America's achievement of independence,—that is most striking to the reader of today. It is interesting to note how thus early Chocano forecasted the change of attitude toward the mother country which was to be definitely indicated as one of the new orientations of the modernist movement in 1906, when Nervo read his *Epithalamium* to the newly wed Spanish monarch.

> Si América venció, fué su victoria
> orgullo maternal para la España:
> árbol que empieza á dar frutos de gloria
> se los debe al torrente que lo baña.

There are still Spaniards who find it difficult to adopt Chocano's rather ingenuous idea that the victory of the colonists over the mother country should be a source of maternal pride to Spain.

Knowing the poet's tendencies, we are not surprised to find the strength of Bolívar exalted above that of Hercules:

> Como en el mito en que Hércules membrudo,
> que no igualó en vigores ni en deseo
> al rebelde Bolívar. . . .

nor to hear the name of the great Liberator palpitate like thunder in the womb of Eternity. (There is something of Hugo in the figure,—of a Hugo that we admire so much in our early days, and then learn to forget for the greater Hugo of the cosmic poems.)

It is at the close of this section that Chocano's address to the mother country occurs. The last four lines were later employed as the conclusion of the *Ofrenda á España* that opens *Alma América*.

> O ancestress of nations, ancient Spain!
> Yield to the lovely law by which life grows—
> Which makes the roses break forth into buds,
> And makes of every bud another rose!

You gave example to America
Of pride maternal, yet are not content
Because you have passed on your courage high
To all the nations of a continent.
Admire the great exploits of your sons!
To wish to punish them in wrath would be
To wish to tear your own deep entrails out.
Our heroes, fit for tales of chivalry
Inherit from their ancestors their blood;
Within their veins the hot life-currents flow
Of all youɪ visionary Quixotes bold
And all your champion Cids of long ago!
O noble Spain, receive me in your arms,
And, to my song, renew the ties of old!
When a gold ring is broken into bits,
Although a ring no more, it still is gold!

For the rest, let us content ourselves with selecting from
the remaining sections an illuminating line here and there.
Apostrophizing Truth, the young poet, most appropriately in a canto that treats of man's scientific search for
truth in the nineteenth century, calls Truth "the x of destiny," which we strive to discover in our manipulations of
the eternal equation. Hegel becomes a Columbus-like
dreamer seeking an America of thought. Nor is it at all
a bad touch when, treating of the Comtian positivism, the
singer declares that the realists have made of matter a
fallen god sunk lower than his very creatures. Schopenhauer looms as

an Attila
Who flays God in the name of Nothingness!

with Nietzsche following close upon his heels, "as if he
were the Quixote of evil." And note this peculiar cosmic

note,—one that sounds, now muffled, now triumphant, from almost everything of significance that Chocano has written:

> ¡Ah! ¿Quién sabe si es sólo un organismo
> el Universo, inmóvil en escencia,
> y que, aunque de apariencia en apariencia
> transformándose va, siempre es el mismo,
> y quién sabe si Diós es su conciencia?
>
> ¡Cuánto organismo bulle en una gota
> de agua, de sangre, de sudor, de llanto!
> ¡Cuánto grandeza flota
> en una pequeñez! Oh Vida, cuánto
> se multiplica tu inmortal reflejo
> que en cada gota de agua reverbera,
> como una eucaristía del espejo
> que en mil pedazos te retrata entera!
>
> ¡Dentro de cada vida hay tantas vidas!
> ¿Ni quien podría refrenar la ola
> que en otras nuevas olas se convierte?
> Las chispas de una hoguera desprendidas
> hogueras pueden ser: cada corola
> es un bosque tal vez; y de esta suerte,
> la vida universal es una sola.

This pantheism, which looks upon us all as atoms of God's consciousness, is a fundamental element of Chocano's outlook upon life. He feels the world beyond the senses; the mystery of the mystic unknown; the prick of doubt for a moment twinges him and he asks, "Who knows, at times, whether there where we seek most we find nothing?" Yet here, as everywhere, he is elementally optimistic, nor is it that melancholy optimism which de Icaza mentions with reference to the poems of González Martínez.

Out of the turmoil will come peace and order; out of the classicism that is Homer, the redeeming Christianity that is Dante, the free thought that is Hugo, will emerge a better world. From his tower (but Chocano's is not an ivory one, and often a red flag floats from the top), the poet gazes toward the future and beholds a harmonious democracy in which Love, "the Host of souls," will rule over all.

El Canto del Siglo is most valuable as a study in the growing mentality of Chocano; it shows that from the very beginning, whatever poetic form his studies assumed, he was imbued with a far stronger social sense than Darío or the other modernist poets of the day,—that he was bound sooner or later to identify himself with continental aspirations,—that not all the scientific lore he imbibed could stifle, though it tempered, his innate poetic gifts,—that his conception of the poet's mission was still a strongly utilitarian one, aiming to teach the multitudes even as it inspired them. As a successor to *La Epopeya del Morro* it represents a poetic retrogression but a mental advance. The national poet of Peru grooms his Pegasus to fly over continents and worlds.

Selva Virgen (1900) is composed of poems written between 1892 and the year of publication. It illustrates all the phases of the poet's art that we have thus far witnessed and contains more material that was later chosen from that literary past which the author rejected than any of the other collections, as may be noted from a comparison of *Fiat Lux!* with the youthful poems. Chocano's virgin forest is virgin only in the author's personal gift of being able to view modernity through the eyes of the primitive; the

author has been called an eternal child; there is something
of this childishness about all genius, although it should
not be cited to excuse the gross exaggeration into which the
poet is liable to fall at times. From the forest issues now
a plaintive note of elegy, now the timorous voice of doubt;
again the singer of love fills the wood with his pastoral
grievances or woos the Byronic muse with a long succession
of Dantesque tercets; there are neo-Hamlet monologues,
summonses to glorious strife, protests, self-assertions, in-
vocations to the Future Verse (see *El Verso Futuro,* addressed to Leopoldo Lugones and Ricardo Jaimes Freyre),
Songs to Zola, to The New Dodecasyllable (addressed to
Amado Nervo), varied sonnets aplenty, Echegarayan dia-
logues between tombs, album verses, quatrains à la Wat-
teau, neo-Hellenic evocations as well as neo-Roman, and
what not else. In the collection as a whole is discernible
a delightful freedom from technical fetters, a liberty that
roves at will through styles and subjects, gathering honey
from every flower in the forest.

Chocano the youthful lover is there, well able to answer
amorous disdain with darts of poesy. He can tell his
scornful lady that though her eyes be heaven, that heaven
lacks both a God and stars; he knows how to pay delicate
compliments in most approved Castilian style (*Ante Un
Estatua Del Amor*) and to lend a sting to farewells
(*Punto Final*).

He is, despite his numerous assertions of having been
born out of his true age, a man of the epoch, responsive to
its conflicting currents, even though he does not allow himself to be swept along hither and thither by them. He, too,
laughs before the trembling idol-worshipper (*Las Voces*

de La Duda), yet recognizes that the priest must always have his cult and the warrior his motto.

> Yo, si duda mi siglo, también dudo;
> yo, si niega mi siglo, también niego;
> pero no tenga liberatad en vano:
> ¡sea el siglo mi ley, no mi tirano!

He doubts and denies, together with his century, but the century can be only his law and never his tyrant. The attitude is characteristic of the poet; somewhere he has referred to himself and to Darío as two of the few who in this age of skepticism dared openly to profess a belief in God. Of the two, he is perhaps the more firm as well as the more joyous believer; Darío's doubt is more deep; it is like the ground bass of the organ over which the player may vary his harmonies and his musical textures, yet ever in consonance with the pedal note; Chocano's doubt is exceptional,—the occasional dissonance necessary for harmonic contrast. He may be moved, at moments, to proclaim that he expects nothing either of the world or of God, —that he is weary of struggles and would gladly plumb the depths of the open abyss, since Life is the road to Death, yet he soon alters his attitude, and at the end of the selfsame poem is ready to declare that it is stupid for the dog of blasphemy to bark before the grave, since Death, to man, is but the child's embrace with the mother. Chocano's doubt is purely intellectual; Darío's is part of his very emotional fibre.

Just as the intellect of Chocano refuses to subject itself to the tyranny of the century whose law it accepts, so the poet in him, for all his passionate love of the crowd, refuses to be encircled by the multitude.

Suya será mi voluntad entera,
mi razón, mi ideal, mi ley, mi brío;
¡pero déjeme, en cambio, que siquiera
puede decir:— ¡Mi corazón es mio! . . .
                          (*Canto de Huelga*)

One may dwell in his ivory tower,—if he must,—in the
midst of the crowd. And Chocano proposes, though his
will, his reason, his ideal, his law, his enthusiasm all belong to the people, to maintain a little corner of his heart
as his very own.

From such as this poem reveals, we are naturally to expect the man more interested in the idea than in the form.
It is the preponderance of the idea that injures so much
of Chocano's early labors as poetry. Without being dogmatic one may express the belief that the best art, like the
best body, is an indissoluble harmony of form and content. The phrase is so trite, but how difficult its realization! With Darío, Chocano's complementary personality,
one may note the reverse: the young Nicaraguan was consciously preoccupied· with technique. Yet in this same
Selva Virgen we come upon such a sterling sonnet as
Arqueología, which flashes upon us with all the bril-
liancy that strikes the eyes of the discoverer in the poem
itself:

ARCHEOLOGY

Searching 'mid Eastern ruins, groping slow,
When some explorer in our modern days
His hand upon a hidden treasure lays—
Gold idols heathens worshipped long ago—
Then with what eager interest aglow
The spirit of the Present backward strays

To that far age when priests raised hymns of praise
To monstrous gods deformed, with foreheads low!

When our age too is dead, from tomb to tomb
Some new explorer, groping in the gloom,
Will search for what the ruins may afford.
How great his fear, how strange his thoughts will be
When, gleaming 'mid the shadows, he shall see,
Rarest, most precious treasure trove, a sword!

In this sonnet's sweep of the centuries one feels something of the similar, if superior, vision in Shelley's sonnet, *Ozymandias of Egypt*. It is a good example of that Parnassianism which Chocano has claimed as his own.

Chocano's ever present dualism is delightfully evident in the pair of poems entitled, respectively, *La Vejez Virgiliana* and *La Vejez Anacreóntica*, in which he sings two opposite views of old age. The English reader naturally thinks of Milton's similar antithetic pair, *L'Allegro* and *Il Penseroso*. As the old man of the soil approaches death, he gazes upon the land and says, "You were mine yesterday . . . Today I shall be yours!" No such autumnal calm for the Anacreontic spirit. He has wine, even though Venus has deserted him, and will wait till his inanimate form falls upon the broken glass. Sometimes the mingling of classic atmosphere and modernity produces a strange climax. Thus Nero, whose god is form, not meaning, who knows that though Venus may be unlearned she is yet fair, who cries "Praised be evil, if evil be beautiful!" can shout, at his death, "I'm dying . . . No, I'm not dying: I am reborn!"

One will meet with disappointment, however, if he tries to distil unity out of the various essences from this virgin forest; it is classic and romantic, idealistic and material, impassioned and impassive,—all at the will of the poet. He writes, not to provide texts for dissection, but from an inner necessity. He is all men, because he is himself. That is the refreshing thing, even amid his most extravagant lines and his most violent metaphors. And, as his later attitude has shown, he who writes in haste may revise at leisure.

El Derrumbe [2] exhibits the characteristic mingling of biblical and classical allusions, violent figures of speech and other well known traits of the early Chocano. As a whole it is a florid, rather prolix composition, not without spots of beauty and power, yet entangled in its own tropical luxuriance, like the fabulous forests of the Amazon. It tells the tale of a savage who is led to civilization by a Christian missionary; the primitive man comes upon the white daughter of a colonist and is smitten with desire for her; she, however, is plighted to another, absent and objected to by her father. In a symbolic dream he speaks to her. "Seek not nobility in origins," he urges, talking strangely like the idealist Chocano; "seek it in the aims of life." His love is vain, however, and he flees the civilization which has only taught him to yearn for that which may never be his.

We are impressed with a sense of the Indian's idealism, yet also with the feeling that conquest was necessary for the sake of progress. The poem, a symbol as an entirety,

---

[2] I use, in this case, the original form of *El Derrumbe*; under the title *El Derrumbamiento* it appears, shortened by almost a third, in *Alma América*. As with *La Epopeya del Morro* in *Fiat Lux!*, there is nothing to indicate that it is the revision of an earlier work.

is likewise set with several passages of intense symbolic beauty.

The opening (*El Salmo de las Cumbres*) is an appealing evocation of the majestic solitude of the mountains and at once provides the setting, both material and spiritual, so to speak.

> ¡Oh murmullos del bosque! ¡oh voz sagrada
> de la Naturaleza! ¡oh, queja honda
> de fiera agonizante! No, no hay nada
> que ensanche más el corazón humano
> que, cuando vibra, el arpa de la fronda
> templada al diapasón del oceano.
>
> Quién descubre una voz que lo enamora;
> Quién, una voz que la recuerda un canto;
> quién, una que lo arrulla ó que implora;
> quién, que nunca oró a Diós, oyendo tanto
> rumor solemne, se arrodilla . . . ¡y ora!

This same religious atmosphere of the forest rises from the opening of the second part (*La Oración de las Selvas*).

With this poem may be said to close Chocano's early period, as distinguished from his own conscious change of direction signalized by *Alma América*. It is a romantic, individualistic, subjective period, in which youthful extravagance, unchecked spontaneity and exuberant imagination run rife. Between *El Derrumbe* and the following collection the poet became aware of a need for more restraint, more artistic control of his gushing inspiration. The definite change from spontaneity to artistry took place; perhaps this is what Chocano means when he calls himself, henceforth, an objective poet. But Parnassian? Neither

his native critic, V. García Calderón, nor his most enthusiastic Spanish commentator, González-Blanco, finds anything of the genuine Parnassianism of a Leconte de Lisle in
him.

3. *Alma América* (1906)

Allowing for personal differences, we may look upon
Alma América as occupying a position of importance in
Chocano's career similar to that occupied by the *Cantos de
Vida y Esperanza* in the career of Rubén Darío; that is,
insofar as each collection stands for the summit of the
poet's achievement and a synthesis of the entire man.
Every element in *Alma América* was already forecasted in
the previous work of Chocano, as was every element in the
Cantos de Vida y Esperanza present in Darío's anterior labors.   But whereas the Darío volume represents an ethical, as distinguished from an æsthetic advance (since his
æsthetics had reached their culmination in *Prosas Profanas*), the Chocano collection stands for æsthetic, as distinguished from ethical progress.   The poet here says nothing he has not uttered before; but how much better he expresses it!   He is the same complex individuality, but he
has mastered his art.

It will be noted that the sub-title of *Alma América* is
Poemas Indo-Españoles.   We have thus, in the title and the
sub-title a synthesis of the chief elements in the book: the
sense of continental destiny, of the natives conquered by
the Spaniards, and of the spiritual bonds that link the
former colonies to the mother nation.   So universal is the
poet in his sympathies, so contemporary with all the factors, that he feels himself at will an Inca, a Conquistador,

a proud American.   Even more: for he can behold, though
not without certain reservations, a union of the Saxon and
the Latin elements.   He possesses an intense race pride
that is at times incompatible with his early protestations
of universal brotherhood.   And although one need not
stress too much the apparent incongruity of an author opening a book of American poems with an address to the
monarch of that nation which long held the colonies in
subjection, one may easily understand why some countrymen should feel that the note produced an element of dis-
harmony.

Some of the prefatory material of *Alma América* (we
should remember that by this time the poet has arrived in
Spain), shows strikingly the change that has come over
Chocano's outlook upon his expressional medium.   For
his heraldic proclamation "O encuentro camino ó me lo
abro" (Either I find a path or I'll open myself one!) we
are well prepared.   The Hugoesque poetic swashbuckling
is an old trait.   But directly after this sword-brandishing
we reach the renunciation: "Ténganse por no escritos
cutantos libros de poesías aparecieron antes con mi nom-
bre."   The poet of "let there be light" here asks "let there
be darkness." . . . "Let all books that have previously appeared over my signature be considered as not having been
written."   And again: "My poetry is objective; and in
such a sense alone do I care to be the Poet of America."
Poets of America, however, are not made by the poets themselves; they are chosen by the people; objective or not objective, Chocano's poetry has made him Spanish America's
poet.   Here, too, appears the motto of Chocano which he
has since repeated with emphasis: "En el arte caben todas

las escuelas como en un rayo de Sol todas los colores,"—
in Art are contained all schools, even as all colors in a
sunbeam." And here we have the refutation of Chocano's
own claims to objectivism. It is true that a more objective
glint shines from some of the author's later poetry, particularly some of the sonnets in *Alma América* and some
of the modernist verse in *Fiat Lux!*; but this is only one of
the colors in Chocano's poetic sunbeam. Why should poets
bother with terminology? Aren't there enough critics to
toy with names?

Yet sometimes the poet makes the best critic—if not of
himself, of his fellow poet. Witness the admirable *Preludio* furnished by Darío to *Alma América*. Not only is
it good poetry, but good criticism; Darío understood Chocano well, and in the thirty lines of his Prelude has said
quite as much as the Peruvian's critics, and how much more
beautifully! Darío sees Chocano's relationship to Pan, to
the Sun, to the Ocean, his spokesmanship for the continent.
He notes his unevenness, his tempestuousness; he notes, too,
the compensatory vigor:

> Pero hay en ese verso tan vigoroso y terso
> una sangre que apenas veréis en otro verso;
> una sangre que cuando en el verso circula
> como la luz penetra y como la onda ondula.

(Do you catch the penetration of the light and the undula-
tion of the waves in Darío's very vowels and consonants of
that last line?) The great Nicaraguan saw that Chocano's
Pegasus was content, "for Pegasus pastures in the meadows
of the Inca." He recognized Chocano's intimate acquaintance with nature, yet realized that the Peruvian's great
power lay in his sonorous trumpeting.

> Pero su brazo es para levantar la trompeta
> hacia donde se annuncia la aurora del Profeta;
> y es hecho para dar á la virtud del viento
> la expresión del terrible clarín del pensamiento. . . .

He saw, too, the poet's essentially dual nature, and that he lived "on love of America and passion for Spain." There is all of Chocano in that Preludio, and not a little of Darío.

Rodó, too, who had at once felt Darío's artistic incapacity (but is incapacity the right word?) for becoming the "poet of America," beheld the right man in Chocano. "I recognized in you," he wrote to Chocano, "the poet who, through a rare and admirable combination, unites the proud audacity of inspiration with sculptural firmness of form; and who, with generous purpose, proposes to return to poetry its arms of combat and its civilizing mission, thus hitting upon the path which, to my mind, will be that of (Spanish) American poetry."

The praise of Darío and Rodó finds its full justification in *Alma América*, which is one of the most notable collections of poems issued by a Spanish American.

Let us consider the volume from three points of view: (1) its Hispanism, (2) its Americanism, (3) its revelations of the poet and his attitude toward his life and art. Its Hispanism, as we have seen from his earlier *Canto del Siglo*, is conciliatory, aiming at a spiritual unity of all the Spanish-speaking peoples; his Americanism is not only political, social, and at times Pan-American, not only concerned with nature, but also with history and the conquered tribes. For that same Chocano who looks forward with hope to the conquered mother country, looks back with atavistic regret at the conquered indigenous tribes; [3] as to his self, it is sufficient here to indicate that it is a complex affair, identifying itself in remarkable degree with all the objects of its interest. Chocano may be objective in style (and that only at times); he is essentially a personal poet.

The opening poem, *Ofrenda A España*, at once strikes the Hispanic note; the poet comes from across the sea,— that sea over which Columbus sailed in quest of the Indies, —and brings greetings from Spanish America. "Oh, Mother Spain, take all my life; for I have given you the Sun of my mountain, and you have given me the Sun of your banner. . . ." Even the language in which he speaks is hers. The same sentiment is brought out by means of a beautiful symbolism in one of the best poems of the collection, the *Crónica Alfonsina*.

On that sea which the poet has crossed to bring his offering to Spain two fantastic ships meet on their opposite course. One of them bears as its figurehead a great golden lion, the other a castle of silver. The lion, of course, is the heraldic animal of León and symbolizes strength; the castle is the emblem of Castile, the symbol of fancy, and castles in Spain. Both crews speak the same tongue: "Oh, lengua del País de la Utopia,"—the language of the Land of Utopia. On one of the vessels, bound for the New World, is Dulcinea, "grave as an Ideal, sad as a Dream, mute as an Enchantment, well wrapped in her cloak." On the other, returning from America, is Jimena (she of the Cid), "on her feet the anklets of the savage, on her shoulder the

[3] The note is common in modern Spanish-American letters. Cf. some of the short stories by Ugarte, Ghiraldo, Ricardo Jaimes Freyre.

skin of the luxurious vicuña, and in her right hand a fan of rarest plumage." . . . The one bears to the New World all the idealism, all the faith, all the passion of the Old Spain; the other carries back from the New World the youthful power, the ardent prowess, the sacred wrath necessary to infuse new life. Don Quixote and Rodrigo (respectively, of course, the lover and the husband of Dulcinea and Jimena), experience a change of heart upon overhearing the mid-ocean colloquy; in Jimena's nature there is something that Don Quixote needs to complete his own; in Dulcinea's nature Rodrigo likewise beholds a complementary personality. Whereupon Don Quixote returns to Spain with Jimena and Don Rodrigo fares forth to America in company of Dulcinea. The Lion of strength and courage has come to the Castle of dreams and ideals; old Spain and the new are once again united.

Such a union of power and delicacy, of strength and grace, are ever present in the poet's mind. When he visits the *Museo del Prado* he beholds in Velázquez and Goya just such a distinction; the first evokes in his memory the scenes of the Conquest; the second, the days of the Colonial epoch. And thinking of his native mountains as he gazes at the gallery of paintings, he feels his double allegiance to America and Spain:

> y quise en el Museo, pensando en mi montaña
> ¡ser la mitad de America y la mitad de España!

A similar, more beautiful evocation of the past occurs in the poem *En La Armería Real,* where the sights in the royal armory more naturally recall to him the glorious deeds of Spaniards on both sides of the Atlantic, thus forming yet

another bond between the heroes in whom flow the same
blood and the same traditions.

It is, quite naturally, the more purely American element
that occupies most of the space of the collection.   Here is
the real Chocano in all his chastened exuberance, yet exuberance none the less.   Here is the lover of the native
fauna and flora, the fellow spirit of Inca and Conquistador
alike, the singer of continentalism, of union between the
northern and the southern neighbors, the trumpeter of
epochs.   Here is the passionate singer of the cities, old and
new; of the rivers and mountains; of a new world within
a New World.   Hear him glorify the Andes, which Darîo
called the vertebræ of a continent:

> As winds along, in snowy marble bare,
> The carven serpent of Laocoön,
> O'er a whole continent the Andes run,
> Braiding their mighty knots in shining air.
> A horror like to Dante's thrills us there,
> Before that crowd of heroes, every one
> Lifting a shield of granite in the sun,
> And crowned with silver helmet gleaming fair.
>
> Each hero's heart is filled with boundless grief
> Because he longs to shout; he trembles, fights,
> Is rent with pain—and yet no shout we hear.
> In sombre ecstasy, his sole relief
> Is to send downward from his farthest heights
> A wandering river, like a silent tear.

Read his epic conception of the Mouths of the Orinoco:

> From prisoning towers of rock, for miles on miles
> Thou fleest through the forest, gliding there
> Like some long dragon borne on wings of air;
> And fifty times thou beatest on thine isles.

Twisting and winding, shifting ceaselessly,
Through fifty gates at last thou rushest free;
Reaching the broad blue spaces of the sea,
Thou through thy fifty mouths dost breathe a sigh.

Thou seemest, when thou meetest Ocean's tide,
The end of some huge rope, outravelled wide,
While fastened to an isle each strand remains.
Hail to thee, Conqueror, who towards the deep
In echoing silver car dost onward sweep,
Holding within thine hand-grasp fifty reins!

Or his sonnet to the Straits of Magellan:

In ocean's perilous night, without a clue,
The daring captain sails.   The straining bark
Sees opening close before it, grim and dark,
A mountain cleft in twain, and ventures through.
The sails are torn, the mad winds rage with might;
Sometimes upon one side a fire they see;
Along both shores hoarse wolves howl stormily,
Sending their voices through the gloomy night.

On the steep sides, the billows bark and bark;
Foam clad, they seem white dogs there in the dark,
Against the black wolves on the lonely shore.
The ship sails on and on—and as of old
The sea kept parting before Moses bold,
The land keeps opening slowly, more and more.

Note how into the simple sonnet form he can infuse the
epic spirit; note the epic conception even in the bold figures.   And note, too, that when he approaches themes in
their very nature less ample, yet no less deep, he can adjust his manner and even his metaphor to the required delicacy.   For example, the beautiful poem on The Magnolia:

Deep in the forest, full of song and fragrance,
Blooms the magnolia, delicate and light,
Like snowy wool among the thorns entangled.
Or, on the quiet lake, a foam-like white.

Its vase is worthy of a Grecian maker,
A marble wonder of the classic days.
It shows its fine, firm roundness, like a lady
Who with bared breast her loveliness displays.

Is it a pearl?   Is it a tear?   We know not!
Between it and the moon, with mystery rife,
There is some unknown story of enchantment,
In which perhaps a white dove lost its life;

For it is pure and white and light and graceful,
Like a soft moonbeam on a snowbank deep,
That rests upon the snow and mingles with it;
Or like a dove upon the branch asleep.

Or that on The Orchids:

Freaks of bright crystal, airy beauties fair,
Whose enigmatic forms amaze the eye—
Crowns fit to deck Apollo's brows on high,
Adornments meet for halls of splendor rare!
They spring from knots in tree-trunks, rising there
In sweet gradation; winding wondrously,
They twist their serpent stems, and far and nigh
Hang overhead like wingless birds in air.

Lonely, like pensive heads, all fetterless,
Lofty and free they bloom; by no dull chain
Their flowers to any tyrant root are bound;
Because they too, at war with pettiness,
Desire to live like souls that know no stain,
Without one touch of contact with the ground.

And do you see how Chocano's rebellious spirit, now chastened, will out in the metaphor of the eleventh line, as translated?

This is the poet in whom González-Blanco would see a teacher of his continent's natural history, its birds and its beasts, quite as instructive as the more sober and less attractive text-books. And this is the background of that New World whose past, present and future are so strongly felt by Chocano.

Of its past he feels himself an organic part; he is an Inca, he is a Viceroy. Who better than he has sung the romantic tales of Inca princesses and Conquistador lovers? Among the best of these stands out *La Ñusta* (Inca Princess), in which the amatory situation of *El Derrumbe* is reversed. The Spaniard García de Peralta loves an Inca princess who herself loves the Inca Hualpa-Cápac. Since, as the poem avers, there is no Spanish soul that does not attain its object, the Spaniard has the fortunate suitor captured and imprisoned, forcing the princess to pay with her virtue for the privilege of visiting her preferred lover. Before surrendering her person, however, she rubs poison over her lips, thus slaying her violator, her sweetheart and herself. Yet even in death she is cheated of her triumph, for she is buried with García de Peralta. Chocano, who has learned the wisdom of brevity, wisely compressed the tale into the limits of some nine pages; there are none of the philosophical intrusions that mar the early versions of *La Epopeya del Morro* and *El Derrumbe*. Similar to *La Ñusta* in inspiration are *Ante Las Ruinas* and *El Tesoro de Los Incas*. When he gazes upon the ruins of the sun-worshippers' temple he feels the royal mantle of the Inca fall upon his shoulders, and an inner voice speaks to him: "Poet, behold your temple. You have been born too late!" The colonial ruins address him with a similar message: "Poet, sing the Past; you were born for that!" And truly, Chocano summons the spirit of the past with a rare artistry that proves him its son; yet because he so poignantly feels it as a past he is by the same token a poet of the present,—a present with which he is discontent, with which he is not in harmony, and of whose fleeting character he is deeply aware. This may help explain his glances both into the past and forward into the future; that is his method of escaping the immediate.

The more universal spirit that grows out of his continental vision,—which is itself an outgrowth of his staunch yet not servile nationalism,—appears in the sonnet to The Isthmus of Panama, in the Epic of the Pacific, in The Song of the Future, and other poems. Here, too, we glimpse the much-mooted Pan-Americanism which so many Spanish-Americans fear is but the lamb's skin over our leonine imperialistic aims. The universalism is no longer the communistic socialism sung by the poet in his juvenile days; that, it would seem, has with his art become chastened.

The Isthmus of Panama, to Chocano, is the symbol of Peace, Union and Harmony, making of two oceans, one. The metaphor of the closing tercets is one of Chocano's most beautiful figures,—beautiful for its symbolism, its organic connection with the subject, its universality.

> Ave que hoy se abre el seno en los prolijos
> cuidados de su amor; ¿de que te extrañas,
> si es por calmar el hambre de hijos?

¡Tu, como esa ave, con tu proprio acero,
te vas también rasgando las entrañas,
para darle la vida á un mundo entero!

A stern beauty, it is true, this rending of the bosom to give life to a whole world, but must all beauty be fragile?

If the *Istmo de Panama* represents the Isthmus as a symbol of union achieved by the blending of two oceans, the *Epopeya del Pacifico* seems similarly to blend the races thus united. In the following collection, *Fiat Lux!*, Chocano, who is fond of issuing little manifestoes a sentence or two long, has written: "My ideal in Life and in Art would be the harmonization of the Latin imagination, Germanic gravity and Saxon energy." It is this Saxon energy that is exalted in the Epic of the Pacific, yet not without a sense of that same fear which has troubled less optimistic spirits. If Spanish America desires to be free, the poet tells his fellow Americans, it must imitate the United States first and equal them afterwards. (Is there not here a reminiscence of Martí's thoughts?) The sense of fear to which we have referred, however, is lulled by a knowledge of continental geography: "Let none grieve about a future conquest; our forests know no better race, our Andes know not what it is to be white, our rivers disdain the bravery of a Saxon; and thus, on the day in which the people of another race dares to explore our countries, it will issue a shriek of horror, for miasma and fever, the reptile and the swamp will sink it into the earth, beneath the fire of the Sun." This, to be sure, is legitimate patriotism of a continental sort, but let us not hasten to call it Pan-Americanism. On the other hand, let us not be blind to the virile spirit which it embodies, and to the determined, if fiery, assertion of a personal Monroe Doctrine, as it were, which the words connote. It is not the race of the blond hair that will break open the canal at last, declares the poet in his fourth stanza. The manual work is brought by the black-haired folk,—the race of the Pyramids, the race that gave its blood to the Roman Circus and its sweat to the Suez Canal. Here, too, the emblem is the white banner of Labor and Peace. In the poem occur two of the noblest lines in modern poetry:

> que el trabajo no es culpa de un Edén ya perdido,
> sino el único medio de llegarlo á gozar.

in which the poet counsels his fellow men to remember that toil is not the curse of a Paradise lost, but the only method of ever attaining to it.

El Canto del Porvenir (The Song of the Future) is equally prophetic and equally reserved upon certain points. Balboa is represented as rising from the past and beholding his ocean. The boa of the Andes has been cut in two, the Canal constructed; Magellan weeps, for how useless is his strait now! Japan and Russia have contended in war, and the United States has become the peacemaker. But out of a disinterested love of peace? Hardly.

> La Paz fué. No era bueno para el País del Norte
> el triunfo decisivo de la amarilla Corte,
> ni menos el temible dominio de los Czares
> en tan ansiadas tierras y codiciados mares.

> Asi, en la Paz, vencieron los Estados Unidos;
> y certeros, astutos, agiles, prevenidos,

trepanaron las tierras, cercenaron los Andes,
unieron dos oceanos . . . y se sintieron grandes.

"Thus, in Peace," reads the fifth line, "the United States conquered." The finale of the poem (which is subtitled Palabras Internacionales—International Words) hints at a defeat for a war-clad Japan and at a bi-continental union of the northern and southern elements. "Liberty!" proclaims this new race, of which the Adam comes from the North and the Eve from the Latins.

And the Land of the Amazons was the Center of the World.

Pan-Americanism of a type, then, there is in Chocano; I would not, however, call him the poet of Pan-America: not by any means. Nor would I be misunderstood as denying him his right to sing his own country in the bold strophes that reveal his love of Whitman and his emulation of the good gray poet. Together with the Darío of the *Canto á la Argentina* he represents the most favorable attitude toward us among the prominent poets.

The essential Chocano, as far as his native America is concerned, dwells in the glorifier of its many-colored epochs. And it is in his personal utterances, as they refer to his own temperament and his views upon art and life, that this glorifier is to be found. He is, as we have long ago guessed, an arrogant, proud, at times boastful, ebullient spirit; in the pomp of his verse (*Símbolo*) there is something Pre-Columbine and aught of the Conquistador; he is doubly epic in nature, a son of the Sun as well as of the Lion, of the Inca as well as of Spain. "I am," he declares in the sonnet *Blasón*, wherein he presents us with his spirit-

ual coat of arms, "the singer of autochthonous and aborig-
inal America; my lyre posseses a soul, my song an Ideal.
. . . When I feel myself an Inca, I render homage to the
Sun, which gives me the scepter of its royal power; when I
feel myself a Spaniard and evoke the Colonial epoch, my
strophes ring out like crystal trumpets. My fancy derives
from Moorish ancestry; the Andes are of silver but the
Lion is of gold, and the two races mingle with an epic
rumble. The blood is Spanish but the pulse is Incaic, and
if I were not a poet, perhaps I should have been a white
Adventurer or an Indian Emperor!" . . . "How many
times I have been born!" he exclaims in *Avatar*. "How
many times I have been incarnated! I am of America
twice, and twice of Spain. If I am now a poet, I was a
Viceroy in the past, a Captain in conquests and a Monarch
of the Sun." He was Yupanqui, he was de Soto, but today
he is more than them all, in the possession of his loved
one. His muse (*La Musa Fuerte*) must have strength as
well as beauty. "I am pleased at the same time with fruits
and with flowers; the concentrated juice, the perfumed essence; and in my song, therefore, in multiple cadence, are
all the graces and all the powers. The viceroys have given
me their lyric skill and the conquerors their august reful-
gence, and so, from verse to verse, there is the heroic difference that existed between the viceroys and the conquerors. I confess that though I love the colonial pomp, I prefer the metals to the finest chords. . . ." It is in the final
poem of the collection, however, that this self-heralding
reaches a worthy climax of identification with his Alma
América. Here the poet becomes the primitive soul of the
Andes and the forests, the rustle of the leaves by night, the

creaking of the trunks, the howling of the beasts.   From
these he learns the secrets of his verses; his lyre, which is
of stone, has an eighth string added to it,—the string of
wild music.   "And thus do I sing with my lyre of eight
strings."   Many times he feels that he is, at bottom, a tree
with gigantic roots and enormous trunk, housing within him
the jaguars of the forest; at others, he is a peak of the
Andes, on which congeals the snow of ten centuries.   And
the voice of the centuries tells him that he is the primitive
soul, "the primitive soul of the Andes and the forests."

This analysis of *Alma América*, long as it may have
seemed, has touched only upon certain characteristics of
outlook and style.   The book is in remarkable degree the
soul of the continent for which it speaks; it is spiritual history.   If the foreign reader seeks a single book that will
communicate to him the complex Spanish-American soul,
here it is.

4. *Fiat Lux!* (1908)

Fiat Lux! is an anthology of the poet's works previous to
Alma América.   It represents a most rigid selection, and
contains besides, some of the later work of the author.
It is divided into four parts: Classic Poems, so called;
Romantic Poems, The Epic of the Morro and Modernist
Poems; it is in this last section that the new poetry occurs,
not unmingled with anterior labors.   Inasmuch as we have
already sampled the earlier poems, it will be necessary
here only to give heed to the later verses.

The Modernist section begins with an interesting bio-
graphical account.   He was born into times of strife, he
tells us, and was lulled by the harmony of trumpets, "of

which all my poetry is but an echo; and as my years of
infancy were years of powder and shot, my mother's kiss
was a purple flower." He played very little as a child,
he writes, and it is easy to believe him, for his childhood
poems reveal a mind almost too sensitive to thought. "Nobody, nobody understands how old within a man must be
who never played as a child. . . ." He recalls how, as a
child, he heard the trumpets of the conquerors blow; he
refers, of course, to the victory of Chile over Peru in
1883; at this time he was but eight years old. "Hear,"
said his mother to him. "And I heard,—I hear it yet, and
shall continue to hear it until a louder trumpet sounds."
He then refers to his revolutionary sentiments, and his
prison experiences; "and I, who was not a child, decided
to become a man." It was the realization of his native
landscape that aroused his poetry to broader visions. And
into this life of turbulence and love of nature, came, "en
medio del camino," the love of a woman. "Woman, you
were like a marine bird fallen upon the bare deck of my
ship!" . . .

Notice how naturally, for all its blasonry and trumpeting, Chocano's poetry blossoms out of his life. Born into
dire days for his native country, he sings a new world and
chants the bravery of his countrymen. Awakened to a realization of the native landscape, he sets its beauty in the
strophes of his verses. Gladdened by love, he wrote,
rarely in the misogynist vein (and then only as a youngster), poems that reveal the lover as a tamed ranger of
the forest. For always it is power, rather than grace,
that is characteristic of Chocano's poetry, as it is of his
outlook upon life in general. As in the sonnet *La Musa*

Fuerte (The Powerful Muse), so in his *Hymn to Will* (*El Himno A La Voluntad*) he likens life to the female who is attracted to the strong man and surrenders to his embrace.

> Como es hembra, la Vida
> ama al fuerte varón;
> y se rinde á su abrazo,
> porque goza en rendirse al vigor.
>
> Voluntad, alma antigua;
> ¡es preciso triunfar!
> Donde ha habido laureles
> ha tenido que haber voluntad.

Laurels go to him of the strong will.   And it is this will that lies at the bottom of Chocano's optimism, as it is Darío's grace that mirrors his doubt.

Two at least of the newer poems are noteworthy for a certain Parnassianism,—a Parnassianism not of thought, but of verbal art: *Danza Griega* and *La Caravana del Sultán*.   In the first, the "monorhythmical sway" of the dancer is delicately conveyed not only by a subtle change of metres, but by a continuous assonance in e; in the second the monotony of the caravan is just as skilfully conveyed by a continuous assonance in a.

For the rest, however, there is nothing essentially new to indicate in the poet's later work.   His first productions pointed unmistakably toward *Alma América,* and while his later ones do not hark back to it exclusively, they are the result of that same inspiration, chastened by a sterner conception of art.

Since it is the effort of every Spanish-American poet, it would seem, to introduce new metrical effects into the lan-

guage, Chocano has sought to do his share. González-
Blanco considers, as the Peruvian's distinct contribution,
'the verse of seventeen syllables, in which are clearly distinguished the hemistichal divisions of a heptasyllable, a
pentasyllable, and a final pentasyllable." (For examples
of this, see *Ante Las Ruinas* and *El Tesoro de los Incas*, both
in *Alma América*.)

Chocano is still a young man,—some forty-five years
old, and it may be too early to summarize his life's labors.[3]

[3] Of all the contemporary Spanish-American authors, Santos Chocano
seems most difficult to follow—from his very birth! Cejador y Frauca, *op.
cit.*, page 284, gives the date of the Peruvian's birth as 1867, with a query
after it. Coester gives 1875, which is more in harmony with the information
received from Manuel González Prada. [See C. Santos González, *Poetas y
Críticas de América*, Paris. Page 512.]

Ventura García Calderón refers to Heredia and Whitman as the chief
influences upon Chocano. Heredia is his master in the classic manner.
In one of his latest poems the Peruvian embraces free metre to the extent
of using lines of twenty-syllables. [See *Fragmento Liminar de una epopeya
cíclica*, in *Nosotros*, February, 1918.]

CHAPTER V

JOSÉ MARÍA EGUREN

It is one of the peculiarities of literature that a nation
like Peru, which up to a relatively short time ago has been
so backward in ideas and so deficient in strong literary figures, should almost at the same time produce two significant
poets that are alike only in their high worth. If one
wishes to acquire quickly, and through a writer who does
not believe in mincing words or ideas, a vivid notion of
what this backward Peru was like, let him have recourse to
Don Rufino Blanco-Fombona—a personality every bit as
formidable as his sonorous name sounds. This writer
opens his essay on Manuel González Prada, the great Peruvian libertarian, with an indictment of early Peru and
the writings produced in its atmosphere; the effect of this
indictment is not only to make the worth of Prada stand
out more shiningly by contrast but also to give the reader
an almost palpable realization of the part played by the
very climate of Lima in the formation of the character of
its inhabitants. Because of Lima's colonial importance
as the seat of the viceroy, which left a tradition of wealth,
sensuality and court-life behind it, and because of the climate of the city, where even the dogs are more gentle and
tame than anywhere else, the court became a breeding-
place for diplomats. "Lima," writes the caustic Venezue-

lan, "is the last capital of America to obtain liberty. Nor does it free itself with its own efforts, but with the aid of Argentines, Chileans, Ecuadorians, Bolivians, Granadans and Venezuelans, who formed the united army of South America, under Bolívar and Marshal Sucre." This colonial heritage remains with the nation's letters until a very late date. "Generally speaking," says Blanco-Fombona, in the same excellent essay upon González Prada, "nowhere have the South American emancipators been written against so bitterly and unjustly as in Peru."

Yet it is Peru of recent days that produces in José Santos Chocano the fearless, proud apostle of Americanism, who, at the death of Rubén Darío, is accorded by many the privilege of wielding that master's sceptre. And it is that same Peru, which in José María Eguren, now seems to have produced a new note not only in the national poetry, but in Castilian verse in general.

José María Eguren is a man of too great modesty. He has been known as a painter of no mean merit,[1] and as a musician. As poet he is new even to his own fellow citizens of Lima, where he has lived all the years of his life, which must now be some forty in number. He is not prolific, and his poetry, again unlike that of his famous countrymen, does not produce the impression of having poured forth like lines of lava from a volcano of inspiration. But despite his modesty he has his pride—an artistic pride, and one that frankly abhors the appeal to the crowd. In this unshakable devotion to his conception of art there

---

[1] For an article upon Eguren as a painter, with illustrations of his canvases, see *Variedades* (Lima, Peru), issue of June 21, 1919. The article is by Teófilo Castillo.

is something noble, even if at times, in his verse, it tends toward a certain ultra-refined complexity. Some artists fear the crowd; some detest it; others ignore it. In all these attitudes there is more than a trace of justice. A certain fear of the masses will act, upon some artists, as a wholesome corrective for their tendency toward abtruseness and obscurity—an obscurity often due, it may be suggested, to the absence of any large number to whom the ideas must be made intelligible. A detestation of the crowd is, as often as not, merely a perverted form of an intense love for art itself, and, like many excesses, to be forgiven for the intense idealism at its root. Ignoring the crowd is perhaps, taking it by and large, the best attitude for the artist to assume; here neither fear nor hatred will operate to destroy the essential humanity of the work, while the man in the artist will perforce strike some note in consonance with the artist in all men. In economic and industrial life the course of betterment may, as we have been told, have to work its way from the bottom upwards. In art it will have to be the other way round, if any way at all. There may be safety in numbers, but art does not travel in crowds.

In other words, we are wrong if we insist upon demolishing the ivory tower. That is the only kind of place in which some spirits can labor. And if their labors bring us a richer life, why need we be concerned with the place of birth? Eguren is an ivory-tower spirit. Something of the pallor of his own countenance has crept into his verses, yet something of his ardent inner self, and something of the color of his own canvases there is, too. And if he is a bad reader of his own works, they are there in print for us to read for our own pleasure. "When he reads his compositions—and they are very badly read," writes Enrique Carrillo in his introduction to Eguren's collection of verse called *La Canción de Las Figuras*, "he interrupts himself and asks, very timidly, with a surprising and touching modesty, 'Do you like it? Do you think it's all right?' Yes, my poor, beloved poet, we like it exceedingly well, we are captivated and enraptured by the soulful music that so sweetly flowers from its tenuous and undulating rhythms. And what a splendid example you present in your retirement, proud and humble at the same time, in the midst of the grotesque array of elephantine vanities that we are forced to behold in our intellectual circles!" The poet's bad reading of his own verses is a very human touch; I believe it was the Russian composer, Chaikovsky, who more than once spoiled his orchestral compositions by conducting them. Creative and intrepretative genius are not always close companions. One thing about Eguren's preferences may prove difficult to understand: his great predilection for Mendelssohn's music. Outwardly, at least, there is no resemblance between the poetry of the one and the music of the other. Mendelssohn is clear, direct, often simple and always sweet, with a sweetness that in these latter days of militant cacophony has unjustly been dismissed as being merely sugary and insubstantial. Eguren is rarely direct or clear; his sweetness is not often companioned by simplicity as it is understood in poetry.

Eguren, in the words of the discerning young Peruvian critic Pedro S. Zulen, is a neosymbolist. Speaking of Eguren's first book, *Simbólicas*, which came out in 1911, Zulen wrote, upon its appearance, "Never have we listened to a genre like that of *Simbólicas,* which now comes to initiate a new tendency in our national poetry, and perhaps a new conception of symbolism in poetry itself." Zulen discerns in Eguren two symbolisms; that of the separate images and that of their combination. That of the separate images is not new in poetry, although Eguren brings his personal contribution to the style; Eguren's novel addition, according to Zulen, consists in a synthesis of the various images. "Each composition of Eguren's is an entire block of ideas and of images, concrete and synthetic in the highest degree. His personality plays no part; it is like the camera, unconscious of the fact that it is producing images; his symbol is something that lives of itself, possessing an independent existence. And in Eguren there is to be admired not only the wealth of his spirit in creative imagination. There is in him not only the sincere soul, the ethical integrity that was for Carlyle one of the conditions that he indicated for the poet if he wishes to rise to something like a kind of earthly deity, but also the other condition laid down by the celebrated English Puritan, as Taine called him: to think musically."

Viewed from this standpoint, Eguren represents a step away from Spanish-American modernism.

To some of his countrymen indeed, Eguren represents the newest aspect of this important movement. His symbolism is a multiple connotation of words, sounds and sense. What he has brought to Peruvian poetry he has, in a way, brought to Spanish-American poetry as a whole; a more suggestive, perturbing and more intimate note—the sensation of the mystery of silent lives, of the tragedy of daily existence, in the manner of Maeterlinck, and the musical transposition of the landscape. "José María Eguren," says Carrillo, "has ben the Moses who made these two fresh streams spring from the rock." Carrillo's praise goes farther still. "I maintain," he asserts, after noting some of the poetic influences that have played upon his poet, and averring that he does not claim for Eguren the foundation of a new poetic art, "that none before him in (South) America has sung as he does."

Just how diverse have been the influences undergone by Eguren may be gathered from names such as our own Poe, Mallarmé, Verlaine, Francis Jammes and Rubén Darío. From influences such as these, plus his own personality, which may not figure visibly in his work but which is there just the same, as it is in the works of all significant artists, Eguren has distilled a symbolic style that merges music and mystery with meanings that must be sought. And herein lies the certainty that he will never be a popular poet. Thus far he has been received either with open arms, by an enthusiastic few, or by ill-worded hostility on the part of certain critics who do not even concede him the right to be called poet. Eguren belongs to that circle of spirits who have been named poets' poets. He either strikes a responsive note in you or he does not. If you are endowed with a capacity for mystic moods (not necessarily a mystic philosophy) you will find durable pleasure in such poems as *El Dios Cansado* (The Weary God), *El Dios de la Centella* (The God of the Lightning Flash), *El Cuarto Cerrado* (The Closed Room) and *Los Robles* (The Oak Trees).

Eguren's poetry possesses a delicate, vibrating sensitiveness to the connotations of colors and sounds and, at its best, a rare flavor which, like a precious attar, is extremely volatile. This is well illustrated by the poem entitled *Las Torres* (The Towers), or in *Los Reyes Rojos* (The Red Kings). Those who have taken delight in watching the changing aspects of a scene under the various colors that play upon it from sunrise to sunset will have seen all that the poet brings to them in his fantastic conception of the distant towers that rise to rage, in the golden, flaming sunbeams, like monarchs in battle, that wound each other in the red glow of sundown and sink to ashes in the black of night.

> Brunas lejanías . . .;
> batallan las torres
> presentando
> siluetas enormes.
>
> Aureas lejanías . . .;
> las torres monarcas
> se confunden
> en sus iras llamas.
>
> Rojas lejanías . . .;
> se hieran las torres;
> purpurados
> se oyen sus clamores.
>
> Negras lejanías . . .;
> hora cenientas
> se obscurecen
> ¡ay, las torres muertas!

Similarly in the poem that is called, too modestly, by the almost anonymous title "Lied III," Eguren evokes the magic of the deep that hovers over all coasts within sight

of which vessels and their brave crews have sunk into the
arms of Neptune's daughters. The conception of the
sunken ships rising from their graves at the sound of the
bell upon the coast, and then sinking back again into "the
Pantheon of the seas" (is that not a beautiful and memorable metaphor?) is embodied in verse of most musical
plasticity; there is an ebb and flow to the five short stanzas
that accords most artistically with the rising of the ships to
the call of the bell and their return to their watery homes.

> En la costa brava
> suena la campana,
> llamando á los antiguos
> bajeles sumergidos.
>
> Y con tamiz celeste
> y al luminar e hielo,
> pasan tristemente
> los bajeles muertos.
>
> Carcomidos, flavos,
> se acercan vagando . . .
> y por las luces dejan
> obscurosas estelas.
>
> Con su lenguage incierto
> parece que sollozan,
> á la voz de invierno,
> preterida historia.
>
> En la costa brava
> suena la campana,
> y se vuelvan las naves
> al panteón de los mares.

It is one of the paradoxes of art that, the more personal

a poet is, the less individuality he allows his reader in the
interpretation of his work; while the less personal the creative artist is in his style, the greater play of interpretative
personality the reader himself may enjoy once he has culti-
vated a taste for the poet.   Providing, of course, the poet is
worth cultivating.   And on that score, I, for one, am pretty
well determined in Eguren's favor.   He is himself.   He
does not affect the sonorous bugle blasts of Chocano merely
because Chocano, doing this style so well, has found immense favor.   For that reason, if you come to him after a
fairly wide reading of Chocano you are apt to feel yourself
in rather rare atmosphere, and find it hard, at first, to catch
your poetic breath, so to speak.   Nor will you find in
Eguren the cosmopolitan versatility of Darío, or the elegiac
sentimentality of Gutiérrez Nájera.   You will find little,
too, suprisingly little, of love.

This is true not only of Eguren, but of others of the
younger poets.   Listen, for instance, to this from the noted
Spanish critic Miguel de Unamuno, in his foreword to
the poetry of José Asunción Silva.   I quote the important
passage because it throws light not only upon Spanish-
American poetry of the past two decades, but also is instructive in a consideration of our own chief poetic spirits.

"Silva is not an erotic poet; strictly speaking, none of
the greatest poets is.   And these great poets, who have not
made of love for woman either the only or even the central sentiment of life, are those who have sung the love of
her with the greatest power, originality and even intensity
. . . It has been said that for those who love but little—
referring to love of woman—that love fills their lives almost completely, whilst in those who love deeply, love is a

subordinate and secondary thing. Nor is this a paradox but rather a question of spiritual capacity. The latter can love three times as intensely as the former and nevertheless accord to love but a third of the spirit. . . ." After speaking of the tendency of young writers to imagine that the eyes of their beloved are the stars about which the universe revolves Unamuno continues: "Nevertheless it is not the beauty of Helen, but the wrath of Achilles that is the basis of the *Iliad;* nor is Beatrice, after all, more than a pretext for the *Divine Comedy,* nor is love the great pivot of Shakespeare's tragedies, nor is Dulcinea more than a spectre in the *Quijote,* nor Gretchen more than an episode in *Faust.* . . . When, in the literature of a people there is a tendency to sing before all and above all of woman for her own sake, it is a sign that people is becoming enervated and lowering itself, even in love."

Whether from some such reasons as Unamuno gives in the foregoing statement, or whether because the love element in Eguren's art finds its vent in music and painting, his poetry thus far is singularly free of anything more than flashes of the grand passion. Nor is it necessary to agree to Unamuno's astoundingly sweeping statement to see his point.

This newest of the symbolists is a highly cultured spirit, too refined for vulgar conquests, yet too sensitive in taste to yield to super-æsthetic extravagances of conception or expression. At his best he is so welcome because of his chaste, cameo-like style and his meaningful visions, that one easily forgives him the higher flights, in which it is hard to follow him. Unless one is case-hardened in the tenets of a particular poetic cult (a most unpoetic attitude towards poetry, and a most unartistic, if not inartistic, attitude toward art in general) he will not deny Eguren a niche in the gallery of significant contemporary poets. Spanish America should hear more of him, and Spain, too.

CHAPTER VI

RUFINO BLANCO-FOMBONA

1874–)

BECAUSE I admire his versatility greatly, because I wish him many years of fruitful labor, in which he may produce an unending succession of spirited works, incidentally learning, too, that not all that is of the United States is necessarily despicable or untrustworthy, and that there is a distinction between a nation as a whole and certain predatory interests within it,—because whatever his faults may be he is one of the most valiant and sincere spirits writing in Europe today, I choose to begin this study of Don Rufino Blanco-Fombona with the necrological notice of himself which he writes at the end of his kaleidoscopic *Lámpara de Aladino*,—Aladdin's Lamp. For surely no epitaph more belied the death it was supposed to chronicle. How throbbing with life it is, and how characteristic of the man who wrote it! How full of self-revelation and self-understanding, of passion and irony. Its epigraph: *Much ado about nothing.* Its substance:

"I would desire, on dying, to inspire an obituary notice of the following style:

"This man, like one beloved of the gods, died young. He knew how to love and to hate with all his heart. He loved fields, rivers, fountains; he loved good wine, he loved marble, steel, gold; he loved nubile women and beautiful verses. He despised the timorous, the presumptuous and the mediocre. He hated traitors, hypocrites, calumniators, venal spirits, eunuchs, servile souls. He was content never to read the manufacturers of trashy literature. In the midst of his injustice he was just. He was prodigal in applause for those by whom he thought it was merited; he admired those whom he recognized as his superiors and held his equals in esteem. Although often he celebrated the triumph of the claw and the impulse of the wing, he felt compassion for the unfortunate, even among tigers. He attacked only the strong. He had ideals, and struggled and made sacrifices for them. He carried disinterestedness to the limits of the ridiculous. Only one thing did he ever refrain from giving: advice. Not even in his most gloomy hours was there lacking, from near or far, the friendly voice and heart of some woman. It is not known whether he was moral or immoral or amoral; but he placed beauty and truth,—his truth,—above all. He enjoyed and suffered much, spiritually and physically. He knew the world and desired everybody to know him. Neither anarchistic nor acratic, he believed that intelligence should govern peoples. As for art, he believed ever that one could and should be original, not forgetting that *nihil novum sub sole*. His life was illogical. His thought was contradictory. His one unchanging attribute was his sincerity, both in feeling and thought. Never did a lie sully his lips or his pen. He never feared the truth or the consequences it entailed. Therefore he faced homicidal daggers; therefore he suffered long incarcerations and longer exiles. He preached liberty by example; he was free. He was a soul of the sixteenth century and a man of the twentieth.

"He rests in peace for the first time. May the earth, which he loved, be propitious to him."

There, in a few hundred words, you have the auto-portrait of one of the foremost Spanish-American figures of today,—a peculiarly human figure, poet in action as well as in thought, complex in soul as well as accomplishment, very much of the present, not a little of the past, and just as much of the future. His life is full of errors, but no less replete with glory; he has lived every moment and lived it hard; he has often been wrong, but never wittingly unjust. Friend and foe alike know where he stands; he is utterly sincere. If, mistaking the attitude of a few for the spirit of a nation, he has been sadistically harsh with the United States, he has been no less stringent and vitriolic with his native and beloved Venezuela; so passionate is he in his adoration of justice and its human symbols, that he even waxes unjust in its defense. His gushing energy has overflowed into countless channels, yet out of the turbulent waters emerges a clear stream of virile manhood flowing onward toward a new and better day.

I

The poet, critic, novelist, sociologist and polemist was born on June 17, 1874, in the city of Caracas, Venezuela. On his father's side he comes of old Spanish aristocratic stock; his maternal line is little less distinguished, his grandfather, D. Evaristo Fombona, having founded the Venezuelan Academy of Languages, and having been a correspondent of the Royal Spanish Academy and coun-

cillor of the Spanish legation in Caracas.   This personage
married a daughter of one of the chief fighters in the war
for Venezuela's independence—a struggle which, Blanco-
Fombona points out, was fiercer and more determined there
than anywhere else on the continent—thus bringing revolutionary blood into the family veins.

The mingling of the aristocratic and the insurrecto strains
is markedly evident in our author. He has himself told
us, in his whimsical necrological note, that he has the soul
of the sixteenth century, and this is no mere metaphor.
The many escapades of his early days, the hot-tempered
spirit of his countless imbroglios in South America and in
Europe alike, the adventuresome wanderlust that has carried him from prisons to virgin forests, from forests to
the effete civilization of contemporary European capitals,
all attest the hidalgo, quick to resent attacks, fancied or
real, quick to recognize bravery, friendly or hostile, and
scornful of life when honor is at stake.   On the other hand
that hidalgoesque spirit is tempered by a passionate revolt
against anything that resembles injustice.   Blanco-Fombona is capable of declaring the exploited Indian of the
Orinoco far superior to his white exploiters; race plays no
part in his prejudices; he has, as we have seen, attacked
his own country as acrimoniously as ours,—in each case
because he has seen a wrong to be righted.   We are not
now concerned with the justice of his views, but with the
white-heat sincerity of his motive.   It may not be urging
the point too far to suggest that the salient traits of Blanco-
Fombona's character are derived from the antagonism
between the two hostile strains in his blood,—an antagonism which seems today to be resolving into something like

harmony. Not that Blanco-Fombona has renounced his youth; but from some of his passages one may gather that he is glad it has past. On the evidence of his friend and critic González-Blanco, we learn that today Blanco-Fombona is a tranquil man, "as far as that is possible," busy with his duties as directing head of the Editorial-America, a publishing house that makes a specialty of issuing notable works by Spanish Americans; "a fine señor who does not even go out at night; a man that shuns all noise; a littérateur who deliberately and insistently flees every literary gathering; a good bourgeois, I repeat, who has his secretary and his book-keeper; a serious gentleman, moderate, courteous, who thinks only of office and home, and who may be seen mornings on horseback in the suburbs of Madrid or afternoons in the Library or the Conference Hall of the Ateneo. . . . None would imagine that this bourgeois, an inhabitant of Madrid, was the same as the 'caballero atorbellinado' of whom Darío spoke; the man of duels, travels, women and cosmopolitan escapades; the poet of *Pequeña ópera lirica*, the author of the lyric prose entitled *Mas allá de los horizontes*." [1]

At the age of eighteen Blanco-Fombona is found enrolled as a volunteer in the revolution against President Andueza, who precipitated the outbreak by trying to prolong his term in office after it had expired. Upon the successful outcome of the revolution, during which he won his way from a position as private to that of aide to general Antonio Fernández, Blanco-Fombona left for the United States, where he remained for two years, devoting himself

---

[1] Andres González-Blanco. *Escritores Representativos de America.* Madrid, 1917. Pages 86–87.

to a rigorous program of self-instruction. And here begins his career of roistering and antipathy to our country;
the first would seem to have subsided, but the second is still
active. It is, let us say at once, a worthy opposition that
must be met, not pushed aside. Blanco-Fombona is listened to in Europe and in Spanish America. He must be
heard here. For the present let it be sufficient to say that
he is alive to the better aspects of the United States, having
translated Prof. Shepherd's book on Latin America into
Spanish; his animosity is the mistaken transference to an
entire people of the dislike he feels,—with more or less
justice, we must admit—for certain policies fostered by certain administrations. But how wrong to erect this motive
into an unthinking hatred of an entire republic,—a people that led the way for Spanish America in shaking off
the fetters of monarchial oppression, and later, in doing
away with black slavery! How puerile, too, is González-
Blanco's glorification of Blanco-Fombona's brawl upon
the streets of New York into a deed of derring-do! [2]

[2] González-Blanco. *Op. cit.*, 88–89. The Spanish critic, fairly safe as
an enthusiastic guide to contemporary literature in Spain and Spanish
America, becomes untrustworthy when he enters the domains of national
character. Take, for a good example, his note on the escapade referred
to. "I have had in my hands," he says, "the newspaper from New York
in which the event is reported, and (italics mine) *nothing can give a better
idea of the cowardice of the yankees before a determined man, in the middle of the street, with a cane in his hand*," whereupon he proceeds to tell
how our author struck out right and left and vanquished—one would imagine—the United States! Shades of logic and González-Blanco's classical
education! So this is what proves "yankee cowardice"! Hardly. Any
more than González-Blanco's words should accuse all Spanish writers of
shallow reasoning.
    Blanco-Fombona was capable of quarreling even with such close friends
as Darío and Enrique Gómez-Carrillo, in a Parisian café. They once
happened to be discussing the smaller nationalities of Spanish America and
our author did not like the supercilious attitude adopted by his friends.

In 1899 we find Blanco-Fombona back in Caracas, where his first book is published, half in prose, half in verse, somewhat after the manner of Darío's *Azul*. . . . But it was not like our author to keep quiet for long; he must needs engage in a duel and flee back to the despised United States, which has so often been the harbor of refuge for Spanish-American revolutionists. Variations of his country's political complexion brought him varied rewards. In 1901 we discover him as Secretary-General of the state of Zulia, one of Venezuela's federal departments. More trouble, in which Blanco-Fombona, forced to defend himself, killed one man and wounded two others of his assailants. For a while he was imprisoned, and when freed of the charge, was escorted to a church of Maracaibo, where the populace sent up thanks to the Lord for his safe delivery. With his consulship to Amsterdam in 1902, and the frequent trips to Paris which this made possible, came another string of duels. We need not enter into particulars. Who gets into so many quarrels in so many parts of the world cannot always be right. The truth must be that young Blanco-Fombona was hasty, arrogant, quarrelsome, too ready for trouble.

Yet this should not mean that he was always in the wrong. His next charge, which carried him to the Territorio Ama-

Whereupon, somewhat overladen with liquor Blanco-Fombona burst into patriotic eloquence: "You both live on that America which you scorn, while this country that you adore (France) wouldn't give you enough to buy a hat with. You, Carrillo, are consul from your country; you, Darío, aspire to be consul from yours. Over there you're somebody; here you are nobody. There you are Rubén Darío and Gómez Carrillo; here you are number 10 or number 25 of the hotel. You are, at bottom, Philistines, bourgeois; you love Paris, France, Europe; power, wealth, established things. Not I. I love America,—our America, even though it be poor, Indian, savage, lousy, leprous, I love it. . . ."

zons, a virgin department comprising between a sixth and a fifth of Venezuela, bordering upon parts of Brazil and Colombia, reveals him in the light of a brave pioneer. Sent thither as governor, he was through motives he has not yet amplified upon, subjected to an attempt at assassination, in which his enemies came out second best.[3]

Blanco-Fombona's European residence, then, has for background a violent life of revolution, adventure and love-making in which poetry seems to be fused with action. The primitive man mingles strangely with the man of culture, —the Spanish hidalgo with the Venezuelan patriot. Somewhat like Darío, he has become legendary in his own day. Poems are inscribed to him,—one by the well-known Argentine poet Leopoldo Díaz, of whose work Blanco-Fombona has written an illuminating exposition. He has been likened, in one of Darío's finest bits of prose, to a denizen of the Italy of Cardinal de Ferrar, of Benvenuto Cellini. (Diaz's sonnet places him in the same company); yet González-Blanco is right in rejecting the imputation of an amoralism of the Renaissance in favor of a more constant, positive guiding principle. His multifarious life has a great purpose and he has given himself unstintingly to it. Not for him the sterility of complacent, negative virtue; life and poetry alike to him have meant action. He has written, and written often, the Word, but his words have flowered from the Deed. Would you understand the man with anything like completeness you must know his Bolivar-olatry,—his intense worship of the Great Liberator, to

[3] For a valuable record of this period read, in *El Lámpara de Aladino* (Madrid, 1915) the section entitled "Viaje de Alto Orinoco," pages 331 to 393.

whom he has tried to be true with pen and sword. Has our own Washington inspired so whole-souled a devotion?

Blanco-Fombona, then, is peculiarly himself in word and deed. Like those who do much, he has committed many an error, but the good far outweighs the bad. He is still a young man, and from his writings may be gleaned, not only a deep understanding of the remarkable man himself, but a better comprehension of the new continental spirit that is forming in Spanish America. Since he himself began as a poet, let us first consider him in that light, afterwards taking up his accomplishments in the fields of criticism, sociology, politics and fiction.

II

It is significant that Blanco-Fombona's first production was a poem entitled *Patria*, and as irony would have it, the poem, which received the prize in competition with other verses written upon the subject of Sucre's centenary, was indited in Philadelphia, where he was then carrying on his studies. "The generation to which I belong," he has informed us in his interesting "Historia de Libros" (*Lámpara de Aladino*) was born into literary life toward 1893. A hundred rose buds opened to the same dawn. In 1893 I was living in Philadelphia, where I was studying, and where I wrote practically in secret, and whence I sent to a contest, originating in Coro (1894) on the occasion of Sucre's centenary, a poem: *Patria*, flaming with youth and enthusiasm, in the lyric-epic vein. The very fact that I participated in a contest shows how young I must have been; I was, in fact, but twenty years old. . . . I won the prize and acquired a reputation . . . in Coro." It seems, then, that Blanco-Fombona started on much the same path as Chocano, with a prize for a lyric-epic poem exalting national pride. *Patria* is today unprocurable, nor does the author seem desirous of resuscitating the poetic corpse. His first book was the collection of verse and prose entitled *Trovadores y Trovas* (1899). It has likewise fallen out of print and is generally recognized as a juvenile performance. "Already," says González-Blanco, "one may discern a constant search for originality in expression and feeling,—an originality which is attested by the recherché metres and an avoidance of the spontaneous feelings that move all poets at that age." Manuel Díaz Rodríguez, now a recognized essayist and novelist—one of the finest prose artists Spanish America has produced in recent years, was at the time of the publication of *Trovadores y Trovas* one of the staff upon the *Cojo Ilustrado*, and greeted his companion's work as the evidence of a nervous, restless, sensual, sad spirit, of superior artistic gifts. It was not until 1904, however, that Blanco-Fombona was to give his true measure as a poet. It was then that the *Pequeña ópera lírica* appeared, in Madrid. It was then that the author became conscious of his art and felt that he had found his path, "which is that of simplicity in expression, truth in feeling, literary sincerity, life truly lived,—in sum, without rhetorical trimmings or verbal tinsel." The passage is important, as are a number of others from *La Lámpara de Aladino*, for with them, it reveals both the virtues and the shortcomings of his poetic work. Now he tells us that the poets, in truth, are the great philosophers, and three pages later (Op. cit. page 10) that "the lie is the gift of poets, priests, kings and soothsayers. We who are neither soothsayers, kings,

priests, nor poets must content ourselves with the truth,
'the humble truth,' as one of its apostles termed it." Do
you find this, as you will find much else in his work, illogical, or inconsistent? "Will you say that what I see within
me, or the spirit in which I gaze upon my surroundings
differs from one day to the next? No matter! That my
eyes lack logic? No matter! I know that they obey a
superior logic. One may ask only the mental and sentimental sincerity of the moment." This is the substance
of Blanco-Fombona's sincerity; his "superior logic" is that
larger truth,—not a dogma but a *becoming*,—which we
have seen in Emerson and in Rodó.

Do you wonder that he should call Unamuno Spain's
greatest living poet? Then wonder no longer when you
read his conception of life and poetry as action. In the
secular parable *La Vida Que Pasa* (As Life Passes By) he
says: "I hear a voice that tells me: you don't write, you
don't think, you don't dream. Yours is not an existence
of contemplation nor of fecund leisure, nor of a taste for
life; it is the hour that flies in childish chatter or in trivial
love-making. Your youth, your energy, wing away, without your realizing it, and they fly off never to return; they
fly off taking with them the sap and bloom of your Aprils,
leaving you—ay!—mouldy, decayed, sterile.

"And I hear another voice which replies:

"Complain not of squandering your life; you are living it."

Both voices are those of the author. It is one of these
voices that later tells him (page 125) that the observer of
Nature will discover nothing if he is not something of a
poet; it is the second that whispers to him during his

memorable trip to his savage seat of government in the *Territorio Amazonas*: "Can it be true that we poets are condemned to dream, while the strong labor and create? No, no. The dream is noble, among other things insofar as it translates itself into action. The greatest poet is he who expresses himself in noble, transcendental acts. Perhaps because of this, and not alone because of his golden speech and his winged fancy José Martí wrote of the Liberator, 'The first poet of America is Bolívar.'" I have before remarked upon the similarity between Martí's conception of poetry and that held by Blanco-Fombona. In Martí's sentence the conceptions crystallize about the figure of their common idol. To them the poet is a doer. In his enthusiasm the poet may often lack the spirit of justice. Indeed, in another of the brief pages that adorn *La Lámpara de Aladino* (page 445, on the "Equity of Poets") our author recognizes that poets lack almost entirely the spirit of justice. Theirs is passion, not equanimity. But, when they are genuine poets and not mere simulators, they instil such impetus, such fire, such passion into their views, that what they hate appears almost as great as what they love. Blanco-Fombona the good hater is in those words, even as he is in his poetry, his novels, his criticisms. For such as he art for art's sake seems a bootless renunciation of human passions. No wonder, then, that he can write, in considering his *Pequeña ópera lírica*, that "more poetry is truly produced, simply as a result of their living, by a Benvenuto Cellini than by a Hugo Foscolo, by a Hernán Cortés than by a Nuñez de Arce, by a Díaz Mirón than by a Darío. . . . The majority of poets are poets only in verse, and have not lived, neither in love nor grief, danger, evil, good, hate, audacity, madness, an hour of true poetry.   Every man whose life lends no material for legends and poetry is a secondary man, even though nature invest him with the gifts of a fabulous goldsmith and an enchanting rhetoric. Darío is the prototype of this captivating poet of the imagination; prosaic, nevertheless, in existence, colorless, meek, calculating, insignificant; null.   But Darío is not alone. A long horde of metrifiers stretches out in both directions of time—past and future—an entire horde that feels art more than life.   Another vast multitude will prefer life and will behold in it the source not only of the beautiful, but of good and evil, which in the hands of an artist are the proper material for art.   To this number I belong."

The man of power in life demands power in poetry.   He is able to conceive only the strenuous life, to the point of momentarily underestimating one of the greatest poets who has sung in the modern Spanish tongue.   Yet at the bottom of his conception is there not a play upon words?   May not beauty be its own excuse for being?   For all Bolívar's glorious exploits could he have penned a glorious collection like the *Canto de Vida y Esperanza?*   Why are worlds to be redeemed if not to grant the Daríos their leisure, that they may in turn beautify our own?   Life is not all action; progress is not all war; there is poetry in the flute as well as in the trumpet, in the blade of grass as well as in the oak.   Nor has Blanco-Fombona been immune to this tenderer aspect; he has written excellent pages of nature love and calm repose.   Essentially, however, he is the man of action; let us grant him his conception of poetry,—and this is all-important,—if that is the banner under which he can sing best.

It was to the *Pequeña ópera lirica* (1904) that Darío prefixed a short, imaginative study which showed its power of grasping the essential element in Blanco-Fombona's spirit. "I enjoy the verses of this Spanish-American poet," he wrote, "who is so much of Italy, so much of the Renaissance, although he is very much of today, and has Spanish blood, and was born in Caracas, and dwells in Paris." The poet of intense personalism, the enemy of exoticism, was capable of an occasional excursion into eighteenth century elegance, despite his masculine, rigorous conceptions of life. The collection, although it has been later surpassed, produced a marked effect upon the youth of the day. A certain deceptive simplicity, as well as an ardent spontaneity, were responsible for this influence. Again like Chocano, there is the epico-lyric tendency united to pantheism,—but characteristically enough, a pantheism that at times is imbued with the same indignation as is felt by the author. This is true especially of the poems that followed in *Cantos de la Prisión y del Destierro* (1911).

The "Songs of Prison and Exile" are the author's favorite writings. They embody, literally, the spirit of the poem *Explicación* in the *Pequeña ópera lirica:*

> El mejor poema es el de la vida;
> de un piano en la noche la nota perdida;
> la estela de un barco; la ruta de flores
> que lleva a ciudades ignotas; dolores
> pueriles; mañanas de riñas; sabor
> de besos no dados, y amor sin amor.

The poems of prison and exile are such stuff as life is made of. "Every stanza is a moment of existence from the ter-

rible days of my last imprisonment between 1909 and 1910,
or from the first hours of my exile, which were the most
bitter of this now so long expatriation." The verses were
written down under the most trying circumstances, with
the author surrounded by spies, manacled in a dungeon,
without pen or paper. More even than Chocano, Blanco-
Fombona imprisons his jailers behind the bars of his lyre.
Like Martí, too, he declares that the lines were written with
his blood. "These verses will avenge me. I trust in them.
While there exists a man of honor, a manly spirit, a victim
of persecutors and a woman in love, my verses will be read,
not because they are beautiful, but because they were written with blood, with tears, with gall, because they are of
flesh and bone, because they are the human outcries of a
man who has suffered." The author, as well as any critic,
touches upon the chief appeal of his lines. They burn
with rage, yet they shine with an occasional spirituality
that lights up the gloom of the cell. Such an illumination
is the *Vuelo de Psiquis* in which the radiant memory of
things beloved eases the bitter burden of the prisoner:

> Me abruma el calabozo. Cruzan mi alma inquieta
>   pensamientos obscuros;
> Y rómpense, al abrirse, mis alas de poeta
>   contra los cuatro muros.
>
> En sepulcro; ¡y viviente!; Son eternos los días
>   y las noches eternas!
> Las Penas me acompañan. En mi torno hay espías
>   y grillos en mis piernas.
>
> Pero al cerrar los ojos: (luz, campo, cielo) miro
>   romperse las cadenas;

> y al brazo de mi novia en al jardín respiro
>   magnolias y verbenas.
>
> Gozo el aire, las nubes, y el chorro del estanque,
>   frescor como mi amada . . .,
> Alguna cosa es bueno que el Despota no arranque
>   ni tenga encadenada.

So passes the poet from vindictiveness to elation, from gloom to sacred ire, ever impelled by an unquenchable thirst for vengeance. The early imprisonment of the author explains in a large measure the development of his pugnacious nature into a torch of patriotism and hatred for every phase of oppression, even as the pugnacity of spirit may explain that inattention to the more graceful aspects of technique which is so often the concomitant of ardent sincerity. Yet it is that very sincerity which renders us willingly forgetful of the more delicate literary traits. Tyrants are not flayed with strips of silk lace or drowned in vases of cologne water. Against his tyrant the very trees turn in indignation; the mountain whither he has fled refuses him shelter; the soil is transformed into rock; the waters are converted into blood. All nature rebels against the supplicating wretch.

But there is a gentler aspect to the poet,—one in which he chooses to appear before us, for more than a moment, in his *Cancionero del Amor Infeliz* (1918). And so great capacity for indignation is that possessed by our singer, that he does not wait for attacks, but in a prefatory note launches forth to meet them. He does not deem it necessary to apologize for a book of love verses. (Why, indeed, should he? And why, indeed, raise the point?) And he very sensibly reminds us that if Plato exiled poets from his Republic, Plato should have been the first to condemn himself to ostracism.   The poems of the *Cancionero* belong to various stages of the poet's career and mirror the changing phases of such love as even a man of action can feel. And despite his yielding to the gentler muse, Blanco-Fombona is still the man of arrogant, pugnacious sincerity. His love verse, he tells us, is not the word of flame that covers the heart of snow, but rather the word of snow that covers the heart of fire.   In all his protestations as to the poetic art Blanco-Fombona himself seems to feel that he lacks certain of the more stylistic attributes, wherefore he combats them instead of remembering that the creative man is the master of his own style and that styles may be as many as men.   He has himself, as a matter of fact, recognized, if not constantly kept this in mind.   Speaking of his artistic ancestry, he has said, "From the French, as from other tongues, I have taken what I should have taken: the example of love of literary independence, a thing which is in accord with my temperament.   This does not signify the imitation of anybody. . . . I hate schools.   Neither in politics nor in literature have I been an *ist* of any sort.   I am I. . . . In the Spanish language Rubén Darío continues, for me, to be higher than the horns of the moon; I admire Lugones, who is in fashion, and Díaz Mirón (his first manner) who is not.   In the various literatures I continue to be fond of Verlaine, Moréas . . . d'Annunzio, without forgetting Byron, Musset, Bécquer, Heine, José Asunción Silva, and above all, Hugo."   The list of names attests a broad eclecticism upon the part of the exiled Venezuelan,—an eclecticism characteristic of his age as well as

of his temperament.   If it is possible to quarrel with a man
for not being himself, my only quarrel with Blanco-Fombona as a poet (or, more exactly, as the critic of poets)
would be for his insistence upon the action element and
his narrowing scorn for sheer beauty in men who have not
been born with his peculiar constitution.   His own poetry
is a torch that transmits his flame to us, thus eminently ful-
filling his conception of its mission.   Even his atheism is
not the calm, philosophical acceptance of a hopeless outlook, but proud, unresigned defiance:

LA PROTESTA DEL PELELE

Locura?   Bien.   No me resigno;
que se resignen los esclavos.
Déme el Destino la cicuta,
el Dolor me clave sus clavos.

Yo no diré; "bendito seas,
mi Diós, tu voluntad acato";
diré: "soy menos que el insecto
bajo la suela de un zapato.

pero no hay que beber mis lagrimas,
ni placerse en mi desventura,
ó asistir con aspecto olímpico
é indiferente á mi tortura;

porque en mi, pelele, hay sufrir,
y tengo un alma yo, el enano,
y puedo pesar la injusticia,
y puedo juzgar al tirano."

I have called this atheism, and we know from plenty of testimony that Blanco-Fombona is not a believer.   Yet do

you see how his very antagonism calls for the personification of the god that he denies?

III

Blanco-Fombona's chief contributions to criticism are contained in two volumes: *Letras y Letrados de Hispano-America* (1908) and *Grandes Escritores de America* (1917). In them appears the fighter, the personalist, the lover of liberty and the patriot that was evident in his very first poems. He is a firm believer in "literary Americanism"; he exalts the autochthonous element, at times unmindful of exaggerations and of enthusiasm that overflows its channel. Yet how discerningly he pierces to the heart of his subject! He possesses a modern, vital sense of the importance of background and epoch; he is deeply sensitive to a host of influences deriving from the past as well as the present; he is patience itself, and not often given to the snap judgments that one might have expected from so impulsive a spirit. He is, above all, creative in his criticism. Out of all his less admirable qualities rises that potent fact; and until mankind shall have become perfect, let us be content with the creative realities that grow as much from error as from so-called infallibility. For is not truth but the sum of errors?

Take, for example, Blanco-Fombona's study of Leopoldo Díaz. At once he signalizes the two dominating traits of the artist,—traits to which the critic himself, as a poet, is often a stranger: delicacy of taste and structural beauty. And no sooner has he made this declaration, à propos of a French translation of Diaz's poems, than he has launched into a miniature disquisition upon the relative poetic potentialities of French and Spanish. "The French language has been fashioned by great artists who imparted to it the flexibility which it possesses today. Not so with our language. It is the rude tongue of the Cid, the heroic tongue of the Romancero. It is we, the (Spanish) Americans who have placed it upon the anvil, who, by dint of much patience have wrought and polished this tongue of iron, and who, by an alchemy less mysterious than conscious, have changed it from bronze to gold. . . ."

(Is not this somewhat exaggerated?)

"We, born in America, sons of that fecund and voluptuous soil, mingled with the indigenous races and with races from the south and north of Europe, are no longer the Spaniard of yore. We are a new race. And within the old tongue we have created a literary language of our own. . . . Rémy de Gourmont—and his phrase has had great fortune—calls our tongue neo-español. And it should be noted and repeated, that Leopoldo Díaz, with the prestige of his name and his talent, has also contributed to this labor of renovation.

"Just as Simon Bolívar, San Martín, Sucre and Hidalgo gave political liberty to America, Leopoldo Díaz, Gutiérrez Nájera, Darío, Casal and Lugones gave it linguistic liberty. The Liberator Bolívar, after the battle of Ayacucho, was able to exclaim: 'Soldiers! You have brought freedom to South America; and a fourth part of the world is the monument to your glory. Where have you not conquered?'

"And the poet-conqueror Leopoldo Díaz may likewise exclaim: 'Comrades! We have given wings to the thoughts of a fourth part of the world. In what lyric emprise have we not conquered?' "

Blanco-Fombona's method is here most adequate to the purpose. It is a question, if not of a new literature, at least of a radical re-orientation. A comprehension of the continental background, political as well as geographical, ethnological and sociological, is more than usually necessary. All the more so since Blanco-Fombona, knowing both South America and the cultural centres of Europe, realizes the one-sided knowledge possessed by outsiders, of Spanish America. "In Europe we are judged very superficially. We are known for our revolutions more than for anything else; revolutions which are not caused by political incapacity, as Europe imagines, and which are explained perfectly by Hispano-American sociologists who should be studied by the European sociologist before we are condemned with the customary doctoral emphasis.

"We are barbarians? Very well: yes, we are barbarous; but like the Italy of the republics. We produce harsh warriors, like Milan; but also wealthy merchants, like Genoa, and great artists, like Florence."

With these patriotic evocations his indignation against political aggression swells. "The United States," he declares, "have seventy million inhabitants": (recall when this was written) "we, not counting Brazil, have as high as fifty. The sentiment of Americanism is very strong in our countries, despite our not being joined by a common political bond. The writer of any of our States, has the entire continent for his public. Offences directed against any of our nations wound us all; and if Europe or the United States, thinking us weak, should one day attack us, this Latin-American race, this race that is the grandchild of the Cid and the daughter of Morazán, Juárez, Sucre,

San Martín, holds tremendous surprises and cruel disillusionments in store for them."

Not all his criticism resolves into polemical digressions, however. Thus, considering Díaz's neo-Hellenism, he makes the very pertinent observation (so self-evident that it is strange how many have overlooked it) that it is after all a neo-Hellenism, a view of Greece through nineteen centuries of Christianity, and not without its stylistic disadvantages. Naturally, then, it is Díaz's collection of sonnets called *Los Conquistadores* which attracts our continental patriot more than the Hellenic evocations. Whereupon another question arises in the critic's active mind: "Has there existed, in America, up to a short time ago, a national literature which is the blood of our blood,— which is ours as are our rivers, our plains, our mountains?"

"What is sure," he replies to himself, "is that we have for a long time lived on borrowings. That we have imitated and rifled the Europeans, above all the Spaniards and the French. I do not censure this. That is our right. Only, from the foreign flowers we must, like skillful bees, make our own honey. Did not the Romans sack the Greeks and did not the Europeans steal from the Latins and Greeks? The first obligation is to live. Then let us live!"

It is easy to note, from what I have translated, the lyric element in Blanco-Fombona's criticism. He does more than elucidate his subject; he maintains a running fire of commentary, suggestion, refutation, threat, glorification; he plunges his entire personality into the task. Little he recks of academic unity and rhetorical prescriptions. But read the essay, then drop it, and you will be astonished to

learn how much you have discovered. Blanco-Fombona
is no Rodó as regards style; but he possesses that irony,
that pugnacity, that variety, which were lacking in the
Uruguayan master. He is, as essayist, the complement of
Rodó, just as we have found Chocano to be the poetic complement of Darío. He has a deep sense of beauty, but it is
a rugged beauty, insofar as it is translated into prose style.
Rodó's prose is the luxuriant, variegated plain; Blanco-
Fombona's is the sturdy sierra. It takes both to produce
the Spanish-American landscape.

For examples of Blanco-Fombona at his best as critic,
I would point to such studies as those on Andrés Bello and
on González Prada in his *Grandes Escritores de America*.
No less than Rodó, he reveals himself in these estimates
of his glorious predecessors,—his fiery passion for truth
and freedom, even if it means, for a moment, to speak
against his idol. And he is aware of this self-revelation.
As he remarks in his prefatory note, "the author observes
with pleasure, as he corrects the proofs, that all the per-
sonages here treated are or were free men and free spirits.
To no adulator of tyrants, no servile pen, no writer in livery
is there here erected an altar. The author, then, without
deliberate purpose, bowed in books, as in his life, only to
those who bear their heads and their consciences erect.
And he also observes, likewise with pleasure, that in his
studies more stress is laid upon the man than upon the
littérateur, and that the life and character of each author
merit as much attention, at least, as his work." Blanco-
Fombona, then, is an auto-critic as well. So widely read a
student as González-Blanco does not hesitate to declare that

the studies upon Sarmiento, González Prada and Hostos may be considered among the excellent pages of Spanish criticism produced in the past twenty years.

As a critic, then (and in this connection the brief, but by no means superficial criticism in the first part of *La Lámpara de Aladino* in the section called Nombres should be taken into account) Blanco-Fombona is the familiar mordant spirit, penetrating in appreciation, lofty in idealism, usually tolerant and never dogmatic in attitude, personal without being merely impressionistic, and above all, creative.

IV

Blanco-Fombona's views upon the development of Spanish America are compressed into a little book of remarkable concision. *The Political and Social Evolution of Hispano-America* was written originally for the *Revue des Revues,* at the instance of its editor, Jean Finot, who found it too long for the purpose and desired to prune it with the editorial shears. Our author took back his contribution and decided to enlarge the essay instead. Out of this labor grew two lectures delivered in Madrid during the month of June, 1911. The book was published in the same year.

The author is thoroughly alive to the dangers of diplomacy and the international character of his apparently Spanish-American subject, and in his introductory remarks, by the simple suggestion of imagining the sudden disappearance of Spanish America, brings the point strikingly home. The study is divided into four main parts: The Colony, Independence, Organization of the New States and the Republic.

Blanco-Fombona deems it essential for the Caucasian element to predominate; the same man who is unsparing in his denunciation of the whites' maltreatment of the natives, finds none the less that posterity has been little just toward the work and the efforts of the conquistadores. It was the Spanish conqueror who brought civilization,—characterized at first by joint theocratic and military power. Despite legislation in favor of the natives, the latter were cruelly treated, as the laws were unheeded. With the importation of negroes from Africa came a new racial element, and the inter-marriage of Spaniards with negro and Indian women produced mulattos and mestizos. "These will merge with one another, the same as the white descendants of the conquistadores, and will produce an inextricable confusion of hybridisms, a scale of colors that begins with the authentic black and the coppery Indian and ends with the white, passing through all the shades of chocolate and coffee with milk. 'It is not known to which branch of the human family we belong,' Bolivar was to write in his message to the Congress of Angostura, in 1819."

As to the population, then, in this era, it is the same throughout America, even as are the methods of the Spanish conqueror. "The adventurers fare forth to conquest, with or without official support. The religious orders form missions and reduce the Indians. The Viceroy or Captain-General does not rule without counter-authority, although his power is great; and the Cabildos, by whom the cities are administered, are a foreshadowing of modern liberties." To the Spanish policy of exclusivism (it was a councillor of Felipe III who branded the interchange of products with any other country than Spain "an invention of the devil")

the spirit of contraband arose. The author quotes the
Brazilian sociologist Manoel Bomfin to the effect that at this
stage both Spain and Portugal were parasitic nations living
upon Colonial America. The truth is, adds our author,
that they were incapable, or at least unskillful, in their
exploitation.

Spain, in its effort to retard the intellectual progress of
the colonies, used religion as its chief weapon. The founding of universities was prohibited, and an embargo placed
upon every manner of book, even though it treated of secular and fictive matter. "But it is impossible to sequestrate
an entire people. The 'noble' Americans, despite the restrictions, exposing their liberty and their lives, read Hume,
Hobbes and even Voltaire, Rousseau and other encyclo-
pedists." Some journeyed to Europe. "Independence
was only a question of time and opportunity." Then
came the great year of 1810 in which the revolution broke
out in all the capitals. "In Caracas, the 19th of April; in
Buenos Aires, the 25th of May; in Bogotá, the 20th of
July; in Quito, the 2nd of August; in Mexico, the 16th of
September; in Santiago de Chile, the 18th of the same
month." Blanco-Fombona feels a fierce pride in that first
date; it is his native city that began the great overturn.

He is too much the historian, however, to reproach Spain
for her conduct. "Besides being futile it is absurd, and
proves ignorance of sociological laws. But," he adds, in
the very next paragraph, "it would be ignorance of those
same laws to condemn the Revolution." It was, in its beginnings, an oligarchic and municipal revolution, in which
the people had no part. It was a superior minority that
accomplished the work, utilizing the municipal power that

had been transmitted to her American sons by Spain, who had inherited it from Rome. "The revolution was municipal because it was in the Cabildos that the revolutionists were found." With striking unanimity the revolutionists decreed the abolition of slavery, the freedom of industries, freedom of commerce, liberty of the press, suppression of nobiliary titles, an open door to the men of every land, race, religions and opinion. Ecclesiastical power was taken away, the tribute of the Indians was abolished. The New World was born anew.

The war which followed was "at the same time civil and international." International as against Spain; civil because of the differences that arose among the colonies. Among the curious phenomena noted during the strife was the infiltration of the revolutionary ideas into the enemy camp. It was in Venezuela, as we have seen, that the battle lasted longest and was waged most violently.

No sooner had the revolution got under way when the question arose as to whether the new states should constitute themselves into a democracy or a monarchy. The Northerners desired a federal republic after our own pattern; the Southerners, a monarchial form. The opposing ideas were incarnated in Bolívar, the Republican, and in San Martín, monarchist. At the historic meeting at Guayaquil they held three secret conferences and then parted forever. The result was a triumph for Blanco-Fombona's idol, Bolívar. And how valiantly and patiently has our author labored in the cause of the Liberator! None better than he has fairly dramatized the vast work and the enduring influence of that epic figure, who anticipated Buckle and Taine in his appreciation of the in-

fluence of environment, who so admired the English constitution, who as early as 1815 formed a great project for a
league of nations, to meet at Panama.

The author offers a thorough explanation of the numerous wars that have been fought upon Spanish-American
territory since the struggle for Independence.   These he
refers to four chief causes: (1) cross breeding; (2) pauc-
ity of population and scarcity of means of communication;
(3) lack of liberty; (4) ignorance.   Coming to the international relations of Spanish America, and its spirit of
solidarity, he finds it convenient to classify under three
headings: (1) the threat of monarchial Europe, which was
answered by a rebirth of Bolívar's continental ideas of
federation and solidarity, and by the Monroe Doctrine,
which was at the time of its promulgation well received in
Spanish America; (2) a growing mistrust of the United
States since 1845–1850 because of its "mutilation of Mexico and its filibusterism in Central America, and a perma-
nent mistrust of Europe, which does not cease to threaten
us."   This endures until the final quarter of the nineteenth
century; (3) hatred and fear of the United States, and a
decreasing suspicion of Europe.   At every outside threat,
the sense of solidarity is reborn.   "The history of our
ephemeral unions is the history of foreign aggression."

During the final quarter of the nineteenth century, notes
Blanco-Fombona, two new currents appear: Pan-Americanism, with Anglo-American influence predominating, and
Pan-Hispanism, which tends to counteract the first.   With
the beginning of the twentieth century comes a spirit of
friendship with Europe at all costs, to offset the imperialism
of the United States and even its mere approach, "since

that country, by its customs, its conception of life, its incapacity for the Fine Arts and its lack of ideals, is the opposite pole of South America." This approach to Europe
itself splits in two, one direction favoring England and
Germany, the other Latin Europe. The last is the more
powerful.

Unfortunately this is the prevailing attitude toward the
United States, so far as one may judge from the utterances
of representative figures. I say unfortunately, for several
reasons. First, because the attitude is not wholly unjusti-
fied, however exaggerated it may become in certain temperaments; Professor Ford, referring to Mexico,[4] speaks of
"the events of a war, which not all our historians find it
easy to regard with complacency." There are other, later
events concerning our national relations with Spanish
America that are equally difficult to regard with complacency. Second, the opponents of the United States seemingly disregard the elements in it that are opposed to the
selfsame spirit of aggrandizement that the Spanish Americans fear from our nation. Third, we have, as a people,
done little to dispel false notions. We have no gifted men
like Blanco-Fombona, Manuel Ugarte and Francisco García Calderón, counteracting the acrimonious utterances and
revealing whatever of fallacy they contain. For the view
that Spanish America is entirely wrong is myopic, fatuous,
dangerous. We are committing the blunder of underestimating Spanish America, and there are many ways in
which that blunder may be driven home to us. We must
know the worst that Spanish America thinks of us and
must strive to change that worst to best. If it takes two

---

[4] *Main Currents of Spanish Literature.* Page 243.

to make a quarrel, it takes two to make a friendship.   For that purpose a little more literature and much less politics will go a long way.   There is as much patriotism in recognizing a wrong attitude as in boasting a right.   By no means do I concede all that Blanco-Fombona says against the United States.   More than once he is grievously wrong. But I insist that such opposition must be met with something more than silence.

We are not alone in our misunderstanding of Spanish America.   The statement made by Clémenceau to Frenchmen on his return from his trip to South America is almost as applicable today: "We judge them more or less superficially; let us not forget that they judge us, too."   This is all the more significant in view of the immense importance of French influence upon the cultural and intellectual development of Spanish America.

Out of this important study by our most fanatic hater (whose attitude I respect because of his undoubted sincerity, even as I deplore it for its too universal application) rises the spirit of a nascent race and a continental soul.   Both race and soul are as yet indistinct, yet acquire homogeneity with each passing year.   Thus, from the continentalism of a merely geographic accident Spanish America is attaining to the continentalism of a new race, a new soul, a new literature, new aspirations.   From our studies of Chocano and Rodó it is easy to see that the politico-economic phase is but the basis for a higher expansion.   The career of Spanish America is yet at its beginning.   It may be as one of the great poets has said: "América es el porvenir del mundo."—(Spanish) America is the future of the world. All signs point to its immediate universal importance.

From Asia to Europe, from Europe to North America, and thence southward, the course of progress wends its way. Our best response to Spanish-American suspicion is to give their fears the lie. Shall we? . . .

In connection with this phase of his labors it is important to keep in mind Blanco-Fombona's incessant researches dealing with every aspect of Bolívar's career. His *Cartas de Bolívar*, 1913 (Letters of Bolivar) are as yet in their first volume, and represent four years of unremitting toil. "Although this work is not mine, but that of the Liberator," he tells us, "it represents an accumulation of effort twenty times greater than that required by any other book hitherto published by me." It is from Bolívar, indeed, that the ardent Venezuelan draws his unflagging fervor of continental patriotism. He is the spirit of Bolívar fighting in the world of contemporary thought. He thinks with a Bolivarian sweep. His conception of the New World and its destinies is that of Bolívar. And he is a worthy paladin.

Of the more purely polemical writings of Blanco-Fombona it is not necessary to speak here at length. He can be withering, sardonic, terrible, at will. Read the Introduction to his *Judas Capitolino* (1912) and you will gather his purpose as fulfilled in the pages that follow. If words can nail tyrants to a cross, Blanco-Fombona wields the mighty hammer.

v

To foreigners whose literary interests are of a general nature it is Blanco-Fombona's fiction that will prove of most intimate appeal. That fiction possesses the double attraction of being autochthonous in inspiration as well as personal (though not subjective) in style.

His very first tales (*Cuentos de poeta*, 1900) displayed his alignment with the modernist reformers of prose. "Today," says the author, in the history of his books which forms by no means the least interesting part of *La Lámpara de Aladino*, "nobody recalls this book, nor do I desire it to be remembered. I repudiate those tales, I disown them, I do not care for them, I do not consider them mine. The only ones among them that I recognize I gathered after submitting them to pruning and orthopedy, in the *Cuentos Americanos* (Madrid, 1904) and in an augmented and definitive edition of Garnier, Paris, 1913." The *Cuentos de Poeta* appeared in a French edition under the title *Contes Americains*, but these are likewise denied by the author. The tales are characterized by a spirit of analysis, irony, even pessimism. As early as their appearance in French, Henri Barbusse recognized in them a touch of Maupassant for their brevity, Daudet for their emotion, and of Villiers d'Isle Adam for their tragic irony.

"I leave to my fair readers," (i.e. *lectrices*, for M. Barbusse then edited the *Femina*) wrote the author who has since given us *Nous Autres, Le Feu, L'Enfer* and *Clarté*, "the trouble of investigating whether it is not a token of personality to summon at the same time the thought of three so divers talents, and I add that the surprising variety of these short tales . . . as well as the picturesque local color that saturates them all in a Venezuelan atmosphere, imparts a highly individual character. . . ."

The tales are told with a most self-critical economy of means and every refinement of contemporary technique.

In such stories as *Molinos de Maíz, El Canalla San Antonio* and *Democracia Criolla* it is not merely the exotic element that appeals to us,—and what, after all, is the exotic, but a lesser known part of ourselves? Behind the exoticism is something peculiarly human,—something we may note in the two novels that follow. The intense fanaticism, the political warfare, the economic transformations mirrored in these tales fuse admirably with the action itself. Not many tales that have come out of South America can match the masterpiece *Creole Democracy*.

It is in his novels that the Venezuelan's power as a writer of fiction may be studied most completely.

The Man of Iron (*El Hombre de Hierro*, 1907) and *The Man of Gold* (*El Hombre de Oro*, 1915) are best considered together. They form an ideological unity; although in no sense is the second the sequel of the first; it is rather a natural outgrowth from the first, or a complement to it.

Blanco-Fombona's novels, like those, for example, of Manuel Díaz Rodríguez, form a delightful contrast, in their limpid, pregnant brevity, to the oceanic tomes of the earlier days,—to the *Amalia* of José Marmol, the *Manuela* of Eugenio Díaz, the *Martin Rivas* of Blest Gana. The change is not only in length, but in style. Yet the inner spirit of revolt is there, etched in firm strokes that leave a cutting impression upon the reader. Blanco-Fombona is everywhere the passionate patriot, and often his passion rises higher than his patriotism. He pierces at once to the heart of his characters; he draws in the background with swift but sure strokes; he wastes little time upon purely literary graces. His pages, at times overdrawn, are never

dull; competent witnesses declare that his pictures of Venezuelan manners are true to life; here, as everywhere else,
you get the impression that whatever else the man may be,
he is intensely, even fanatically, sincere.

Who is his "man of iron"?   A mere creature of wax.
Who is his "man of gold"?   A creature of dross, being of
the earth most earthy.   The very titles of his two novels
reveal the ironic substructure of so much of the author's
work.   He is deeply sensitive to the irony of life; he has
undergone it in no small degree.   More, indeed, than any
of the writers considered in this book he possesses the
gift of the scorpion sting.   As often as not, whether in his
poetry or his prose, it is his indignation, his rancor, that
speaks its heart.   His irony, however, is not that of a contemplative Hardy, with a smile in his eye and a very delicate, scornful curl upon his lip.   Nor is it, on the other
hand, a carping, withering sarcasm.

It is true that the background of both novels is the writer's
native Venezuela, and more particularly the city of Caracas.
But the inner tale unfolded has all humanity as the pro-
tagonist and the world as milieu.   The triumph of evil over
good is as old as sin,—precisely as old; the portrayal of
this triumph in a work of art utterly devoid of preachiness
and bringing to us a new, poignant realization of the old
knowledge, is a triumph for Blanco-Fombona's skill.

Nor should it be imagined that the noted exile from
Venezuela is lacking in the more tender traits.   There are
pages of simple, haunting pathos in the two novels that are
difficult to match for their directness, their unadorned,
straightforward manner.   One suspects, and not on the
evidence of these pages alone, that for all his early bragga-

docio and swashbuckling, Blanco-Fombona has, at bottom, a tender heart, laden with as much sorrow as venom, as much honey as gall.

El Hombre de Hierro was written in prison. The author, who had in 1904 given up his position as Venezuelan consul in Amsterdam, had returned to his native land, or, as he calls it, "mi convulsiva tierruca." In 1905 he was named governor of the Territorio Amazonas, a wild district bordering upon Brazil, and it was here, as we have seen, that he underwent a series of strange adventures. Out of the attack upon the administration building grew charges against him for murder and assault. He was imprisoned in Ciudad Bolívar, and later freed, having been found innocent. "The Man of Iron," then, was born in the cell, which has nurtured many a masterpiece. The writing took eight weeks; the result was one of the author's most enduring books.

Crispín Luz is the highly trusted book-keeper of the firm Perrín and Company. He is not only a model employee, but a model person altogether. He is deeply devout; he is the incarnation of self-sacrifice; he respects, even worships, authority. He not only gives of his best to his employer within working hours, but takes work home, where he occupies a dubious position, because of his humble, submissive nature. He is by no means the favorite child of his mother, a novel-devouring, yet practical woman who keeps an open eye upon the family budget.

When the time comes for Crispín to marry, he is brought together with his future wife, by much the same method as plotting matchmakers may learn from "Much Ado About Nothing." María herself, though not so meek as Crispín, is colorless and imitative enough to desire a husband because it is the regular thing,—because most maidens marry, because her giddy cousin is happily engaged to a vivacious dandy; because, in short, she is talked into the match.   Crispín, however, worships her with the worship of the meek for unexpected joys.   Yet early he feels, rather than detects, that all is not as it should be.   Perhaps the advent of a child will tighten the bonds between husband and wife; yet when the child comes, it brings with its ugliness only more sorrow.

The truth is that María has never known real love until it has been revealed to her through Julio de Nájera, a Brummelesque Don Juan whose voluptuous epicureanism takes delight more in the quest than in the conquest, and who, once he has attained his egotistic ends, forgets María for another.   In the meantime Crispín, blind to everything, toils away slavishly, undermining his fragile constitution.   The inevitable occurs; he is stricken with tuberculosis of the lungs and soon dies as humbly and as meekly as he has lived.   Life has made sport of him from the beginning to the end; in his family he was but a footstool; in business he was a tool; in love he was a dupe; he was the victim of the sum of his virtues, which consumed him like an overmastering vice.

The man of iron, so named by Mr. Perrín because of his reliance upon the faithful employee,—his right arm,— was really but a man of putty.   Yet could anyone have pointed to a single characteristic of his and said "This is evil"?   While he himself was saintly, all too saintly, he was victimized by the all too human.

The author makes no concessions to the reader of popu-

lar novels. He begins at the end, after the funeral of
Crispín, and very skillfully glides back into the chronicle
of events, leading at last to the death and burial in the final
chapter, thus completing the circle. His characterization
is rapid, but by no means superficial; his scenes are brief,
but not blurred. From its technical aspect, indeed "The
Man of Iron," together with its successor, is athletic both
in strength and freedom from superfluity. There is not a
character, a scene, a situation, that may be dispensed with;
every word, indeed, contributes its necessary share to the
whole. From this standpoint, there is a world of difference
between Blanco-Fombona's novels and an *Amalia* or a
Martin Rivas. His ability to compress a characterization,
at its best, is indicative of intimate acquaintance with de
Maupassant; at its worst it degenerates into caricature,
though happily not very often.

The patriot is evident in his satire against natives who
have travelled abroad and must vent their superiority by
depreciating the limitations of Caracas; the fair-minded
critic is likewise revealed by the fact that one of the noblest
figures in the book is a Roman Catholic priest, Father Iz-
nardi,—so noble, indeed, that he is forced out of the country by the hostile attitude of the organized church, which
will have none of his civic and patriotic virtues.

Whether he is describing an earthquake or the inception
of a revolution, an excursion to the country or the death of
one of the meek who did not obtain his share of the inheritance of the earth, Blanco-Fombona seizes unerringly upon
the essential traits. The earthquake is no mere piece of
description,—it reveals the temper of the populace, the
bravery of the priest; the inception of the revolt is likewise

illuminating as to the Venezuelan background against which
Crispín Luz plays his eminently virtuous, eminently ludicrous rôle.

Who are the happy in *El Hombre de Hierro?*   The persons with hearts of iron.   Julio de Nájera, flitting from
woman to woman, only occasionally piqued by a more determined resistance than he is wont to encounter; Rosalia,
María's cousin, wilful, wily, superficial, unscrupulous;
Ramón, Crispín's brother, ever scheming for new acquisitions, ready to squander his money upon dancers and act-
resses; Perrín, the employer, in whose interest even Crispín
consents to wink at wrong-doing.   Virtue alone is victimized, by itself as much as by others; it becomes, not its own
reward, but its own hangman.

This is not all of life; no novel can hope to be.   Crispín
is not all of virtue, because he is too much of it.   He forms,
however, a notable type in modern fiction.   We say an
Oblomov when we refer to the Russian Hamlet, prodigal
in words, fruitful in genuine intelligence, yet sterile or
abortive in deed; we think of Cæsar Moncada (Pío Baroja's
Cæsar or Nothing) as the opposite type,—equally sterile in
the end, yet as prodigal in busy-body futilities as in epigrams; with such as these Crispín Luz belongs as the representative of victimized virtue.   In this novel of Venezuelan
life the author has epitomized a world,—a world filled
with Crispíns in every walk of life.

And what of María?   Is she any the less a victim for
not being possessed of her husband's docility?   In one
trait,—an important one,—she resembles him; her lack
of will.   And one may question whether she or her husband
is essentially the less "moral" of the two.

But I am entering a province which does not concern the author. His aim was to present a slice of life, not to sit in judgment, which is one of mankind's most ludicrous postures. In this novel he produced not only a notable piece of fiction, but a notable work of art, untainted by any too evident purpose of propaganda, yet illuminated by a human glow that warms the heart for all its cynicism; *El Hombre de Hierro* attests a deep, if unostentatious, knowledge of human passions and motives; it may not bring hope, but it brings understanding.

The Man of Gold was begun in the summer of 1913 at Pornichet, a Breton seashore retreat; after an interruption it was finished at Madrid in the winter of 1914–15. "Perhaps," the author tells us, "it is up to the present moment my best book. . . . Its background presents a picture which those will recall who desire to study the political and social customs of Venezuela during the epoch of Castro. There are many portraits from life."

The Man of Gold, however, is far more; it is just as universal in application as its predecessor. Its generating spirit is essentially the same, only it presents the question from a different angle. In the preceding novel it is the virtuous man who succumbs to rascality and vice; in *El Hombre de Oro* the passive saint yields to the active sinner. Blanco-Fombona himself, commenting upon the protagonists of the novels, contrasts them thus: "The first lacks the personal elements of combat, necessary in the society in which he dwells,—and fails; the second possesses qualities lacked by the society in which he lives,—and imposes his will."

We first meet the man of gold as a rising book-keeper,—

Crispín's own profession.   But Señor Irurtia is a genuine, not a metaphorical, man of iron.   His one passion is gain, and to this he subordinates every human attribute.   He loans money at exorbitant interest; he cuts down his personal expenses to the lowest margin, he drives the hardest bargains and at last becomes wealthy.   During all this time, however, he has been, as most of his kind must be, anti-social in character.   His fellow man existed only to be exploited; the government was an institution to be defrauded; woman,—the only woman he really knew was his rheumatic old housekeeper Tomasa, whom he had inherited along with other domestic articles.

Yet it is a strange group of women that is destined to affect Irurtia's career.

The three old-maid Agualonga sisters, a religious, high-minded trio whose ancestry contains noble as well as revolutionary blood, live entirely absorbed in their niece: Olga Emmerich, an eighteen-year-old pampered creature whose thoughts are centered only upon herself.   Ever since she was left on their hands she has worked her will upon them; all their repressed maternal instincts vent themselves upon her,—they are, indeed, her three mothers.   Does Olga conceive a violent desire for an Andrés Rata,—a spineless, subservient, fawning creature who yields to her every caprice?   They may object, but they yield, too.   Does she need money to settle down with?   They will sell their old mansion, peopled with so many treasured memories, or exchange it for a smaller place and give Olga the cash received for the difference in value.   Thus they have recourse to Irurtia, who deals in real estate.

It suddenly enters Olga's head that this Irurtia would

make a good match for Rosaura, one of the three sisters,
with whom he seems somewhat pleased. But this thought
is by no means connected with any concern for Rosaura's
happiness. Olga is thinking of—Olga. Old Irurtia is
repulsive, inwardly and outwardly; but he is rich. Should
he marry Rosaura, who has a special fondness for Olga,
the latter will have access to much more money than that
which will be realized by an exchange of the old manse for
a smaller place. To accomplish this end the young
Machiavelli in petticoats sets a complicated human ma-
chinery in motion. It is the story of Crispín and María
over again, only with more malice, more cruelty. Rosaura
is thrust toward the old miser,—made to feel that it is a
necessary sacrifice,—that it would be selfish of her to
refuse. Irurtia, as much as it is possible, falls in love
with her quite genuinely, but she cannot countenance him.
Not all the knavery of Olga, of the ridiculous "General"
Chicharra, of the rodent-like Andrés Rata, with his flattering newspaper roguery, can bring about the union out of
which the conspirators hope to reap profit at the expense
of Rosaura's misery. Irurtia himself weighs Rosaura in
the balance against his ounces of gold, and the gold wins.
Besides, this man, whose entire career has been one of
parasitical feeding upon society, is invited, because of his
riches, to a post in the President's cabinet, and we leave him
at the close of the tale undermining the very office of the
President.

Like the previous book, this one is etched rather than
written. The vitriolic characterization of Chicharra and
Rata as well as parts of Olga's portrayal, fail of effect by
the very excess of the author's passion. Without his own

testimony, it is easy to detect personal animosity against real characters. The portions dealing with local politics are, if true to life, a terrible condemnation of conditions in Venezuela. Yet the book as a whole suffers little by the caricature of a Chicharra. In every sense it is worthy of the volume to which it forms a spiritual companion.

If one or two of the characters be somewhat overdrawn, where, on the other hand, is it possible to find so well delineated, so neatly sketched, yet so fully vivified a trio of women as the three Agualonga sisters? As the last remnants of an old family, they form a tragic trio that stands out in luminous contrast against the self-seeking creatures who play upon their pride and their good nature. Like Crispín, they, too, are the victims of their virtue. For Olga they abandon their mansion, for Olga they abandon their ideals, and in the end are left to face old age without even the presence of the scatter-brained, self-willed maiden for whom they have made one sacrifice after the other. It is the old triumph of evil over good. Cirilo Matamoros, the native doctor who refuses to accept money for his services, lands in prison as a reward for all his public benefactions; Eufemia, oldest of the three sisters, dies of a broken heart caused by the abandonment of the family home; Rosaura, who in her maiden days refused a man she really loved, because he would not take Olga to live with them, is deserted at last by that Olga who tried to force her into marriage with the abhorrent, money-grubbing Irurtia. Irurtia, on the other hand, works his way up to the shadow of the presidential chair; Chicharra acquires new power in the government; Olga satisfies her every whim, unmindful alike of wifely duty or human consideration.

The chapter depicting the departure of the three sisters from their ancestral homes is one of the most affecting in modern fiction. It reveals, as do similar scenes in the preceding book, a Blanco-Fombona that, one hopes, will be more in evidence in his future works,—a writer who is master of the deeper human emotions, prober into the deeper wells of feeling.

El Hombre de Hierro and *El Hombre de Oro* are a notable couple; they contain, largely, the author's outlook upon life,—a life by no means devoid of what have been called the finer things, yet in which evil is triumphant more often than good. In such a sense, if we must use names, Blanco-Fombona is a pessimist. But not in the sense that includes a resigned acceptance of things, for Blanco-Fombona's entire life is a denial of such resignation. He is a born fighter against the evil he discerns, and by that very token in a certain sense an optimist. These books are not mere "literature"; they are life,— throbbing life. If they are not all of life it is because Blanco-Fombona is not all humanity, any more than are you and I. No greater tribute can be paid to his novels—and the statement applies to his work as a whole, except where he vents those purely personal grudges that other writers repress so far as letters are concerned—than to say that while we read them we accept his world, his creatures, his attitude, and live through the scenes under the spell of his word. There is a great novelist in Blanco-Fombona,—a greater novelist, I believe, than poet or even critic. His two works establish his position firmly.

It is *La Lámpara de Aladino*, 1915 (Aladdin's Lamp) that contains the quintessence of the author's rich personal-

ity. His diabolic spirit, in all its acrimony is here; his
mundane curiosity, raised to a creative power, is here; the
book,—one of the most curious of literary collections,—
is the man in all his aspects. Though it is composed of
bits written at various times and with not a thought of
later assembling, it is strangely revelatory of the complex
author behind the pen. Here is Blanco-Fombona the critic,
the fiction writer, the poet, the sociologist, the polemist,—
the multiple man.

Why "Aladdin's Lamp"?

Because whenever you choose to rub it, the jinni appears.
And because, like Aladdin, we may turn the page instead of
rubbing lamps, and at each page find a new spirit awaiting
us. But let the author interpret himself:

"Aladdin, capricious Aladdin, rubs his magic lamp.
The jinni appears. Aladdin desires festive garb. The
spirit accedes, and Aladdin, the orphan of a botching tailor,
the son of an indigent widow, shines resplendent like a
lord. He rubs his magic lamp again. The jinni appears
submissively. Aladdin asks a palace. And the most opu-
lent castle is his. The ambitious youth rubs once more.
The spirit asks him: 'What do you desire?' The ambitious youth desires to behold the Sultan's daughter in his
arms, languishing for love, and by virtue of the jinni the
sultan's daughter languishes for love in his arms. But
Aladdin is insatiable. He desires more, ever more, and
more still.

" 'Unhappy one, your desire will slay you,' warns the
spirit. 'Your present desire spells death; if I should satisfy it, you would die.'

"We are all, at times, are we not, the covetous son of the tailor? We all have our Aladdin's lamps.

"But not always does famishing Desire, Insatiability, rub it.

"At times, more frequently, Aladdin's lamp is Imagination, of which we do not ask all because its gifts please only chimerical, unbalanced men, without any practical spirit, whom we call poets. As we rub the magic instrument the miracle occurs, and out of the clouds come women we love, landscapes gazed upon by our eyes, peoples that opened their doors to our curiosity. . . . Do you understand now how evocation of past life—memories, travels, emotions, readings—may be christened with an Oriental title?"

Accordingly the strange collection is divided into (1) Names, (2) Thoughts and Emotions, (3) Cities and Panoramas, (4) Italy, (5) The Trip to the Upper Orinoco, 1905, (6) Commentaries, (7) Confessions. Let us rub the lamp a few times and sample the jinni's compliance.

Such an array of names as files by our eyes in the opening section! And despite the brevity of his treatment, the author unfailingly presents us with a thought that lingers. There is a rich vein of imaginative humor, now gay, now punning, now ironic, now swashbuckling, but never dull. With equal grace he flits from Maeterlinck to Loti, to Wilde, to Lamartine, to Isadora Duncan, to Anatole France and whom not else, in a half dozen literatures, with a refreshingly international outlook. For, despite the intense patriotism he can feel and the intense national hatred that is the outgrowth of that patriotism, Blanco-Fombona is very much of an internationalist.

Discussing Maeterlinck he can throw off the observation that France has never produced a single really great drama because it does not love exaggeration even in passion. "I am surprised that nobody should have observed this before. Shakespeare could not have been born in France." In similar fashion he predicts (this was before the war, which has now delayed the fulfillment of his prophecy) a theatre that will be the glory of Russia and the envy and despair of other nations. So, too, referring to Oscar Wilde, he cannot resist a slap at the British pharisaic, "holier-than-thou" attitude and at literary sanctimoniousness. "Grief converted Wilde in his last days, to Christianity, without such Christianity having anything to do with sects, Protestant or otherwise. The author of *De Profundis* was the last Christian." Speaking of Isadora Duncan he is led to his rarely forgotten topic,—the United States. "The United States, which still lack a national music and poetry, likewise lack a typical dance. (The cake-walk is not Yankee, it is negro.)" Like Rodó, he considers the will our great virtue. From a consideration of Gogol's sparkling comedy *Revizor* he arrives at a definition of genius: "converting the small things of every day into the great things of all the centuries."

I shall not make a minute analysis of his *Names*; it is sufficient to indicate that the man is peculiarly alive to every impulse of art and science; one need not agree with all he says to admire his many-faced curiosity,—a curiosity that, as I have said, is creative. This is no merely superficial versatility; it is the full utilization of the full man that, as we have learned from Rodó, we all carry within us. It is literature with a deep root in contemporary life; it is

not Darío's lyric contemporaneity or Chocano's all ages
in one; it is a passionate, belligerent contemporaneity that
is strewn with the errors that accompany man's striving.
It is representative of a type of mind that we lack in our
own nation.

Pensares y Sentires (Thoughts and Emotions) is no less
suggestive. Indeed, Blanco-Fombona cannot write detach-
edly. "The whole man thinks," said Lewes in his biography of Goethe; when Blanco-Fombona works, the whole
man writes.

In his cynical moments he is capable of a bit like his
"best definition of a man,"—"The best definition of a man
would be this: the only animal who can laugh, cry, and get
drunk. Perhaps others have given it before. As I have
lived in England, Germany, Holland and the United States,
I find it a gem." At other times his cynicism combines
with his sociological interest, and he gazes at the human
panorama from an elevation of mingled scorn and
optimism:

"The survival of the fittest," he declares, in his *Los
Arboles Sobre el Monte* (The Trees Upon the Mountain),
"is a natural law in so far as it applies to all of nature. But
in this vile, bourgeois society the fittest to live are the vilest.
To change the environment, revolutionizing it with whatever means science places at our disposal, is to prepare a
better world, whence better men will perforce issue, without any other equality being necessary than that of the right
to eat and the right to forge ahead.

"The serf desired to become a citizen and succeeded.
The citizen of today lacks necessities and laughs at the sin-
ister situation of going to the ballot box with an empty

stomach. The modern man is hungry. The great revolution of the future is the revolution for bread. And when man will possess bread and rights, he will place his happiness in something else and will strive to obtain it. This is how humanity endures, through movements, change and interchange of ideals. Stagnant waters produce only slime and miasma.

"When the people desired to conquer rights it flocked to the banners of a Mirabeau and listened to the great voices of the philosophers. Now it throngs about doctrines,—pregnant with the future,—of a Karl Marx; and always the people will seek a guide and will rally around some guiding banner. For, despite the fact that personalities are nothing without the group, the Carlylean conception of history contains much truth.

"The people are mountains, but the great trees grow upon them."

His views of democracy is the aristodemocratic view of Rodó, only that Blanco-Fombona is outspokenly socialistic. At times, indeed, his cult of the free personality leads him to what many would shrink from as anarchy.

It is in this section that the author presents in succinct form his views upon Spanish America's contribution to Castilian literature. First of all, he contends, Spanish America has brought a revolutionary fermentation; then a deep love of nature, a more vivid feeling for landscape, the mountain coolness, the breath of pampas, virgin forests and seas. Too, a cult of form, a love of elegant things, a dynamic prose, and verses free of the old, pneumatic eloquence. Finally, an intense æsthetic emotion,—tenderness and sensualism in art. "In this last respect, Manuel Guti-

érrez Nájera, for example, is the Castilian poet without
predecessors. . . . One of the most pithy and disturb-
ing of contemporary thinkers, Don Miguel de Unamuno,
has truly written: 'Our tongue speaks things to us
from beyond the great sea that it never spoke here.' "

We will pause long enough upon the *Ciudades y Pana-
romas* to note that Blanco-Fombona is no mere parlor tour-
ist. He sees beyond the lithographed pamphlets of the
traveling agencies. Commenting upon Mother Spain he
returns to his favorite themes. He entertains high hopes
for a genuine renaissance of Hispanic grandeur. He sees,
too, the undoubted influence of the younger Spanish-Amer-
can writers upon Spanish literature, especially the effect of
Darío, Lugones, José Asunción Silva, Herrera Reissig, and
of Ricardo Palma, the venerable Peruvian scholar, poet and
chronicler. With perspicacious patience he indicates
cases of almost servile imitation, and reproves Spain for
its neglect of the Spanish-American intellect, not to speak
of its envy and jealousy. Yet these words, so easily misunderstood, are not mere acrimony for its own sake. Underneath them, as the writer himself assures us in a note,
lies a genuine desire for a mutual understanding. Blanco-
Fombona is not so black as he paints himself with his
caustic habit of utterance.

More interesting than the Italian travels is the exception-
ally vivid account of his trip to assume charge of his guber-
natorial duties in the wilds of Venezuela. The tale reads
like fiction, with a background as exotic as it is picturesque.
The entire expedition had something of the Quixotic about
it. Blanco-Fombona the roisterer is there, becoming drunk
and endangering the life of his few companions; the poet

is there, too, inspired by the ambient into the extemporiza-
tion of poetry,—into Alexandrian ecstasies—à la Chocano:

> Yo tengo el alma antiguo de los conquistadores;
> Orinoco, los Andes. . . .

the economist is there, with the realization that here may
be situated the future centre of the world's commerce.   So
is the sociologist.   What is the first thing Blanco-Fombona
does in his official capacity?   He constitutes the Muncipal
Council amid his desert territory; he founds schools; he
studies the various Indian dialects with the purpose of publishing vocabularies of the indigenous tongues.   And here
we come upon one of the numerous instances of the fairness that underlies all his proud extravagances,—a fairness
comparable with that of Blasco Ibáñez, whose social ideas
run in similar channels.   Blanco-Fombona at once sets
about to protect the exploited Indians; as a reward for his
civilizing influences he is made the target of assassination,
which he escapes by his own right arm.   The governors
of the province have rarely enjoyed great ease.   Venancio
Pulgar was slain; Meléndez Carrasco was wounded; Tavera
Acosta was put to flight; Díaz, whom Blanco-Fombona succeeded, was poisoned, and Blanco-Fombona's own successor,
Maldonado, was shot to death.   While correcting the proofs
of his book the author learned that the new governor, General Roberto Pulido, had been assassinated together with
twenty-five or thirty companions.   Is it any wonder, then,
that our writer inveighs against the lawless whites of the
dangerous territory?   He finds the Indians, on the whole,
an industrious kind, contrasting most favorably with the
riff-raff of the Caucasians that have there assembled from

all the corners of the earth.   There is a grim humor in his
statement that despite the undoubted existence of gold
mines in the East, the whites frequently rob from one another and even slay, all joining in the plundering and the
persecution of the Indians.   The author while defining
man, might have added another attribute: the sole creature
who robs his fellow in plenitude, impelled by desire of gain
rather than hunger.   For a moment, in his quasi-Chateau-
briandian exaltation of the Indian, he becomes a sort of
devil's advocate.   "As to their religious beliefs," he remarks, "the Indians are more logical than other peoples.
They give feasts to the Devil.   They aver, and with reason,
that since the Almighty is the Supreme Good, He is incapable of wishing evil upon His creatures, so that it is unnecessary to present Him with adulation or feasts.   These
they reserve for the Spirit of Evil, who must be maintained
propitious. . . ."

The *Viaje al Alto Orinoco* (1905) is a moving, novel-
esque, at times poetic description of a madcap, if patriotic,
epoch in the writer's multifarious career.   All of the writer
is in its colorful pages.

The *Comentarios* are often words turned swords, glisten-
ing before they stab.   Ask not Blanco-Fombona for consistency; ask of him the self of the moment.   Do you
imagine that his anti-United States utterances are the
product of a blind, unreasoning hatred?   Then read what
he can say of all Europe and its hypocritical cant about
civilization when the purpose of diplomats is to be effected
(*La Justicia Inmanente*, page 398) ; read what he can say of
France, the nation he adores, in his article upon Xeno-
phobia (page 431) ; the truth is that, without fear he attacks

evil wherever he sees it. His sight may often err, but rarely his aim or his sincerity. In this connection, easily one of the finest of the *Comentarios* is his virile attack upon *Frasas Hechas* (Stock Phrases). "Sound Germany," "Tranquil Holland," "The Model Republic," "Spanish Indolence" and "Mad France" rouse his ire. Is it not because at bottom, these stock phrases represent, as do most, a crystallization of thought that is the enemy of fluid opinion and that deeper knowledge without which no lasting national friendship may be effected?

Confesiones presents a difference only of degree; almost everything that has come from the author's pen is in one way or another a confession. The writer may, at times, achieve a certain Parnassianism of form; essentially, however, he is personal,—one might almost say, at the risk of adding to the intricate mesh of terminology, that he is essentially projective. Yet he is such a master of word and style that we are very apt to be carried along in the current of his thought.

It is number XV of the Confessions that contains the probable keynote to Blanco-Fombona's personality as it is revealed in his literature. "There comes from Colombia a letter that produces a powerful impression upon us," he writes, "in that it recalls the hours of anguish spent in torture in the prison of Caracas (1909–1910). And I who, illumined by a ray of love, thought myself five hundred years away from that darkness of yesterday! But no. My heart cannot forget. That unmerited and protracted grief, that violent and hate-blinded persecution, this exile that cuts my life in two, all this drama of barbarocracy let loose against me, has darkened my character, poisoned my soul. . . ."

Here, then, is one of the sources of a virulence that disturbs many a page of our author,—that renders him unwittingly unjust,—that alienates the reader who seeks merely the amenities of "polite" literature. Some may wish it absent, but that is to wish Blanco-Fombona to be somebody else. We must accept him for what he is, a thoroughly human, sincere, passionate fighter in causes that he deems just.

From the same letter (sent by Saturio González) we obtain an interesting glimpse of that prison life which Blanco-Fombona has sung in his poems. There was many a sleepless night, in which the noted author read manuscripts of his own which were later confiscated and lost for good, including a diary of his imprisonment.

The book concludes with a history of the author's works. The account is rich in anecdote, in humor, in self-analysis, in literary interest. It seems organically impossible for Blanco-Fombona to be dull. Following the account is that short obituary note with which I opened this chapter,—a note of death that rings with life.

It is too early to attempt a definite evaluation of Blanco-Fombona's position in Spanish-American literature. He is yet a young, if altered, man. Unless future events should embroil him in pure polemics, he seems destined to produce fiction and poetry of distinctive and lasting worth. He is a man of the new age, and that age is emerging from the chaos of battle and international misunderstanding.

TRANSLATIONS

The poetry quoted in the text and not made clear by the surrounding matter is here translated quite literally. The citations are indexed under the author in whom they occur, preceded by the first line of the original.

MANUEL GUTIÉRREZ NÁJERA

No soy poeta, etc.

I am not a poet; you can see that. In vain you flatter me with such a title, for neither is the nest a thrush or a nightingale, nor is the piano a tenor or a baritone!

Por qué es preciso, etc.

Why is it necessary for happiness to end? Why does the sweetheart remain at the window, and to the note which says, "Till tomorrow," why does the heart reply "Who knows?"

Recordar . . . perdonar . . . haber amado. . . .

To recall, to pardon, to have loved, to have been for a moment happy, to have believed . . . and then, to recline wearily upon the snowy shoulder of oblivion.

El templo colosal, etc.

The colossal temple, with its immense nave, is dank and dreary; there are no flowers upon the altar; all is dark, so dark. The candles are extinguished! Lord, where art thou? I seek thee in vain! . . . Where art thou, O Christ? I call thee in fear, because I am alone, even as the frightened child calls his father! . . . And there is nobody at the altar! Nobody in the nave! All is submerged in sepulchral gloom! Speak! Let the organ sound! Let me see the candles burn upon the altar! . . . I am drowning in the darkness. . . . I am drowning! Arise from the dead, oh my Lord! "

JOSÉ MARTÍ

Un beso! etc.

"A kiss."—"Wait."—That day as they parted, they loved each other. "A kiss!"—"Take it!" That day as they parted, they wept.

Entró la niña en el bosque.

The maiden entered the forest arm in arm with her wooer, and there was heard one kiss, and another, and then nothing more was heard. She was in the woods an hour, and emerged without her lover. There was heard a sigh;—a sigh, and then nothing more.

JULIÁN DEL CASAL

Ver otro cielo, otro monte.

To behold another sky, a different mountain, another shore, another horizon, a different sea. Other peoples, other races, with different habits of thought.

Ignea columna sigue mi paso cierto!

A pillar of fire follows my certain steps! A redeeming faith saves my soul! I know that beyond the waves the haven awaits me! I know that after the night will rise the dawn. . . . If we had lived longer together, our separation would not be so painful. You cultivate your ills, and I forget. You see everything black, and I see it rose color!

JOSÉ ASUNCIÓN SILVA

Infancia, valle ameno.

Childhood, fair valley of blessed repose and coolness, where the ray of the sun that scorches the rest of life is gentle. How saintly is your pure innocence, and your fleeting, transitory joys; how sweet it is in hours of bitterness, to look to the past and evoke your memories!

cuentos más durables que las convicciones
Tales more enduring than the convictions of solemn sages
and sapient schools, and who surround with your fictions the
gilded cradles of our great-grandmothers.

campanas plañideras
. . . plangent bells that speak to the living of the dead.

Una noche
On a night, on a night permeated with murmurs, perfumes
and the music of wings; on a night in which the fantastic
glow-worms gleamed in the moist and mystical shadows. . . .

SALVADOR DÍAZ MIRÓN

No intentes convencerme de torpeza
Attempt not to convict me of baseness with the delirium of
your madness! My reason is at once light and firmness,
firmness and light, like the rock crystal! Like to the nocturnal pilgrim, my immortal hope does not gaze upon the
ground: beholding on my path naught but shadow, I con-
template only the splendor of the heavens! . . . Erect under
all blows, in my persistence I feel superior to victory. I have
faith in myself: adversity may cheat me of triumph, but not
of glory! Let the abject persecute me! I desire to attract
envy, though it vanquish me! The flower to which the
insects swarm is rich in colors and in perfume. . . . To illuminate is to burn! A burning inspiration will be the
flame that consumes me! . . . The pearl blossoms from the
wounded mollusc, and Venus is born of the bitter
foam! Conform, then, woman! We have come to this vale
of tears that overwhelms us,—You, like the dove, for the
nest and I, like the lion, for the combat.

En mí el Cosmos intima señales.
In me the Cosmos suggests tokens and is a congeries of
mental impressions. . . . For me, as an objective spirit,
everything exists as I behold it. And the nuance lends its

own lyric element to the gay talent; this it is that imparts
character and tone, novelty and worth to the product.

AMADO NERVO

Sois rey, etc.
You are king of America, still, in a certain manner, even as
before. King, as long as the divine tongue of Cervantes
sweetens the lips and sings in the songs of eighteen republics
and fifty millions of beings; as long as the austere ideal of
Castilian honor guides our souls and our hands.

ENRIQUE GONZÁLEZ MARTÍNEZ

Busca en todas las cosas.
Seek in all things a soul and a hidden meaning; limit not
yourself to mere appearances; scent and follow the trail of
the secret truth, with a piercing glance and a sharp ear.
Love life's tender aspect,—the calm of the swaying flower,
color, the landscape; gradually you will learn to decipher
their language. . . . Oh, divine colloquy of things and the
soul! There is in all things a tender smile, an ineffable
grief or a sombre mystery. Do you know whether the drops
of dew are tears? Do you know what secrets are sung by
the zephyrs?

RUBÉN DARÍO

Murió tu padre, es verdad . . .
Your father has died, it is true; you weep for him, and are
right; but resign yourself, for there exists an eternity where
there is no suffering . . . and the just dwell in song amid
white lilies . . .

Este del cabello cano . . .
This sage with hair as white as ermine, merged his childhood
candor with his old age's experience. When you hold such
a man's book in your hands, each expression is a bee, which,
flying from the paper, leaves its honey on your lips and its
sting in your heart.

Decidme si he de alzar voces altivas.

Say whether I shall raise my voice proudly in praise of the modern spirit, or whether, casting these times into oblivion, I shall give myself up entirely to recollections. . . . Today the bolt of Olympic Jupiter is the slave of Franklin and of Edison; nothing remains of the glorious thyrsus, and vile champagne has dethroned Falernian wine. . . . All is over. Tell me, sacred muses, how shall I sing in these gloomy days, in which human pride attempts to cast God out of heaven.

Noble ingenio: la luz de la palabra . . .

Noble spirit, the light of the word touches the soul and imparts new life to it, revealing to it unknown wonders in the infinite world of beings. Eternity appears in all its majesty, attracting the eager spirit, and anxious hope grows in the human bosom at the distant splendor of the dawn. You, inspired, yearnful, raise your brow and, with the diapason of harmony, wisely follow a fruitful course, extending the standard of the language, forming the flash of thought, producing uniform melodies like the immortal rhythm of the spheres.

Eres artista?   Te afeo.

Are you an artist?   I disfigure you.
Are you worthy?   I criticise you.
I abhor you if you are rich
and if you are poor I stone you.
And pillaging honor,
and wounding everything in sight,
it appears certain that
man is a wolf unto man.

Vivió el pobre en la miseria.

The poor man dwelt in poverty,
none gave ear to him in his misfortune;
when he asked an alms
they cast him from the house.

After he died a pauper
they raised a statue to him. . . .
Long live the dead, for they have neither
stomach nor jaws!

No quiero el vino de Naxos.
I ask not the wine of Naxos, nor the urn of those beauties,
nor the glass in which Venus woos handsome Adonis. I
wish to drink love only from your crimson lips, oh beloved
mine, in the sweet springtide.

Fué acaso en el Norte ó en el Mediodía? . . .
Was it perchance in the North or in the South? I do not
know the day nor the season, but I know that Eulalia still
laughs, and her golden laughter is cruel and eternal!

Amor, en fin, que todo diga y cante.
Let love, then, say and sing all: let love enchant and fascinate
the serpent with diamond eyes that is coiled about the tree
of life. Love me thus, fatal, cosmopolitan, universal, vast,
unique, alone, and all; mysterious and erudite: love me, sea
and cloud, crest and wave.

No es demacrada y mustia. . . .
It is not emaciated and withered, nor does it grasp a crooked
scythe, nor does it wear an anguished expression. It resembles Diana, as chaste and virgin as she; in its countenance there is the grace of the nubile maid and on its
brow a garland of starry roses. In its left hand it holds
green, triumphal palms, and in its right, a vase filled with
the water of oblivion. At its feet, like a dog, lies a love,
asleep. *Amico.* The gods themselves seek the sweet peace
Death sheds. *Quirón.* The grief of the gods is their inability to die.

Inclitas razas ubérrimas, sangre de Hispania fecunda . . .
Glorious, numerous races, blood of our fertile Hispania,
Valiant fraternal spirits, luminous souls, all hail!

Come is the moment long yearned for, when voices aquiver
  with gladness
New hymns will chant. All about us the air is alive with
  vast portents,
Magical waves of life surge in the immanent throes of new
  birth.
Backward oblivion totters, backward flees death in her error;
Heralds proclaim a new kingdom,—the sybilline dream is
  fulfilled,
And here in the box of Pandora, whence issued so many
  misfortunes,
Suddenly we have discovered, smilingly pure, talismanic,
As our divine Vergil might say it, writing his verses im-
  mortal,
The heavenly queen of light,—Hope that descends from the
  skies!

Mientras el mundo aliente, mientras la espira gire . . .
  While the world endures and the sphere rotates, while the
  cordial wave nourishes a dream, as long as there is a live
  passion, a noble task; an impossible quest, an impossible
  deed, a hidden America to discover, Spain will live!

Jwentud, divino tesoro . . .
  Youth, divine treasure, now you are leaving never to return!
  When I desire to weep, I cannot, and at times, without wishing to, I weep. . . . The heavenly tale of my heart has been
  plural.[1]

Y para mí, Maestro, tu vasta gloria es esa:
  To me, Master, your vast glory is this: you loved the fleeting
  deeds of the hour; above groping science, dense history,
  you loved eternal Poesy, brighter than the dawn.
  Glory to you, who, driven about at the whim of destiny, lived
  to the clearest and most beautiful old age; your enormous

[1] See the translation of this entire poem in *Eleven Poems of Rubén Darío.*
G. P. Putnam's Sons, New York, 1916.

catafalque would be that of Victor Hugo, if there were in
Buenos Aires an Arch of the Stars!

Pluguiera á Dios las aquas, antes intactas . . .
Would to God that the waters, before untouched by man, had
never reflected the white sails; that the astounded stars had
never witnessed the arrival of your caravels upon these
shores!

JOSÉ SANTOS CHOCANO

Siempre al cantar Victor Hugo.
Ever, when Victor Hugo sang, Napoleon Third trembled.

vano, vano será que una Dalila.
in vain, in vain, will it be for a Delilah to shear my poet's
locks.

yo quiero la igualdad, ya que la suerte.
I ask equality, since our lot is the same at the beginning; if
we are all equal in death, let us all be equal in life.

crucificádme, y bién?   ¿Yo hablo al presente?
Crucify me—Well? Do I speak to the present? No; I
speak to the future. Sacred equality will be the ideal of the
future race. . . . Oh, Equality! Brother, have you not seen
the sun, shedding its rays upon all? Thus, too, does the
God of Christ illuminate; therefore, levelled in greatness,
you have the same right of receiving the sun on your forehead, as of holding God in your bosom!

Lee mis pobres versos, ya que el yugo.
Read my poor verses, since I wear the constant yoke of love
for you; devour them and extract all their sap, for the greatest of my pleasures is to see them die like those flowers
which women tear apart as they play with them.

Traemos desde otros mundos.
We bear from other worlds, like recollections of former days,

ineffable sympathies, deep-rooted antipathies. The wrathful waves,—do they break against the rock for the mere sake of breaking? Is love but loving? Where is the point of departure of our life,—the shore or the sea?

debe de ser hermoso y eloquente.
It must be beautiful and eloquent to behold entering the heavens anew, a Satan redeemed and pardoned.

Entonces canté amor.
Then I sang love. I rent the veils of the profound genesis. I opened my book, as God his heavens, and beheld my verses, as God his worlds.

En medio de la noche, en que camina. (Note to *La Epopeya del Morro.*)
Amid the night in which the world journeys toward tomorrow's dawn, each hero, crowning each ruin, is like each torch that illumines Nero's nights. Human torch, infernal flame, divine light!

Cinco veces.
Five times greater, at last, has the encamped enemy grown. . . . And five times within himself grows every soldier.

Y esa mujer.
And that woman, her flesh rent by an infamous dagger, with the glance of a glowing sun in her wavering pupil; that woman, sacrificed upon the cannon,—is the image of the dead Fatherland.

y el patrio pabellón.
and the nation's flag, stained in red, when the glorious pyre shall be extinguished, will float above the dying embers like a flame become a banner!

porque el gran Bolognesi.
For the great Bolognesi was the sum of Agamemnon, Nestor,

Achilles. Thus the American incarnated the majesty of Atreus's Agamemnon, the experience of Nestor the old, and the fearlessness of Peleus's son.

Si América.
If America conquered, her victory was a source of maternal pride to Spain; the tree which begins to give forth fruits of glory, owes it to the stream that bathes it.

Como en el mito.
As in the myth in which sinewy Hercules, who neither in strength nor in desire equalled the rebellious Bolivar. . . .

¡Ah! Quién sabe. . . .
Ah, who knows whether the universe is only an organism, immovable in essence, and which, although from appearance to appearance it keeps on undergoing transformation, is ever the same,—and who knows whether God is not its consciousness. . . . How many organisms stir in a drop of water, of blood, of sweat, of tears! How much greatness floats in littleness. Oh, Life, how much is your immortal reflection multiplied, which in each drop of water reverberates like the eucharist of the mirror which in a thousand fragments reflects you entire! . . . Within each life there are so many lives! Who could prevent the wave from changing into other waves? The sparks from a flame may become fires in themselves; each corolla is a forest perhaps; and thus universal life is one complete existence.

Yo, si duda mi siglo.
I, if my century doubts, doubt too. I, if my century denies, likewise deny. But not in vain do I possess liberty. Let the age be my law, but not my tyrant.

Suya será mi voluntad.
To it will belong all my will, my reason, my ideal, my law, my spirit. But let me at least be able to say, on the other hand, "My heart is my own!"

¡Oh murmullos!

Oh, murmurs of the forest! Oh, sacred voice of Nature! Oh, deep plaint of the agonizing beast! No, there is nothing that more swells the human heart than, when it vibrates, the harp of the foliage, attuned to the ocean's diapason. . . . One discovers a voice that enchants him; another, a voice that recalls a song; another, a voice that lulls or implores; yet another, who never prayed to God, hearing such solemn sounds, falls to his knees and prays!

Pero hay en ese verso.

But there is in this vigorous, terse verse a blood that you will scarcely find in any other,—a blood that, when it circulates in the verse, penetrates like light and undulates like the wave.

Pero su brazo.

But his arm is made for lifting the trumpet toward there where the Prophet's dawn appears. And he is made to give to the winds the expression of the terrible trumpet of thought.

y quise en el Museo.

And in the Museum, thinking of my mountains, I wished to belong half to America and half to Spain.

Ave que hoy se abre.

Bird that today rends its bosom in the numerous cares of its love,—why be surprised, if it is to still the hunger of your children? You, like that bird, with your own beak, are rending your entrails to give life to an entire world.

La Paz fué.

Peace was made. The decisive triumph of the yellow Court was not good for the Republic of the North, nor was the former rule of the Czars over such eagerly-sought lands and coveted seas. . . . Thus, in the making of peace, the United States conquered,—and with sure aim, astute, agile, fore-

seeing, they trepanned the lands, cut the Andes, united two
oceans and felt their greatness.

Como es hembra.

Since Life is a female, she loves the strong man; and yields
to his embrace because she rejoices to surrender to strength.
Will, ancient soul; we must triumph! Where there have
been laurels, there must have been will-power.

RUFINO BLANCO-FOMBONA

El mejor poema es el de la vida.

The best poem is that of life; the lost note of a piano in the
night; the wake of a vessel; the flowery road that leads to
unknown cities; childish sorrows; mornings of quarrel; the
taste of ungiven kisses, and loveless love.

Me abruma el calabozo.

The dungeon crushes me. My soul is crossed by dark
thoughts. My poet's wings, as they open, break against the
four walls. In a tomb, and alive! The days are eternal,
and eternal the nights! The Griefs keep me company.
About me are spies, and chains upon my legs. . . . But as I
close my eyes (light, fields, sky) I feel my fetters break;
arm in arm with my sweetheart in the garden I breathe the
scent of magnolias and verbenas. . . . I take delight in the
air, the clouds, the waters of the pond, as refreshing as my
beloved. . . . There is yet something good that the Despot
cannot take from me or fetter.

Locura? Bien. No me resigno.

Madness? Very well. I refuse to resign myself. Let slaves
do that. Let Destiny make me drink hemlock, and Grief
drive its nails through me. . . . I will not say; "blessed art
Thou, my Lord, Thy will be done." I will say, "I am less
than the insect under the sole of a shoe. But there is no use
in gulping down my tears, nor in trying to make a pleasure
of my misfortune, or to look upon my torture with an

Olympic, indifferent expression. For in this puppet that I am, there is the capacity for suffering, and I, the dwarf, possess a soul and can weigh injustice and can judge the tyrant."

THE END

INDEX